10/08

Dungeo

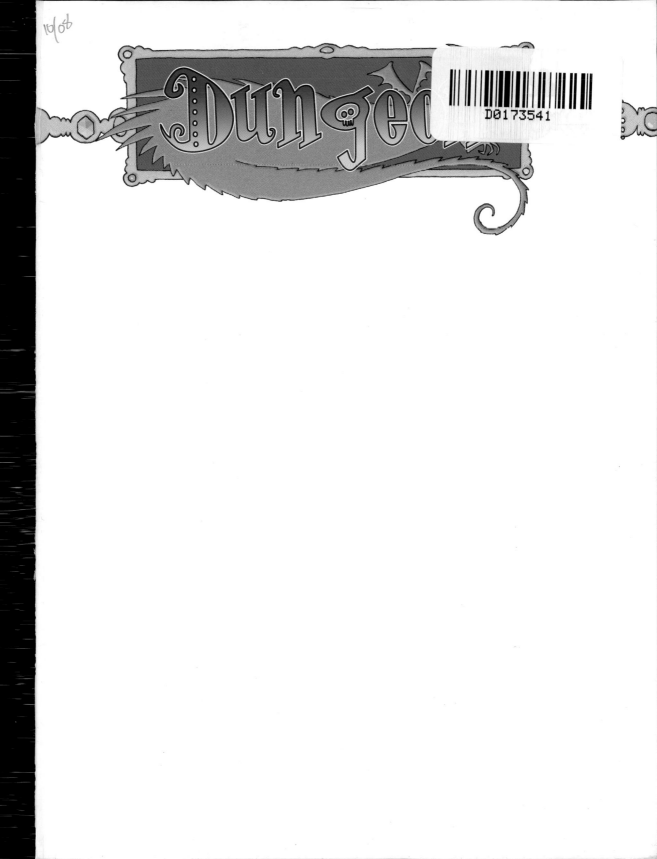

Also available from Trondheim:
Dungeon, vol. 2, $14.95
Mr. O, $13.95
with Thierry Robin:
Li'l Santa, $14.95
Happy Halloween, Li'l Santa, $14.95
With Manu Larcenet:
Astronauts of the Future, vol. 1, $14.95

Add $3 P&H first item $1 each additional.

Write for our complete catalog
of over 200 graphic novels:
NBM
555 8th Ave., Suite 1202
New York, NY 10018
www.nbmpublishing.com

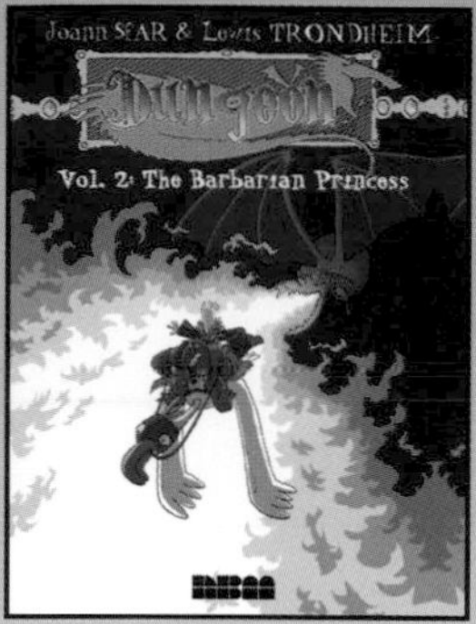
SFAR & Lewis TRONDHEIM
Vol. 2: The Barbarian Princess

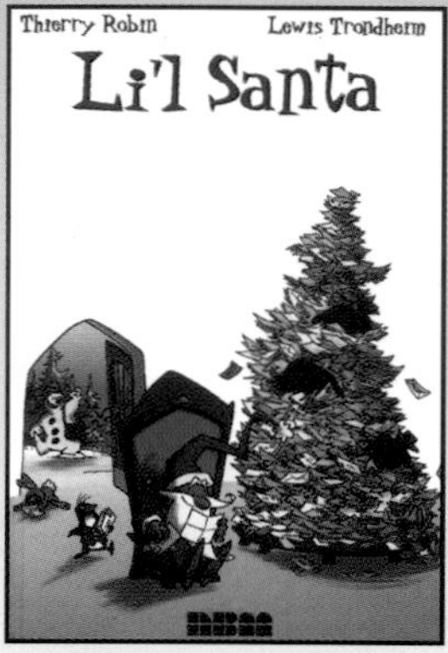
Thierry Robin
Lewis Trondheim
Li'l Santa

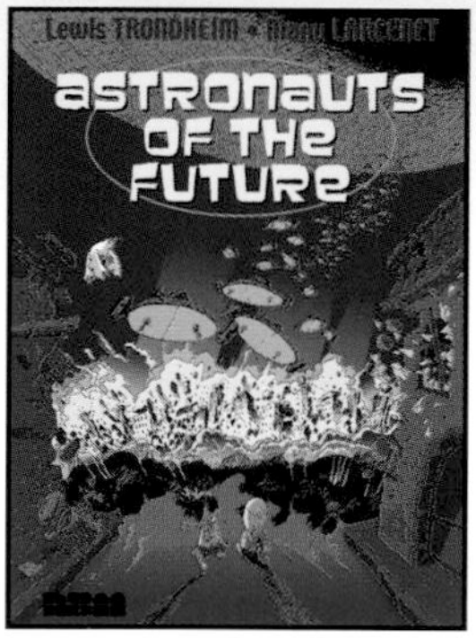
Lewis TRONDHEIM
LARCENET
ASTRONAUTS OF THE FUTURE

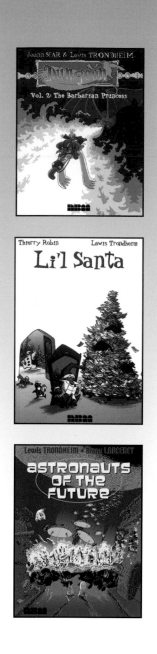

Zenith

Volume 1:

Duck Heart

Joann SfAR &
Lewis TRONDHEIM

NANTIER · BEALL · MINOUSTCHINE
Publishing inc.
new york

ISBN 1-56163-401-8
© 1998 Delcourt Productions-Trondheim-Sfar
© 2003 NBM for the English translation
Translation by Joe Johnson
Lettering by Ortho

Printed in China

3   2

GRAPH SFAR v.1

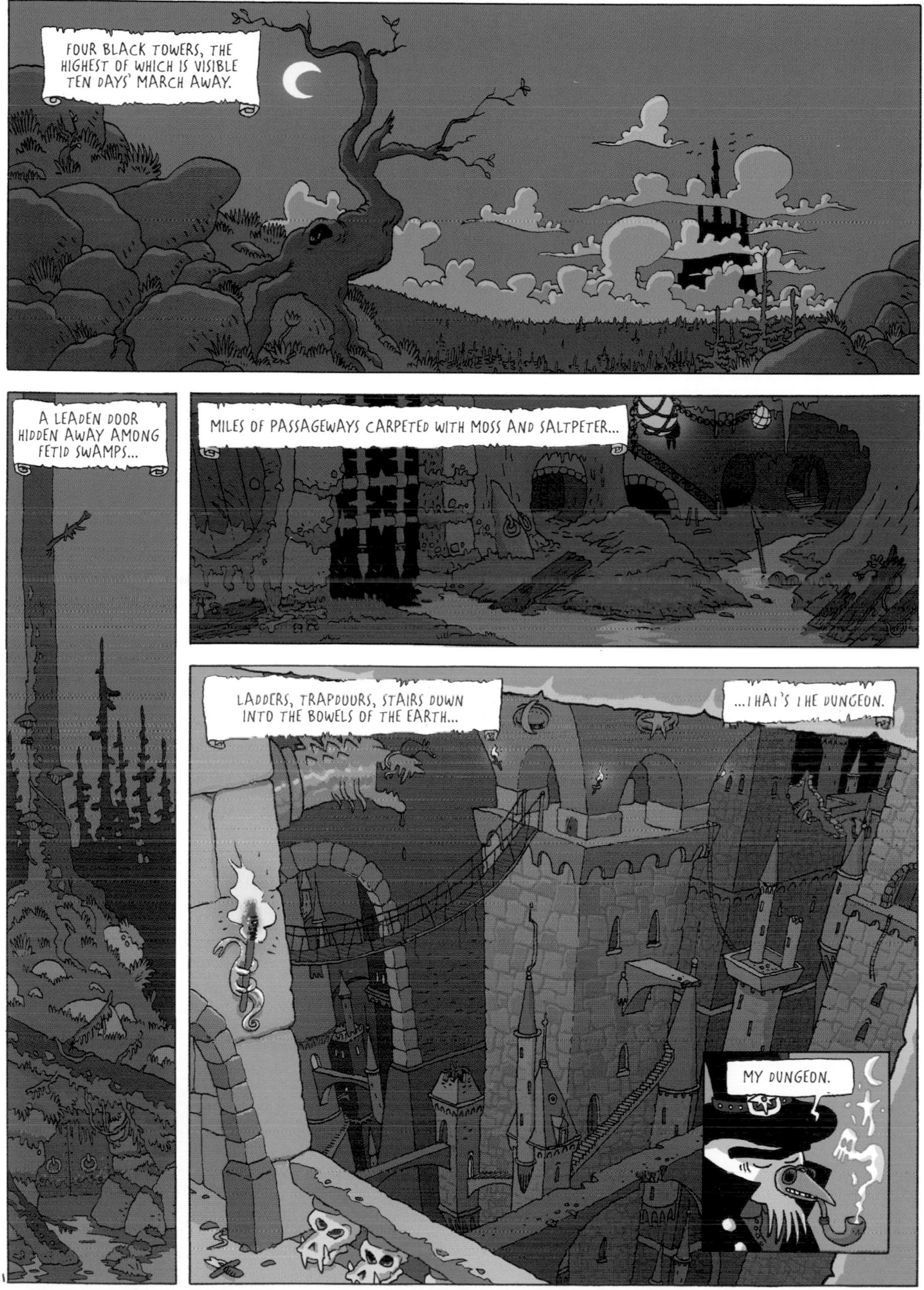
FOUR BLACK TOWERS, THE HIGHEST OF WHICH IS VISIBLE TEN DAYS' MARCH AWAY.
A LEADEN DOOR HIDDEN AWAY AMONG FETID SWAMPS...
MILES OF PASSAGEWAYS CARPETED WITH MOSS AND SALTPETER...
LADDERS, TRAPDOORS, STAIRS DOWN INTO THE BOWELS OF THE EARTH...
...THAT'S THE DUNGEON.
MY DUNGEON.

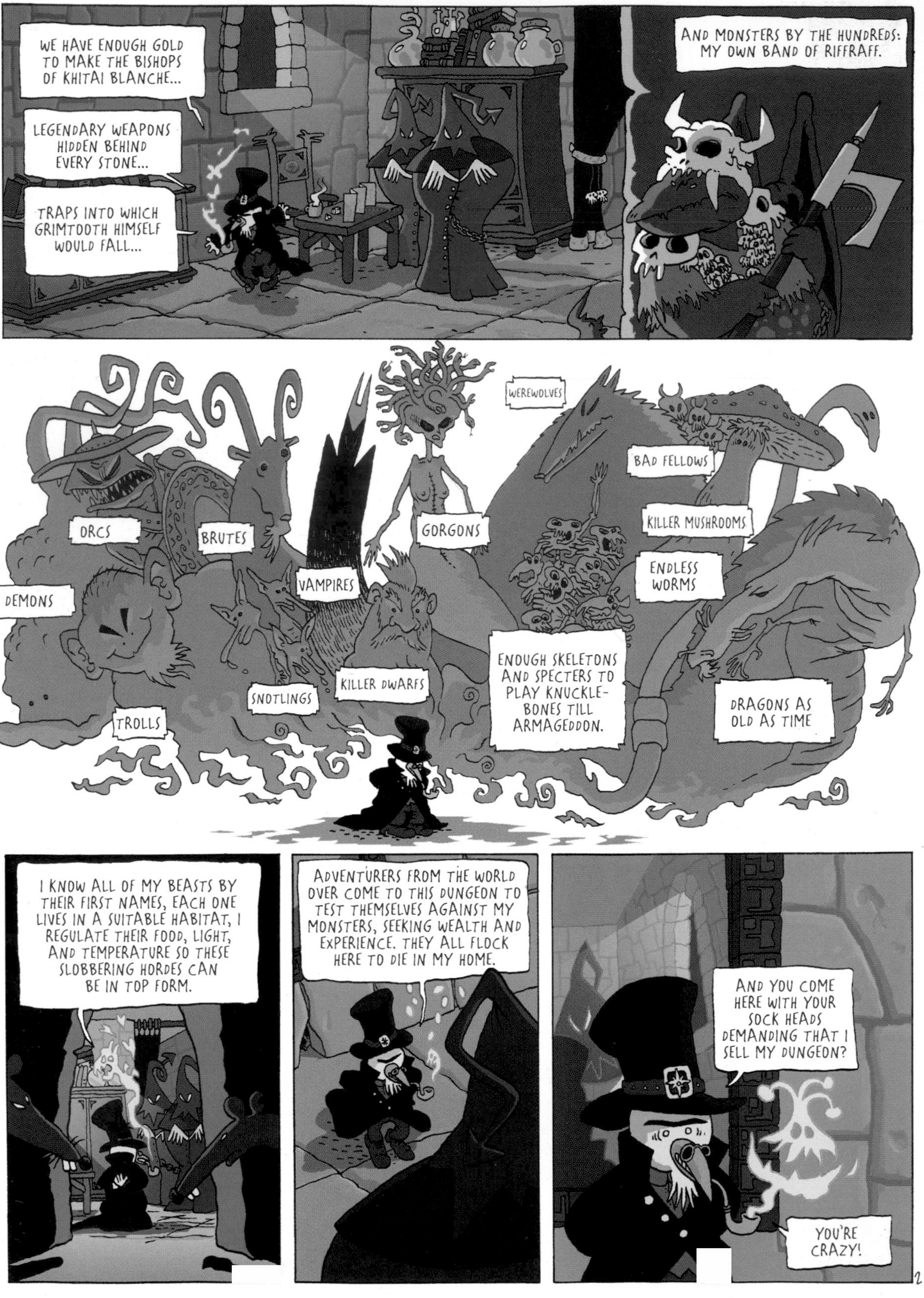
WE HAVE ENOUGH GOLD TO MAKE THE BISHOPS OF KHITAI BLANCHE...
LEGENDARY WEAPONS HIDDEN BEHIND EVERY STONE...
TRAPS INTO WHICH GRIMTOOTH HIMSELF WOULD FALL...
AND MONSTERS BY THE HUNDREDS: MY OWN BAND OF RIFFRAFF.
WEREWOLVES
BAD FELLOWS
KILLER MUSHROOMS
ORCS
BRUTES
GORGONS
DEMONS
VAMPIRES
ENDLESS WORMS
ENOUGH SKELETONS AND SPECTERS TO PLAY KNUCKLE-BONES TILL ARMAGEDDON.
KILLER DWARFS
SNOTLINGS
TROLLS
DRAGONS AS OLD AS TIME
I KNOW ALL OF MY BEASTS BY THEIR FIRST NAMES, EACH ONE LIVES IN A SUITABLE HABITAT, I REGULATE THEIR FOOD, LIGHT, AND TEMPERATURE SO THESE SLOBBERING HORDES CAN BE IN TOP FORM.
ADVENTURERS FROM THE WORLD OVER COME TO THIS DUNGEON TO TEST THEMSELVES AGAINST MY MONSTERS, SEEKING WEALTH AND EXPERIENCE. THEY ALL FLOCK HERE TO DIE IN MY HOME.
AND YOU COME HERE WITH YOUR SOCK HEADS DEMANDING THAT I SELL MY DUNGEON?
YOU'RE CRAZY!

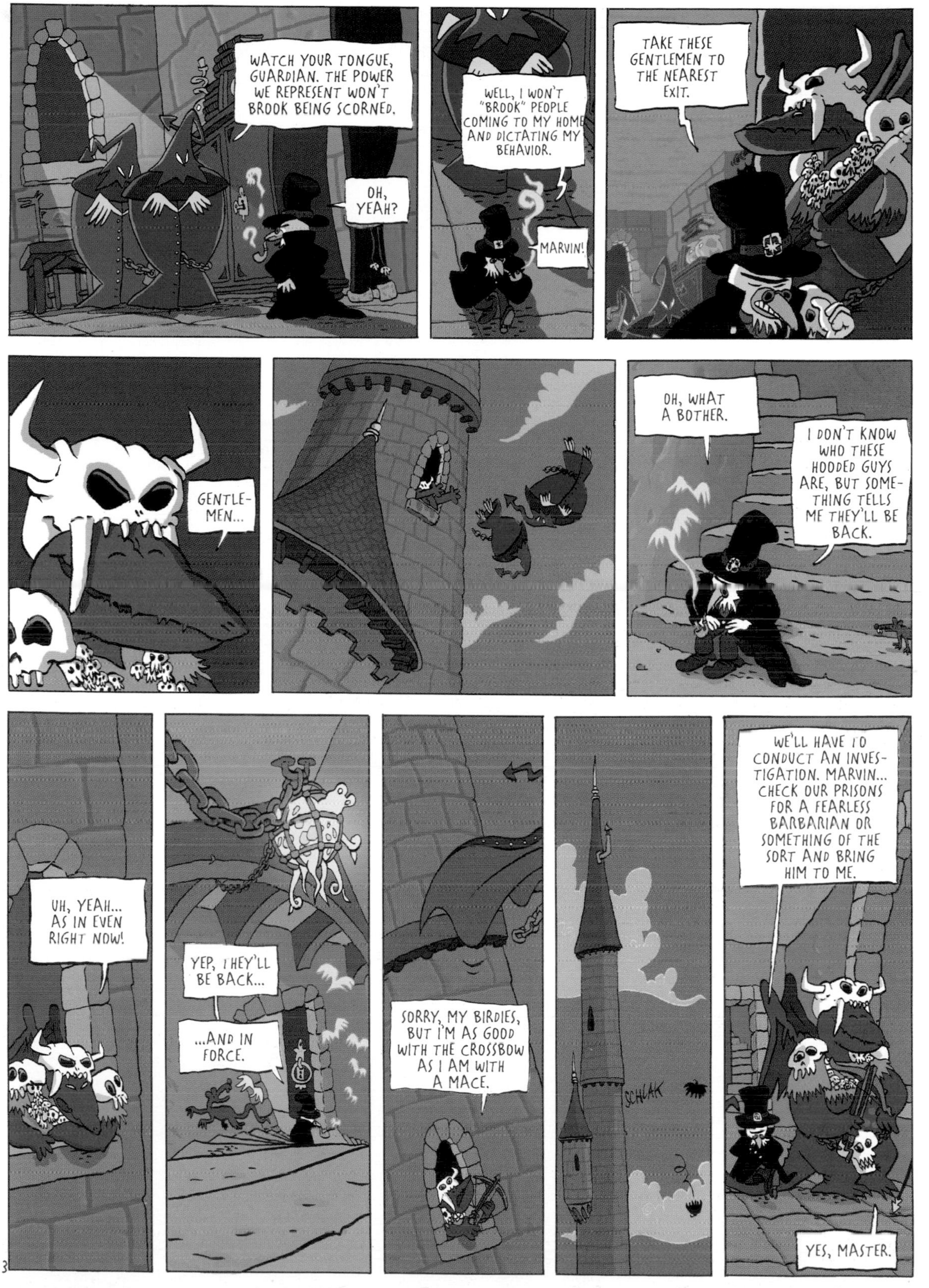
WATCH YOUR TONGUE, GUARDIAN. THE POWER WE REPRESENT WON'T BROOK BEING SCORNED.
OH, YEAH?
WELL, I WON'T "BROOK" PEOPLE COMING TO MY HOME AND DICTATING MY BEHAVIOR.
MARVIN!
TAKE THESE GENTLEMEN TO THE NEAREST EXIT.
GENTLE-MEN...
OH, WHAT A BOTHER.
I DON'T KNOW WHO THESE HOODED GUYS ARE, BUT SOME-THING TELLS ME THEY'LL BE BACK.
UH, YEAH... AS IN EVEN RIGHT NOW!
YEP, THEY'LL BE BACK...
...AND IN FORCE.
SORRY, MY BIRDIES, BUT I'M AS GOOD WITH THE CROSSBOW AS I AM WITH A MACE.
SCHLAK
WE'LL HAVE TO CONDUCT AN INVES-TIGATION. MARVIN... CHECK OUR PRISONS FOR A FEARLESS BARBARIAN OR SOMETHING OF THE SORT AND BRING HIM TO ME.
YES, MASTER.

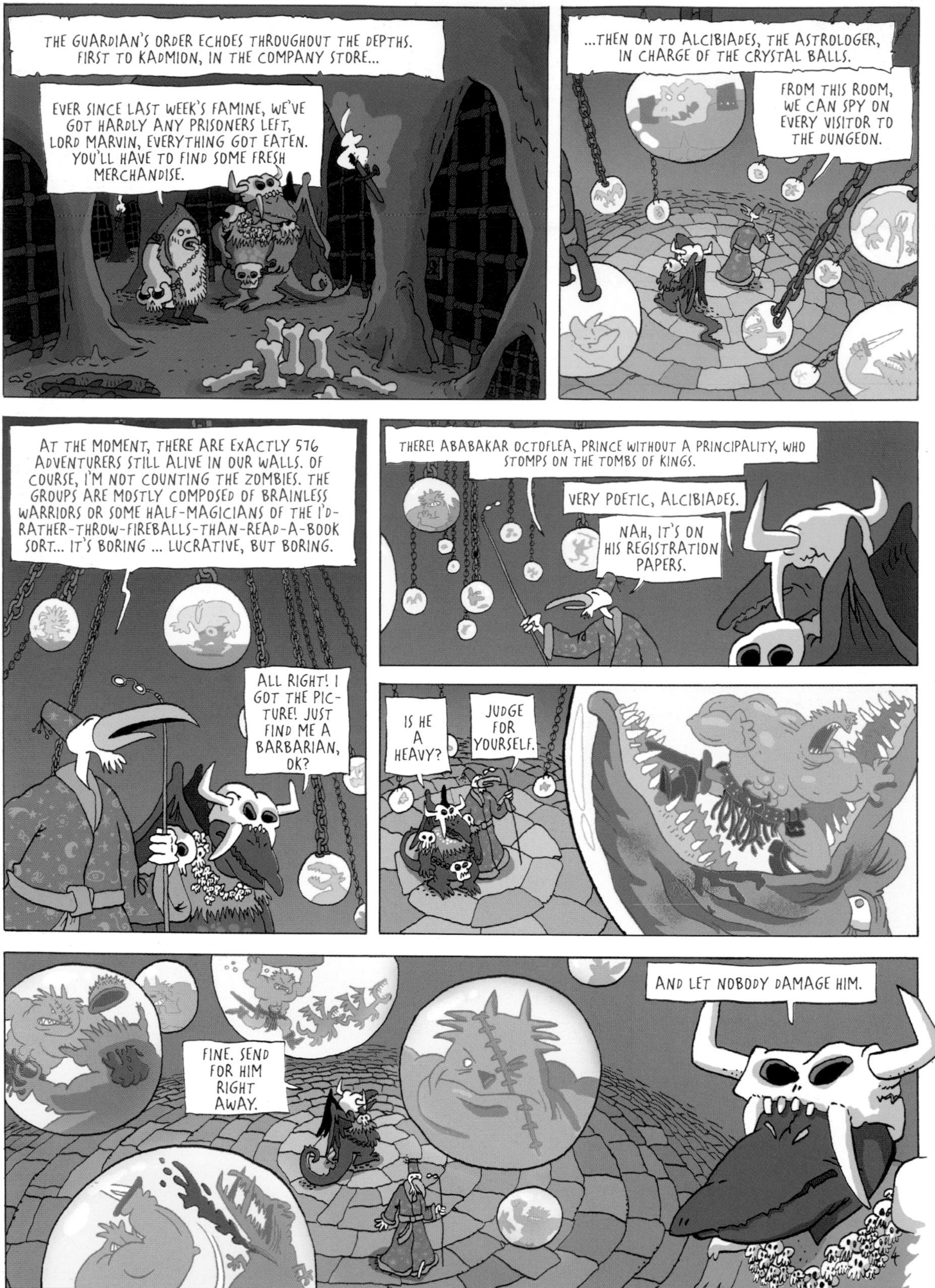
THE GUARDIAN'S ORDER ECHOES THROUGHOUT THE DEPTHS. FIRST TO KADMION, IN THE COMPANY STORE...
EVER SINCE LAST WEEK'S FAMINE, WE'VE GOT HARDLY ANY PRISONERS LEFT, LORD MARVIN, EVERYTHING GOT EATEN. YOU'LL HAVE TO FIND SOME FRESH MERCHANDISE.
...THEN ON TO ALCIBIADES, THE ASTROLOGER, IN CHARGE OF THE CRYSTAL BALLS.
FROM THIS ROOM, WE CAN SPY ON EVERY VISITOR TO THE DUNGEON.
AT THE MOMENT, THERE ARE EXACTLY 576 ADVENTURERS STILL ALIVE IN OUR WALLS. OF COURSE, I'M NOT COUNTING THE ZOMBIES. THE GROUPS ARE MOSTLY COMPOSED OF BRAINLESS WARRIORS OR SOME HALF-MAGICIANS OF THE I'D-RATHER-THROW-FIREBALLS-THAN-READ-A-BOOK SORT... IT'S BORING ... LUCRATIVE, BUT BORING.
ALL RIGHT! I GOT THE PICTURE! JUST FIND ME A BARBARIAN, OK?
THERE! ABABAKAR OCTOFLEA, PRINCE WITHOUT A PRINCIPALITY, WHO STOMPS ON THE TOMBS OF KINGS.
VERY POETIC, ALCIBIADES.
NAH, IT'S ON HIS REGISTRATION PAPERS.
IS HE A HEAVY?
JUDGE FOR YOURSELF.
FINE. SEND FOR HIM RIGHT AWAY.
AND LET NOBODY DAMAGE HIM.
4

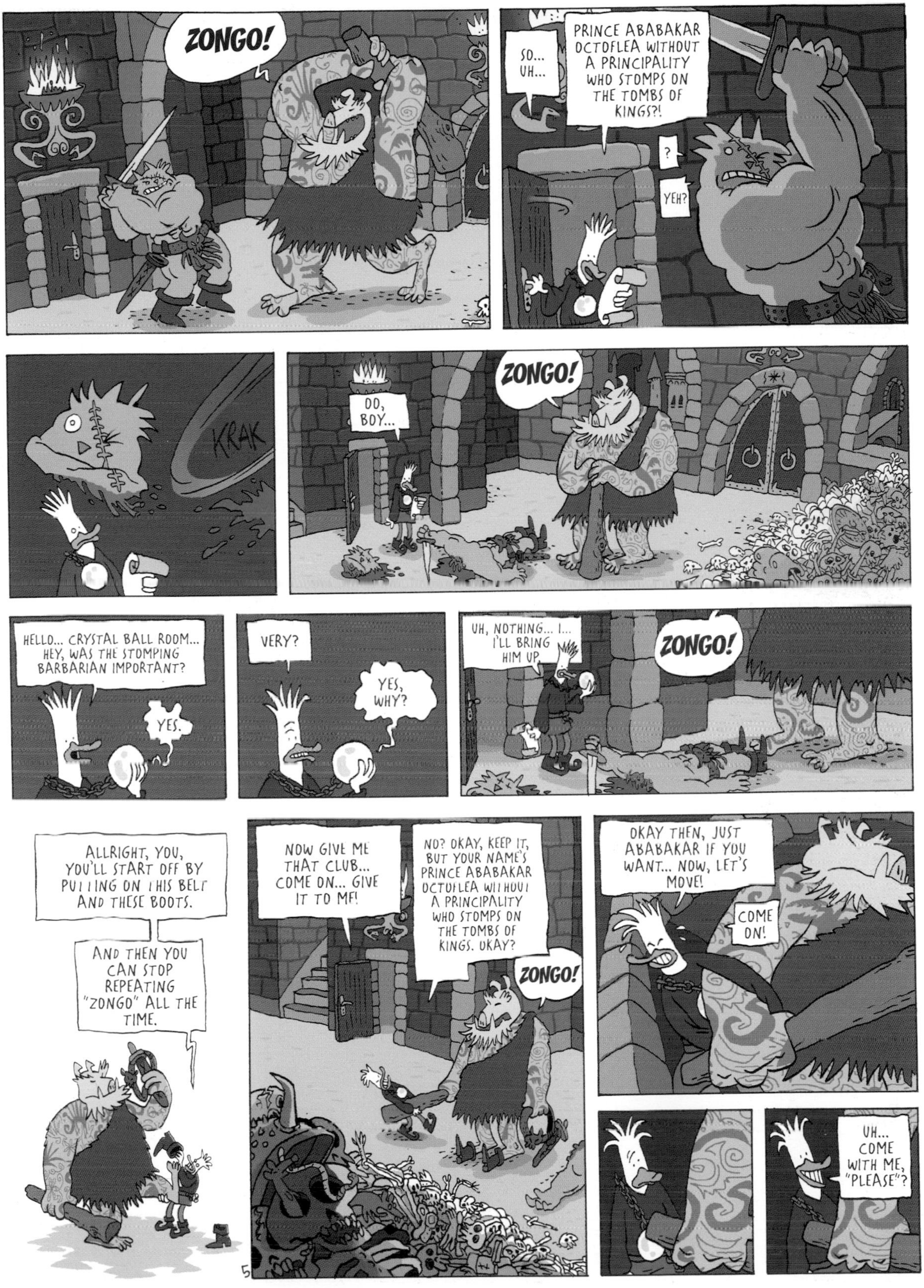
ZONGO!
SO... UH...
PRINCE ABABAKAR OCTOFLEA WITHOUT A PRINCIPALITY WHO STOMPS ON THE TOMBS OF KINGS?!
?
YEH?
KRAK
OO, BOY...
ZONGO!
HELLO... CRYSTAL BALL ROOM... HEY, WAS THE STOMPING BARBARIAN IMPORTANT?
YES.
VERY?
YES, WHY?
UH, NOTHING... I... I'LL BRING HIM UP.
ZONGO!
ALLRIGHT, YOU, YOU'LL START OFF BY PUTTING ON THIS BELT AND THESE BOOTS.
AND THEN YOU CAN STOP REPEATING "ZONGO" ALL THE TIME.
NOW GIVE ME THAT CLUB... COME ON... GIVE IT TO ME!
NO? OKAY, KEEP IT, BUT YOUR NAME'S PRINCE ABABAKAR OCTOFLEA WITHOUT A PRINCIPALITY WHO STOMPS ON THE TOMBS OF KINGS. OKAY?
ZONGO!
OKAY THEN, JUST ABABAKAR IF YOU WANT... NOW, LET'S MOVE!
COME ON!
UH... COME WITH ME, "PLEASE"?

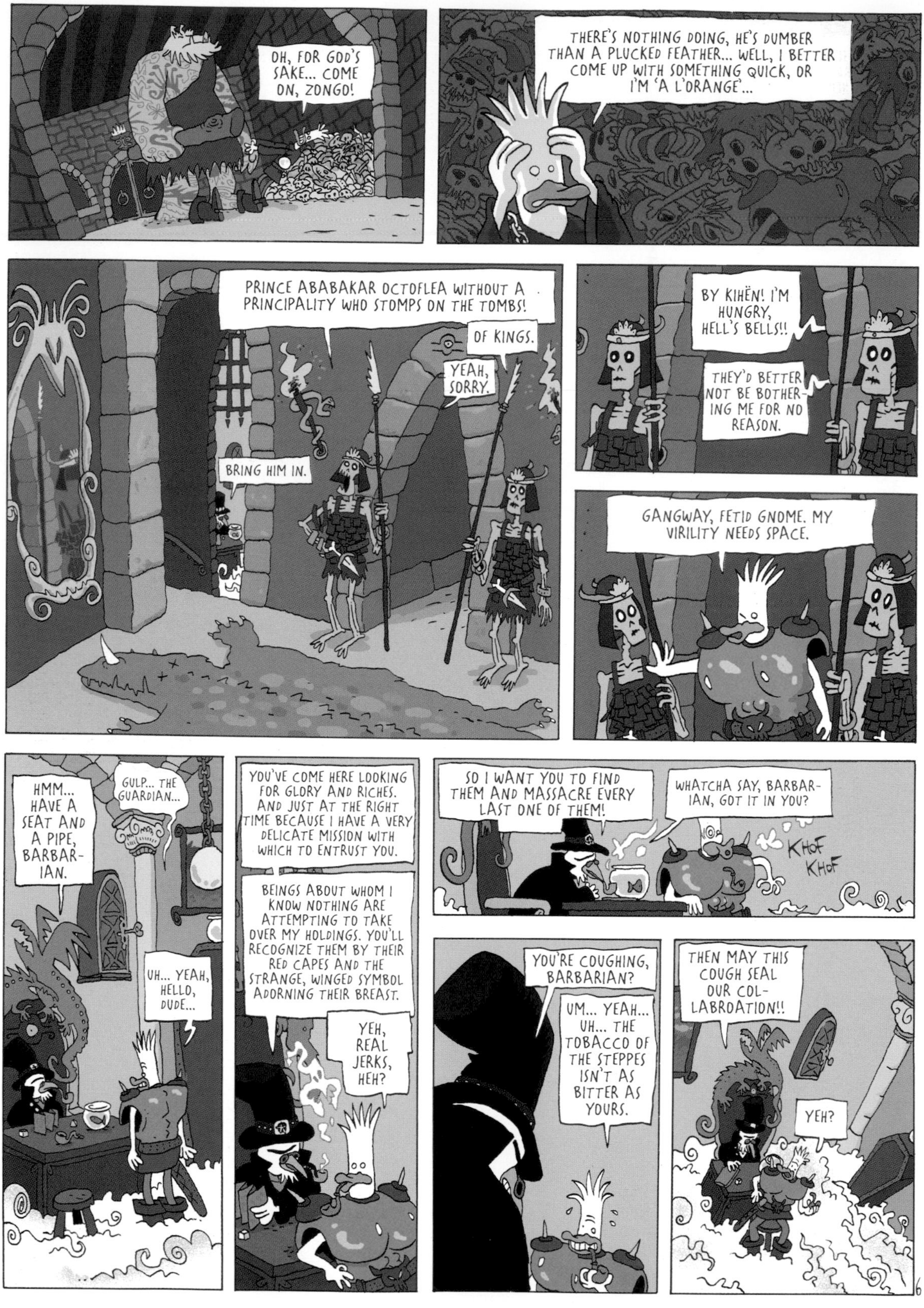

OH, FOR GOD'S SAKE... COME ON, ZONGO!
THERE'S NOTHING DOING, HE'S DUMBER THAN A PLUCKED FEATHER... WELL, I BETTER COME UP WITH SOMETHING QUICK, OR I'M 'A L'ORANGE'...
PRINCE ABABAKAR OCTOFLEA WITHOUT A PRINCIPALITY WHO STOMPS ON THE TOMBS!
OF KINGS.
YEAH, SORRY.
BRING HIM IN.
BY KIHËN! I'M HUNGRY, HELL'S BELLS!!
THEY'D BETTER NOT BE BOTHERING ME FOR NO REASON.
GANGWAY, FETID GNOME. MY VIRILITY NEEDS SPACE.
HMM... HAVE A SEAT AND A PIPE, BARBARIAN.
GULP... THE GUARDIAN...
UH... YEAH, HELLO, DUDE...
YOU'VE COME HERE LOOKING FOR GLORY AND RICHES. AND JUST AT THE RIGHT TIME BECAUSE I HAVE A VERY DELICATE MISSION WITH WHICH TO ENTRUST YOU.
BEINGS ABOUT WHOM I KNOW NOTHING ARE ATTEMPTING TO TAKE OVER MY HOLDINGS. YOU'LL RECOGNIZE THEM BY THEIR RED CAPES AND THE STRANGE, WINGED SYMBOL ADORNING THEIR BREAST.
YEH, REAL JERKS, HEH?
SO I WANT YOU TO FIND THEM AND MASSACRE EVERY LAST ONE OF THEM!
WHATCHA SAY, BARBARIAN, GOT IT IN YOU?
KHOF KHOF
YOU'RE COUGHING, BARBARIAN?
UM... YEAH... UH... THE TOBACCO OF THE STEPPES ISN'T AS BITTER AS YOURS.
THEN MAY THIS COUGH SEAL OUR COLLABROATION!!
YEH?

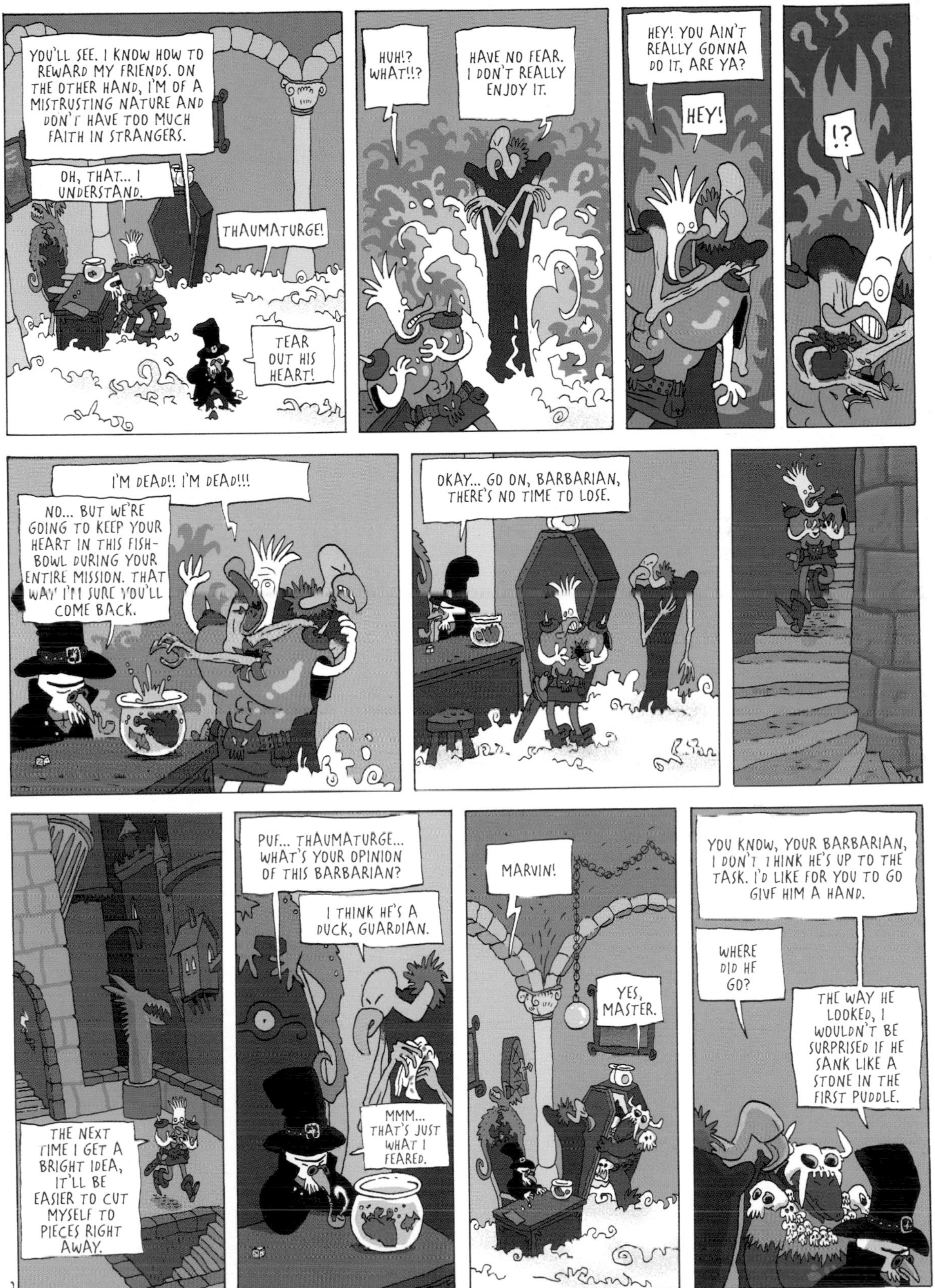
YOU'LL SEE. I KNOW HOW TO REWARD MY FRIENDS. ON THE OTHER HAND, I'M OF A MISTRUSTING NATURE AND DON'T HAVE TOO MUCH FAITH IN STRANGERS.
OH, THAT... I UNDERSTAND.
THAUMATURGE!
TEAR OUT HIS HEART!
HUH!? WHAT!!?
HAVE NO FEAR. I DON'T REALLY ENJOY IT.
HEY! YOU AIN'T REALLY GONNA DO IT, ARE YA?
HEY!
!?
I'M DEAD!! I'M DEAD!!!
NO... BUT WE'RE GOING TO KEEP YOUR HEART IN THIS FISH-BOWL DURING YOUR ENTIRE MISSION. THAT WAY I'M SURE YOU'LL COME BACK.
OKAY... GO ON, BARBARIAN, THERE'S NO TIME TO LOSE.
THE NEXT TIME I GET A BRIGHT IDEA, IT'LL BE EASIER TO CUT MYSELF TO PIECES RIGHT AWAY.
PUF... THAUMATURGE... WHAT'S YOUR OPINION OF THIS BARBARIAN?
I THINK HE'S A DUCK, GUARDIAN.
MMM... THAT'S JUST WHAT I FEARED.
MARVIN!
YES, MASTER.
YOU KNOW, YOUR BARBARIAN, I DON'T THINK HE'S UP TO THE TASK. I'D LIKE FOR YOU TO GO GIVE HIM A HAND.
WHERE DID HE GO?
THE WAY HE LOOKED, I WOULDN'T BE SURPRISED IF HE SANK LIKE A STONE IN THE FIRST PUDDLE.

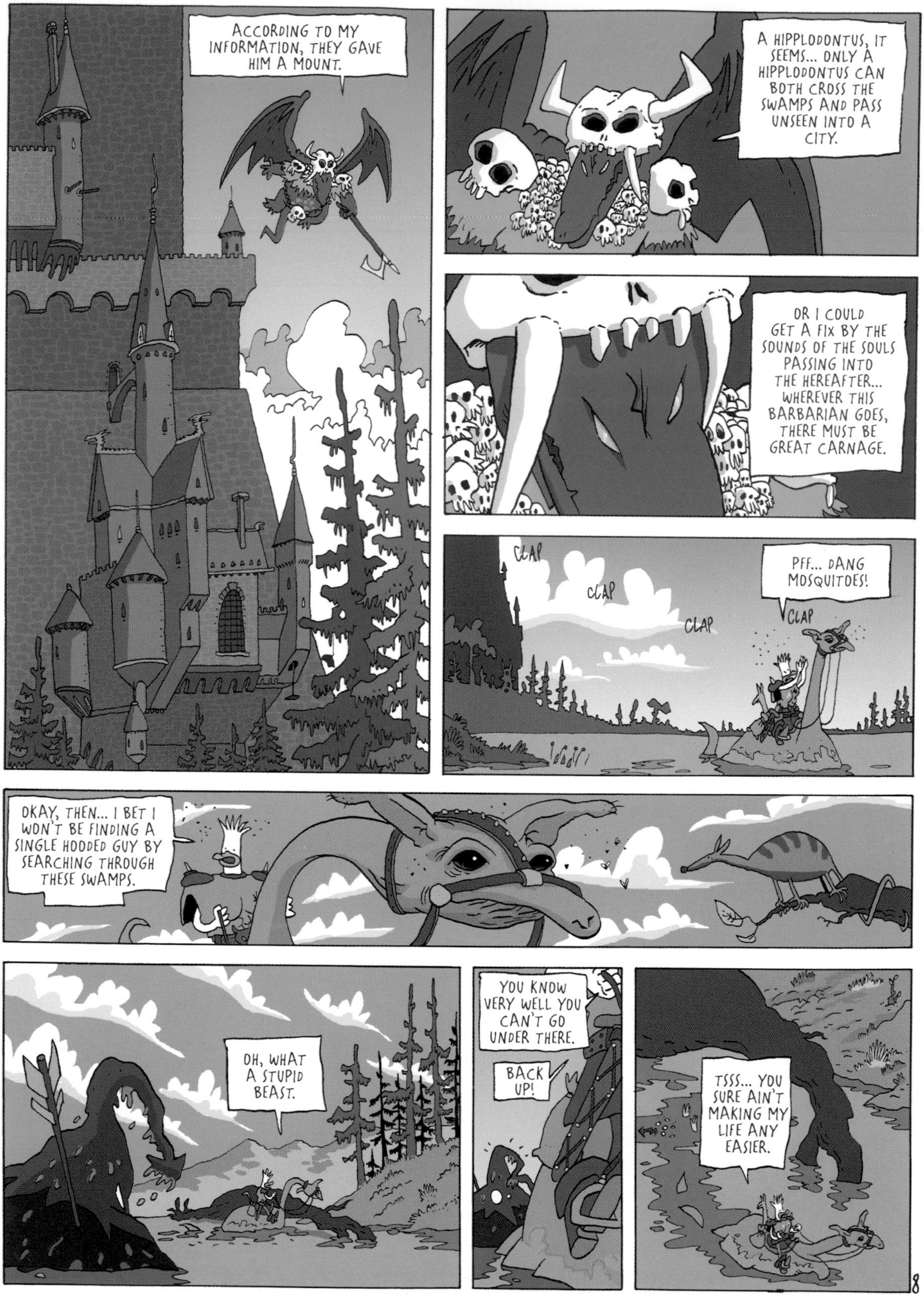
ACCORDING TO MY INFORMATION, THEY GAVE HIM A MOUNT.
A HIPPLODONTUS, IT SEEMS... ONLY A HIPPLODONTUS CAN BOTH CROSS THE SWAMPS AND PASS UNSEEN INTO A CITY.
OR I COULD GET A FIX BY THE SOUNDS OF THE SOULS PASSING INTO THE HEREAFTER... WHEREVER THIS BARBARIAN GOES, THERE MUST BE GREAT CARNAGE.
CLAP
CLAP
CLAP
PFF... DANG MOSQUITOES!
CLAP
OKAY, THEN... I BET I WON'T BE FINDING A SINGLE HOODED GUY BY SEARCHING THROUGH THESE SWAMPS.
OH, WHAT A STUPID BEAST.
YOU KNOW VERY WELL YOU CAN'T GO UNDER THERE.
BACK UP!
TSSS... YOU SURE AIN'T MAKING MY LIFE ANY EASIER.

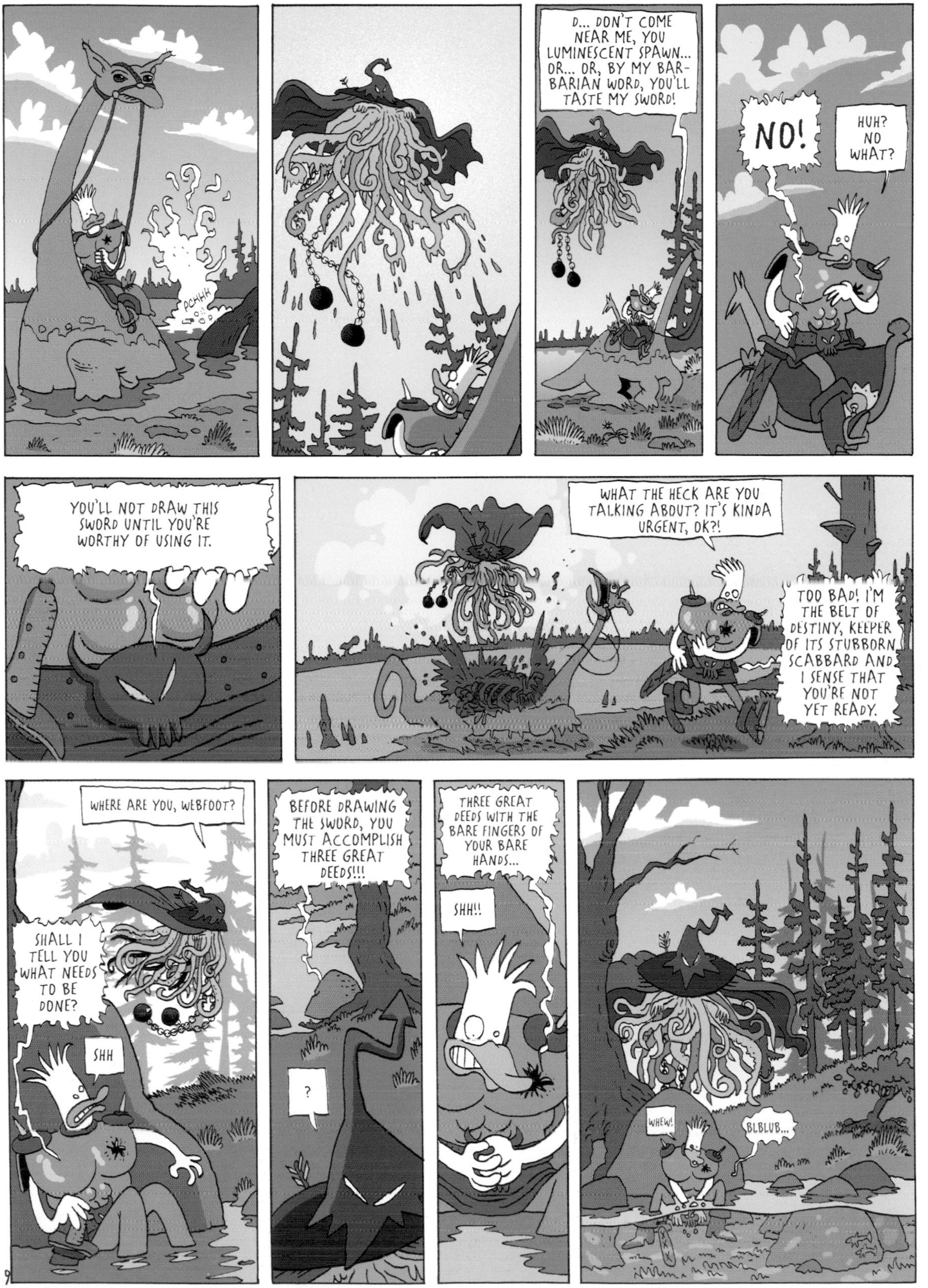
PCHHH
D... DON'T COME NEAR ME, YOU LUMINESCENT SPAWN... OR... OR, BY MY BARBARIAN WORD, YOU'LL TASTE MY SWORD!
NO!
HUH? NO WHAT?
YOU'LL NOT DRAW THIS SWORD UNTIL YOU'RE WORTHY OF USING IT.
WHAT THE HECK ARE YOU TALKING ABOUT? IT'S KINDA URGENT, OK?!
TOO BAD! I'M THE BELT OF DESTINY, KEEPER OF ITS STUBBORN SCABBARD AND I SENSE THAT YOU'RE NOT YET READY.
WHERE ARE YOU, WEBFOOT?
SHALL I TELL YOU WHAT NEEDS TO BE DONE?
SHH
BEFORE DRAWING THE SWORD, YOU MUST ACCOMPLISH THREE GREAT DEEDS!!!
?
THREE GREAT DEEDS WITH THE BARE FINGERS OF YOUR BARE HANDS...
SHH!!
WHEW!
BLBLUB...

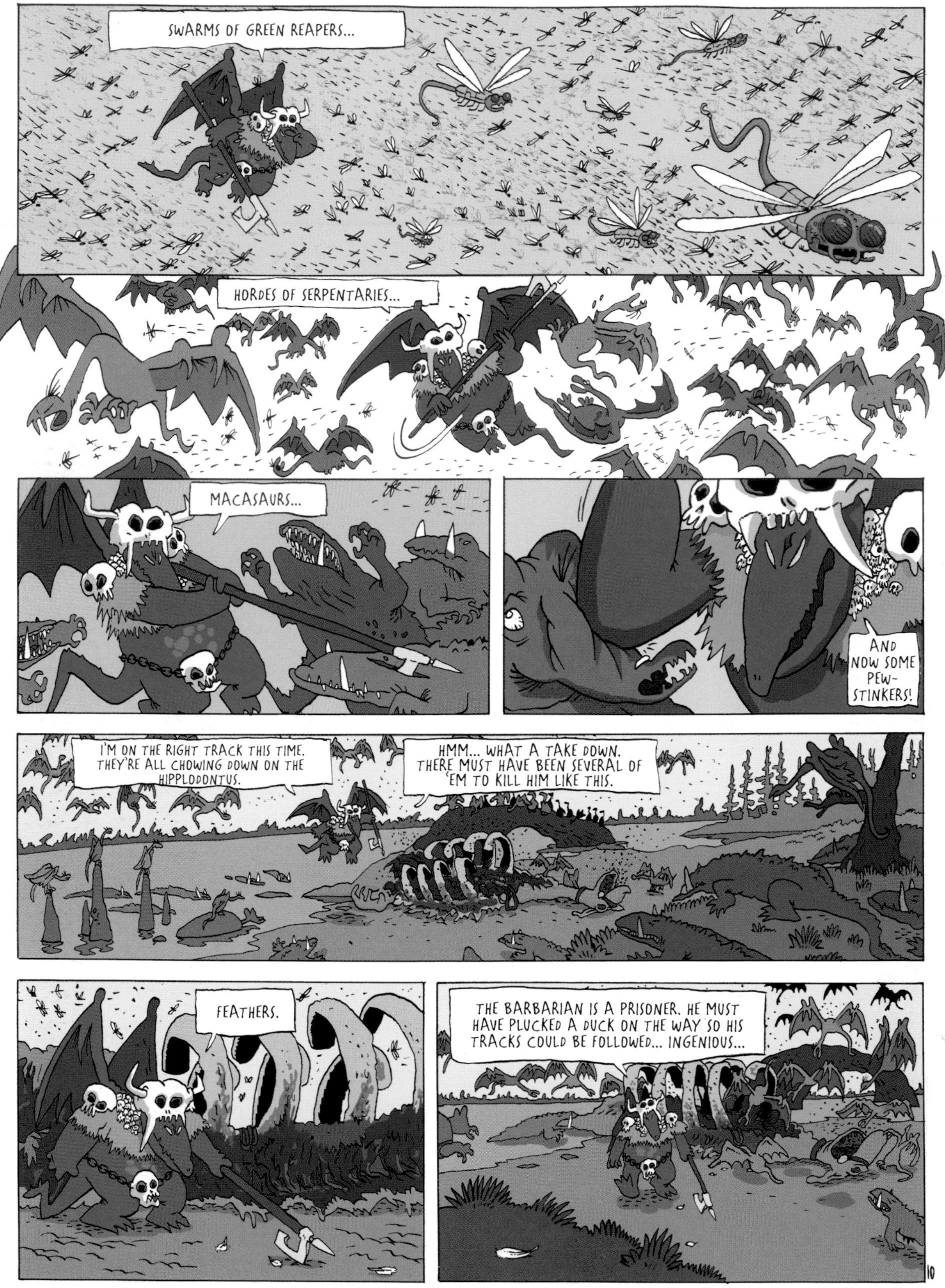
SWARMS OF GREEN REAPERS...
HORDES OF SERPENTARIES...
MACASAURS...
AND NOW SOME PEW-STINKERS!
I'M ON THE RIGHT TRACK THIS TIME. THEY'RE ALL CHOWING DOWN ON THE HIPPLODONTUS.
HMM... WHAT A TAKE DOWN. THERE MUST HAVE BEEN SEVERAL OF 'EM TO KILL HIM LIKE THIS.
FEATHERS.
THE BARBARIAN IS A PRISONER. HE MUST HAVE PLUCKED A DUCK ON THE WAY SO HIS TRACKS COULD BE FOLLOWED... INGENIOUS...

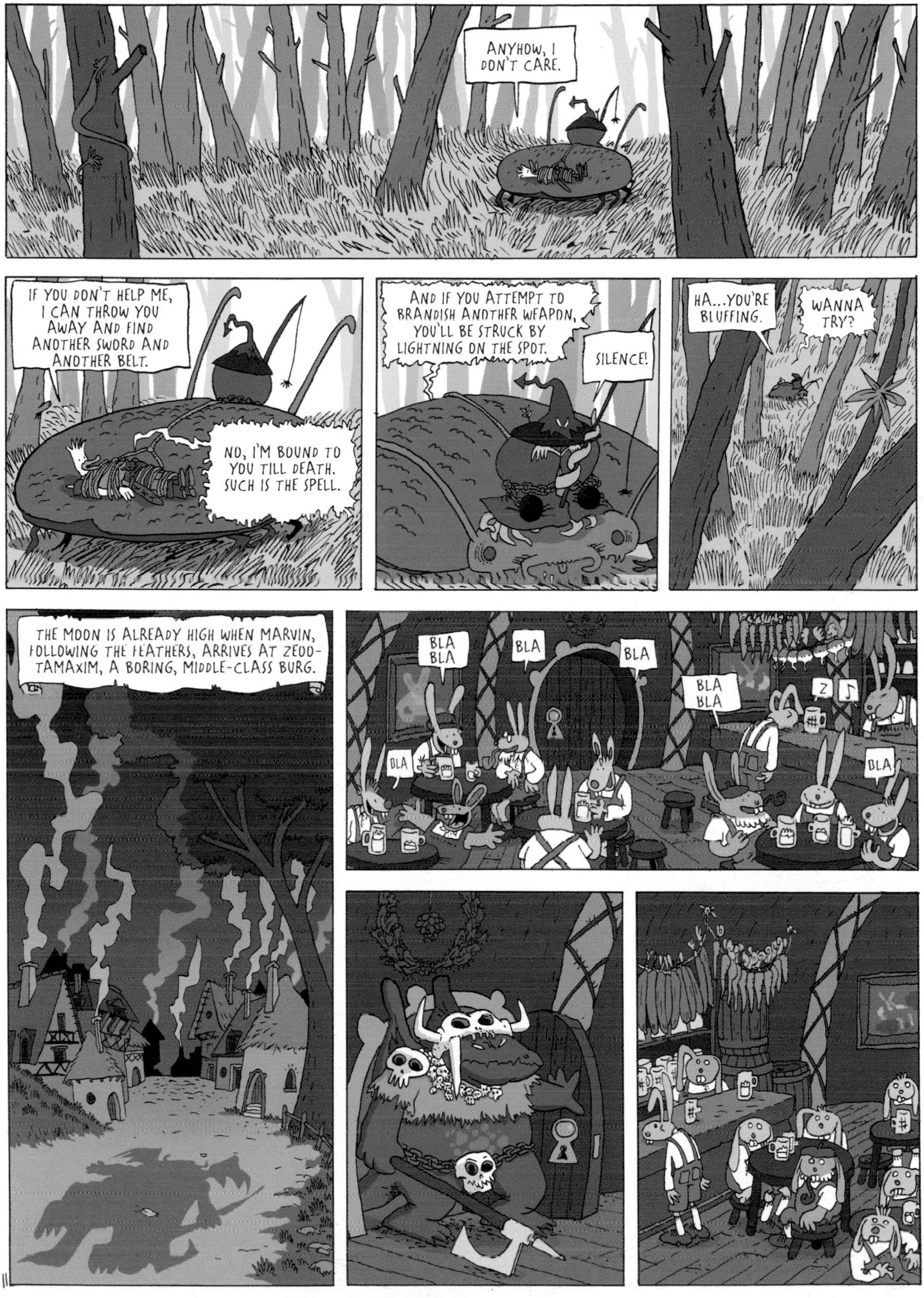
ANYHOW, I DON'T CARE.
IF YOU DON'T HELP ME, I CAN THROW YOU AWAY AND FIND ANOTHER SWORD AND ANOTHER BELT.
NO, I'M BOUND TO YOU TILL DEATH. SUCH IS THE SPELL.
AND IF YOU ATTEMPT TO BRANDISH ANOTHER WEAPON, YOU'LL BE STRUCK BY LIGHTNING ON THE SPOT.
SILENCE!
HA...YOU'RE BLUFFING.
WANNA TRY?
THE MOON IS ALREADY HIGH WHEN MARVIN, FOLLOWING THE FEATHERS, ARRIVES AT ZEDD-TAMAXIM, A BORING, MIDDLE-CLASS BURG.
BLA BLA
BLA
BLA
BLA BLA
Z ♪
BLA
BLA

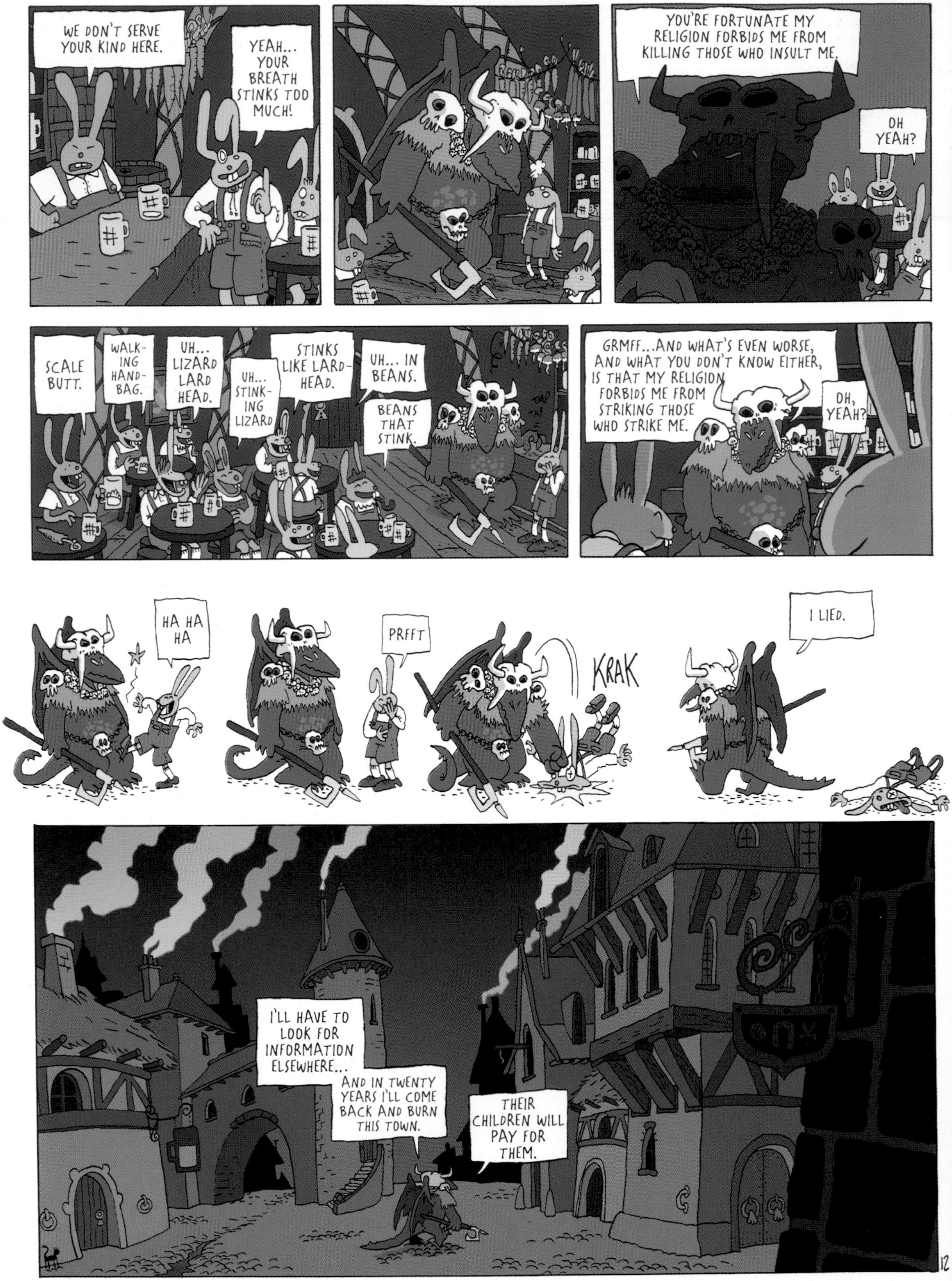
WE DON'T SERVE YOUR KIND HERE.
YEAH... YOUR BREATH STINKS TOO MUCH!
YOU'RE FORTUNATE MY RELIGION FORBIDS ME FROM KILLING THOSE WHO INSULT ME.
OH YEAH?
SCALE BUTT.
WALK-ING HAND-BAG.
UH... LIZARD LARD HEAD.
UH... STINK-ING LIZARD
STINKS LIKE LARD-HEAD.
UH... IN BEANS.
BEANS THAT STINK.
GRMFF...AND WHAT'S EVEN WORSE, AND WHAT YOU DON'T KNOW EITHER, IS THAT MY RELIGION FORBIDS ME FROM STRIKING THOSE WHO STRIKE ME.
OH, YEAH?
HA HA HA
PRFFT
KRAK
I LIED.
I'LL HAVE TO LOOK FOR INFORMATION ELSEWHERE...
AND IN TWENTY YEARS I'LL COME BACK AND BURN THIS TOWN.
THEIR CHILDREN WILL PAY FOR THEM.

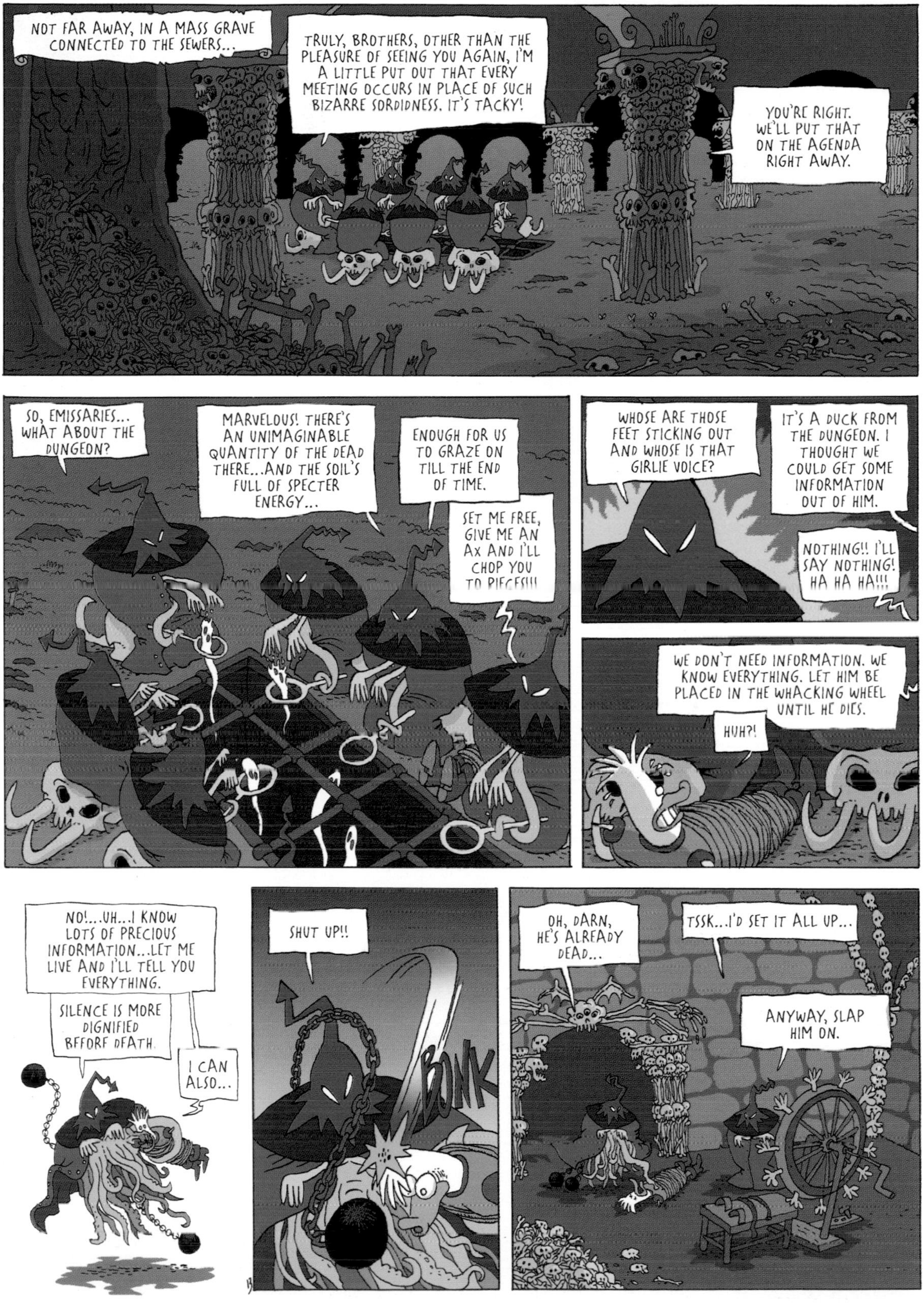
NOT FAR AWAY, IN A MASS GRAVE CONNECTED TO THE SEWERS...
TRULY, BROTHERS, OTHER THAN THE PLEASURE OF SEEING YOU AGAIN, I'M A LITTLE PUT OUT THAT EVERY MEETING OCCURS IN PLACE OF SUCH BIZARRE SORDIDNESS. IT'S TACKY!
YOU'RE RIGHT. WE'LL PUT THAT ON THE AGENDA RIGHT AWAY.
SO, EMISSARIES... WHAT ABOUT THE DUNGEON?
MARVELOUS! THERE'S AN UNIMAGINABLE QUANTITY OF THE DEAD THERE...AND THE SOIL'S FULL OF SPECTER ENERGY...
ENOUGH FOR US TO GRAZE ON TILL THE END OF TIME.
SET ME FREE, GIVE ME AN AX AND I'LL CHOP YOU TO PIECES!!!
WHOSE ARE THOSE FEET STICKING OUT AND WHOSE IS THAT GIRLIE VOICE?
IT'S A DUCK FROM THE DUNGEON. I THOUGHT WE COULD GET SOME INFORMATION OUT OF HIM.
NOTHING!! I'LL SAY NOTHING! HA HA HA!!!
WE DON'T NEED INFORMATION. WE KNOW EVERYTHING. LET HIM BE PLACED IN THE WHACKING WHEEL UNTIL HE DIES.
HUH?!
NO!...UH...I KNOW LOTS OF PRECIOUS INFORMATION...LET ME LIVE AND I'LL TELL YOU EVERYTHING.
SILENCE IS MORE DIGNIFIED BEFORE DEATH.
I CAN ALSO...
SHUT UP!!
BONK
OH, DARN, HE'S ALREADY DEAD...
TSSK...I'D SET IT ALL UP...
ANYWAY, SLAP HIM ON.

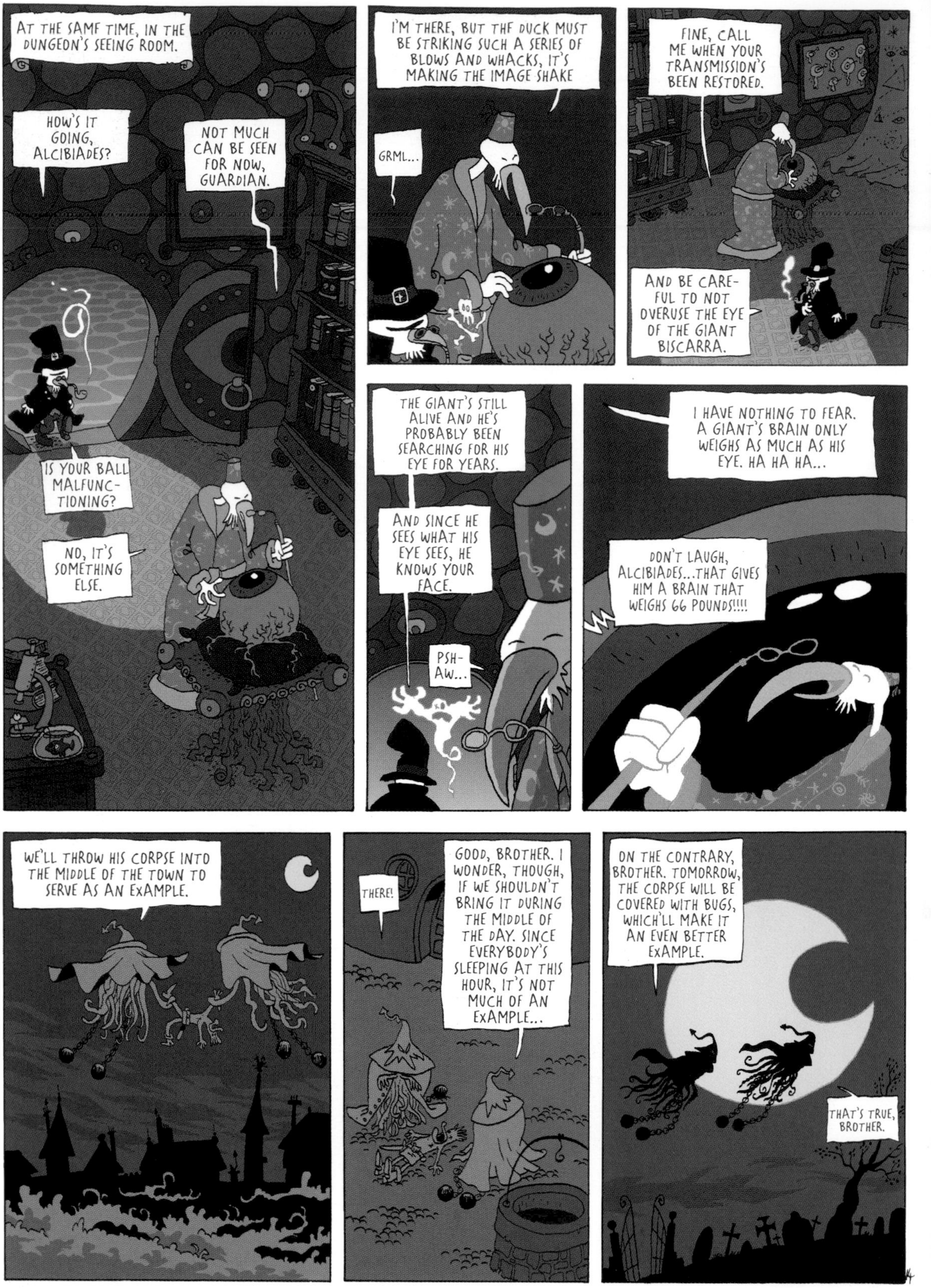
AT THE SAME TIME, IN THE DUNGEON'S SEEING ROOM.
HOW'S IT GOING, ALCIBIADES?
NOT MUCH CAN BE SEEN FOR NOW, GUARDIAN.
IS YOUR BALL MALFUNCTIONING?
NO, IT'S SOMETHING ELSE.
I'M THERE, BUT THE DUCK MUST BE STRIKING SUCH A SERIES OF BLOWS AND WHACKS, IT'S MAKING THE IMAGE SHAKE
GRML...
FINE, CALL ME WHEN YOUR TRANSMISSION'S BEEN RESTORED.
AND BE CAREFUL TO NOT OVERUSE THE EYE OF THE GIANT BISCARRA.
THE GIANT'S STILL ALIVE AND HE'S PROBABLY BEEN SEARCHING FOR HIS EYE FOR YEARS.
AND SINCE HE SEES WHAT HIS EYE SEES, HE KNOWS YOUR FACE.
PSH-AW...
I HAVE NOTHING TO FEAR. A GIANT'S BRAIN ONLY WEIGHS AS MUCH AS HIS EYE. HA HA HA...
DON'T LAUGH, ALCIBIADES...THAT GIVES HIM A BRAIN THAT WEIGHS 66 POUNDS!!!!
WE'LL THROW HIS CORPSE INTO THE MIDDLE OF THE TOWN TO SERVE AS AN EXAMPLE.
THERE!
GOOD, BROTHER. I WONDER, THOUGH, IF WE SHOULDN'T BRING IT DURING THE MIDDLE OF THE DAY. SINCE EVERYBODY'S SLEEPING AT THIS HOUR, IT'S NOT MUCH OF AN EXAMPLE...
ON THE CONTRARY, BROTHER. TOMORROW, THE CORPSE WILL BE COVERED WITH BUGS, WHICH'LL MAKE IT AN EVEN BETTER EXAMPLE.
THAT'S TRUE, BROTHER.

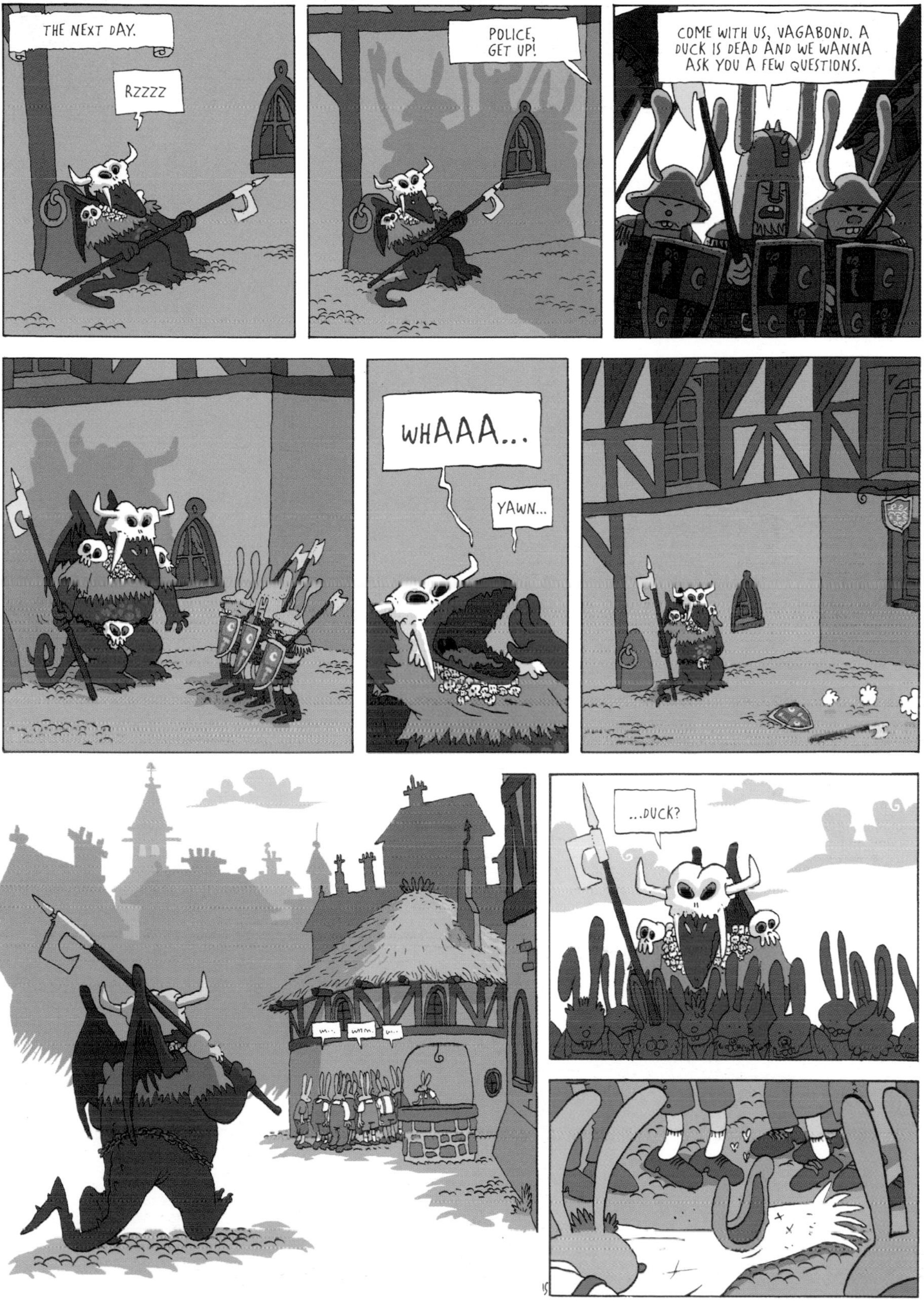
THE NEXT DAY.
RZZZZ
POLICE, GET UP!
COME WITH US, VAGABOND. A DUCK IS DEAD AND WE WANNA ASK YOU A FEW QUESTIONS.
WHAAA...
YAWN...
...DUCK?

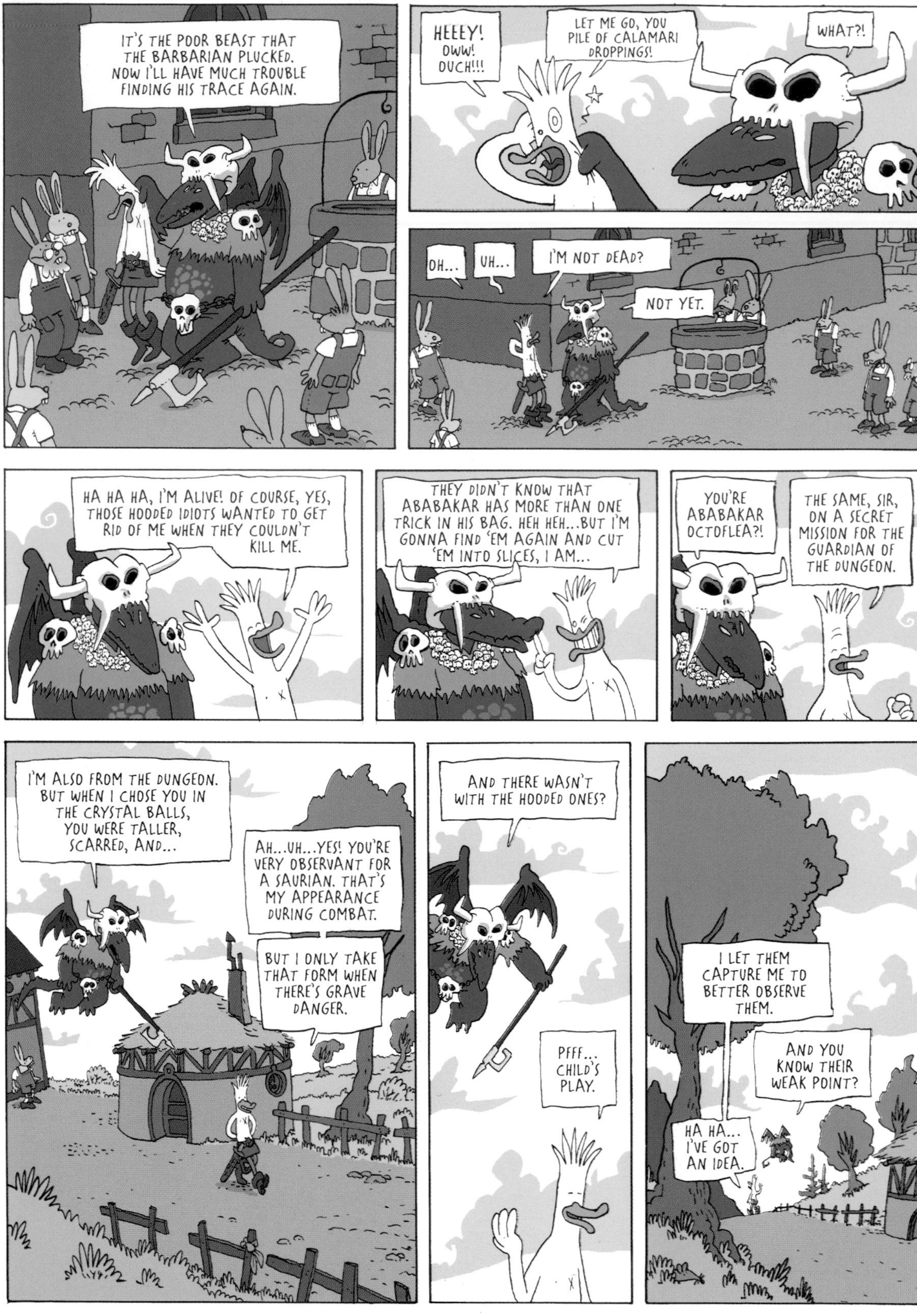
IT'S THE POOR BEAST THAT THE BARBARIAN PLUCKED. NOW I'LL HAVE MUCH TROUBLE FINDING HIS TRACE AGAIN.
HEEEY! OWW! OUCH!!!
LET ME GO, YOU PILE OF CALAMARI DROPPINGS!
WHAT?!
OH...
UH...
I'M NOT DEAD?
NOT YET.
HA HA HA, I'M ALIVE! OF COURSE, YES, THOSE HOODED IDIOTS WANTED TO GET RID OF ME WHEN THEY COULDN'T KILL ME.
THEY DIDN'T KNOW THAT ABABAKAR HAS MORE THAN ONE TRICK IN HIS BAG. HEH HEH...BUT I'M GONNA FIND 'EM AGAIN AND CUT 'EM INTO SLICES, I AM...
YOU'RE ABABAKAR OCTOFLEA?!
THE SAME, SIR, ON A SECRET MISSION FOR THE GUARDIAN OF THE DUNGEON.
I'M ALSO FROM THE DUNGEON. BUT WHEN I CHOSE YOU IN THE CRYSTAL BALLS, YOU WERE TALLER, SCARRED, AND...
AH...UH...YES! YOU'RE VERY OBSERVANT FOR A SAURIAN. THAT'S MY APPEARANCE DURING COMBAT.
BUT I ONLY TAKE THAT FORM WHEN THERE'S GRAVE DANGER.
AND THERE WASN'T WITH THE HOODED ONES?
PFFF... CHILD'S PLAY.
I LET THEM CAPTURE ME TO BETTER OBSERVE THEM.
AND YOU KNOW THEIR WEAK POINT?
HA HA... I'VE GOT AN IDEA.

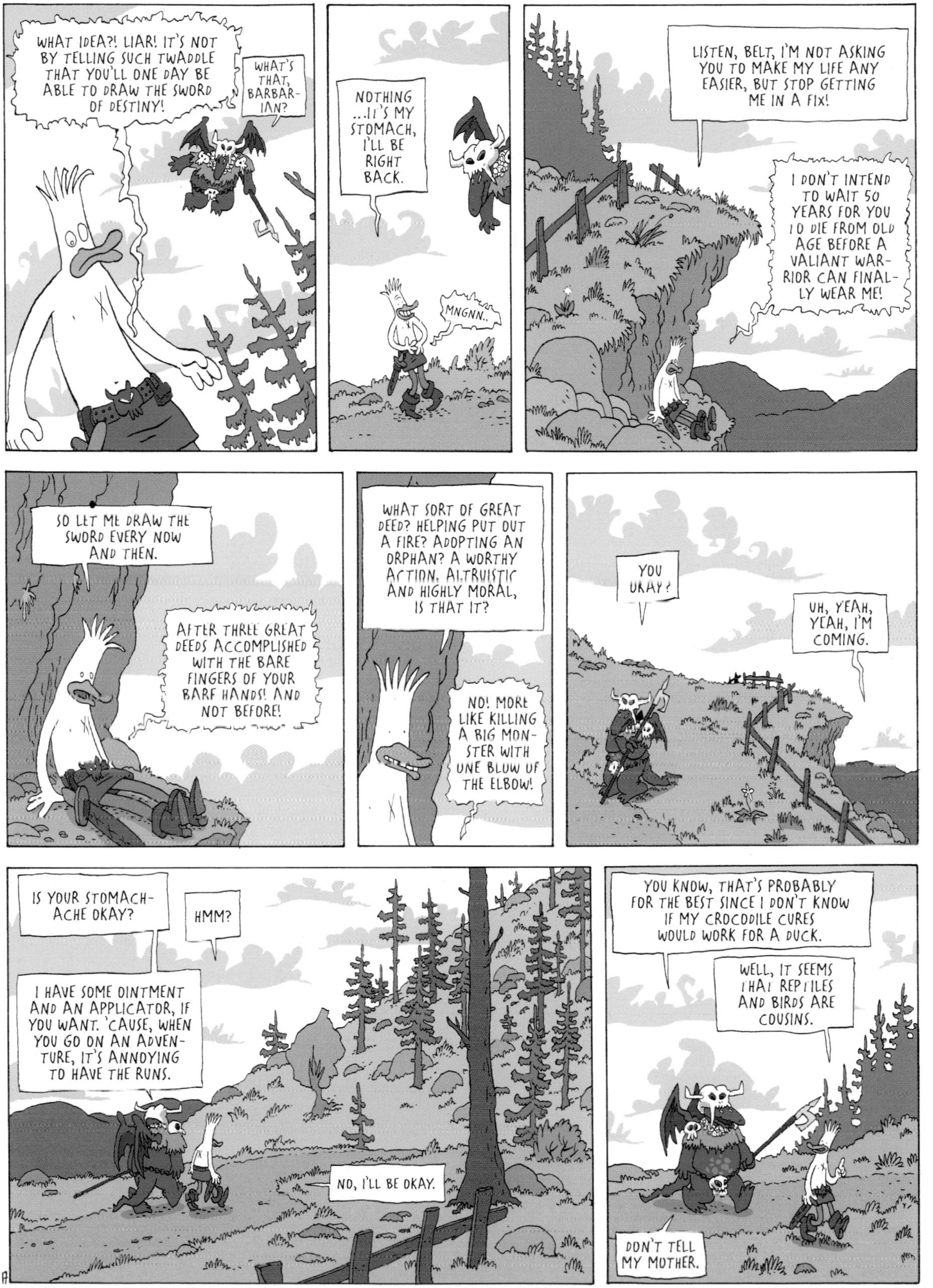
WHAT IDEA?! LIAR! IT'S NOT BY TELLING SUCH TWADDLE THAT YOU'LL ONE DAY BE ABLE TO DRAW THE SWORD OF DESTINY!
WHAT'S THAT, BARBARIAN?
NOTHING ...IT'S MY STOMACH, I'LL BE RIGHT BACK.
MNGNN..
LISTEN, BELT, I'M NOT ASKING YOU TO MAKE MY LIFE ANY EASIER, BUT STOP GETTING ME IN A FIX!
I DON'T INTEND TO WAIT 50 YEARS FOR YOU TO DIE FROM OLD AGE BEFORE A VALIANT WARRIOR CAN FINALLY WEAR ME!
SO LET ME DRAW THE SWORD EVERY NOW AND THEN.
AFTER THREE GREAT DEEDS ACCOMPLISHED WITH THE BARE FINGERS OF YOUR BARE HANDS! AND NOT BEFORE!
WHAT SORT OF GREAT DEED? HELPING PUT OUT A FIRE? ADOPTING AN ORPHAN? A WORTHY ACTION, ALTRUISTIC AND HIGHLY MORAL, IS THAT IT?
NO! MORE LIKE KILLING A BIG MONSTER WITH ONE BLOW OF THE ELBOW!
YOU OKAY?
UH, YEAH, YEAH, I'M COMING.
IS YOUR STOMACHACHE OKAY?
HMM?
I HAVE SOME OINTMENT AND AN APPLICATOR, IF YOU WANT. 'CAUSE, WHEN YOU GO ON AN ADVENTURE, IT'S ANNOYING TO HAVE THE RUNS.
NO, I'LL BE OKAY.
YOU KNOW, THAT'S PROBABLY FOR THE BEST SINCE I DON'T KNOW IF MY CROCODILE CURES WOULD WORK FOR A DUCK.
WELL, IT SEEMS THAT REPTILES AND BIRDS ARE COUSINS.
DON'T TELL MY MOTHER.

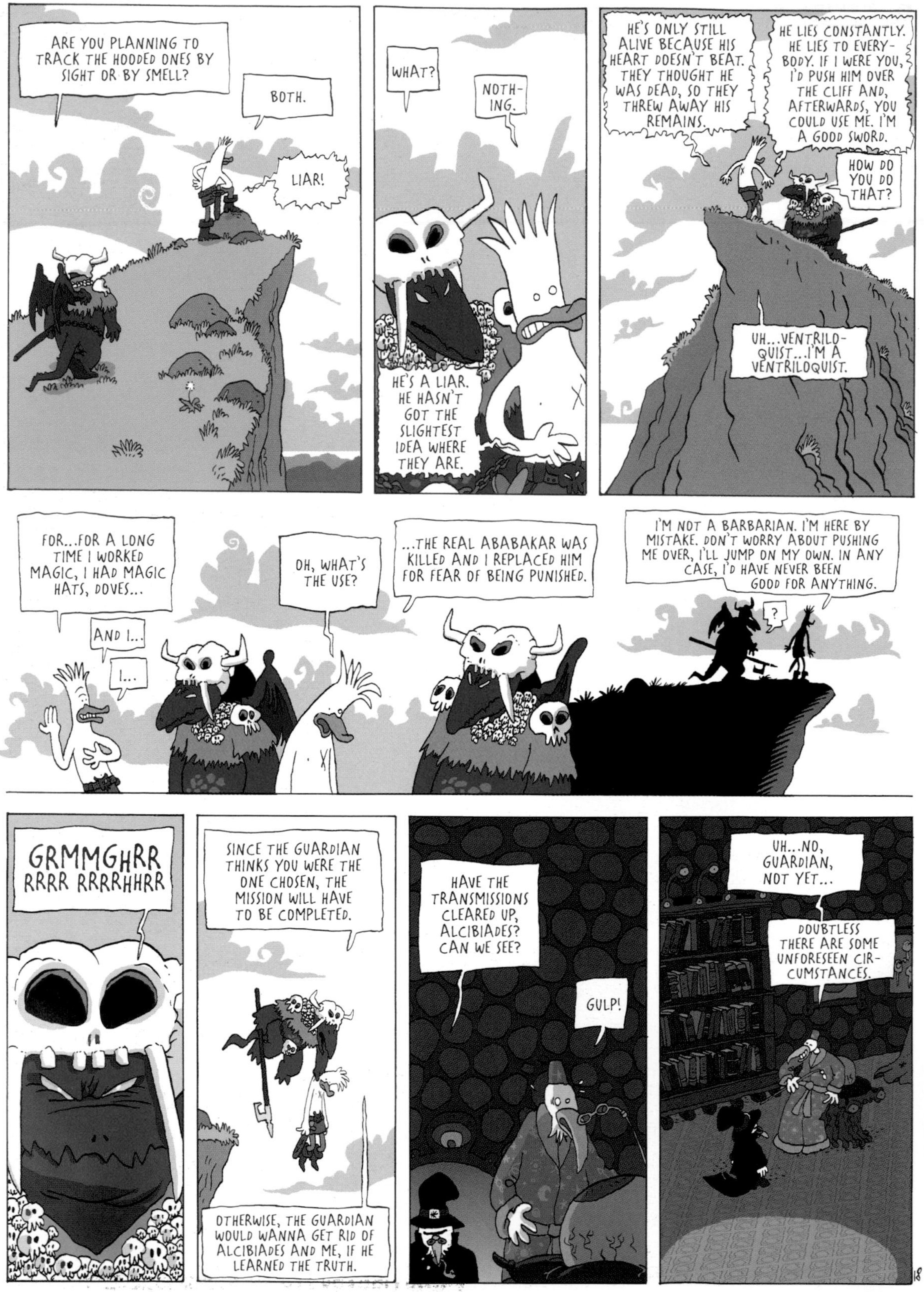

ARE YOU PLANNING TO TRACK THE HOODED ONES BY SIGHT OR BY SMELL?
BOTH.
LIAR!
WHAT?
NOTHING.
HE'S A LIAR. HE HASN'T GOT THE SLIGHTEST IDEA WHERE THEY ARE.
HE'S ONLY STILL ALIVE BECAUSE HIS HEART DOESN'T BEAT. THEY THOUGHT HE WAS DEAD, SO THEY THREW AWAY HIS REMAINS.
HE LIES CONSTANTLY. HE LIES TO EVERYBODY. IF I WERE YOU, I'D PUSH HIM OVER THE CLIFF AND, AFTERWARDS, YOU COULD USE ME. I'M A GOOD SWORD.
HOW DO YOU DO THAT?
UH...VENTRILOQUIST...I'M A VENTRILOQUIST.
FOR...FOR A LONG TIME I WORKED MAGIC, I HAD MAGIC HATS, DOVES...
AND I...
I...
OH, WHAT'S THE USE?
...THE REAL ABABAKAR WAS KILLED AND I REPLACED HIM FOR FEAR OF BEING PUNISHED.
I'M NOT A BARBARIAN. I'M HERE BY MISTAKE. DON'T WORRY ABOUT PUSHING ME OVER, I'LL JUMP ON MY OWN. IN ANY CASE, I'D HAVE NEVER BEEN GOOD FOR ANYTHING.
?
GRMMGHRR RRRR RRRRHHRR
SINCE THE GUARDIAN THINKS YOU WERE THE ONE CHOSEN, THE MISSION WILL HAVE TO BE COMPLETED.
OTHERWISE, THE GUARDIAN WOULD WANNA GET RID OF ALCIBIADES AND ME, IF HE LEARNED THE TRUTH.
HAVE THE TRANSMISSIONS CLEARED UP, ALCIBIADES? CAN WE SEE?
GULP!
UH...NO, GUARDIAN, NOT YET...
DOUBTLESS THERE ARE SOME UNFORESEEN CIRCUMSTANCES.

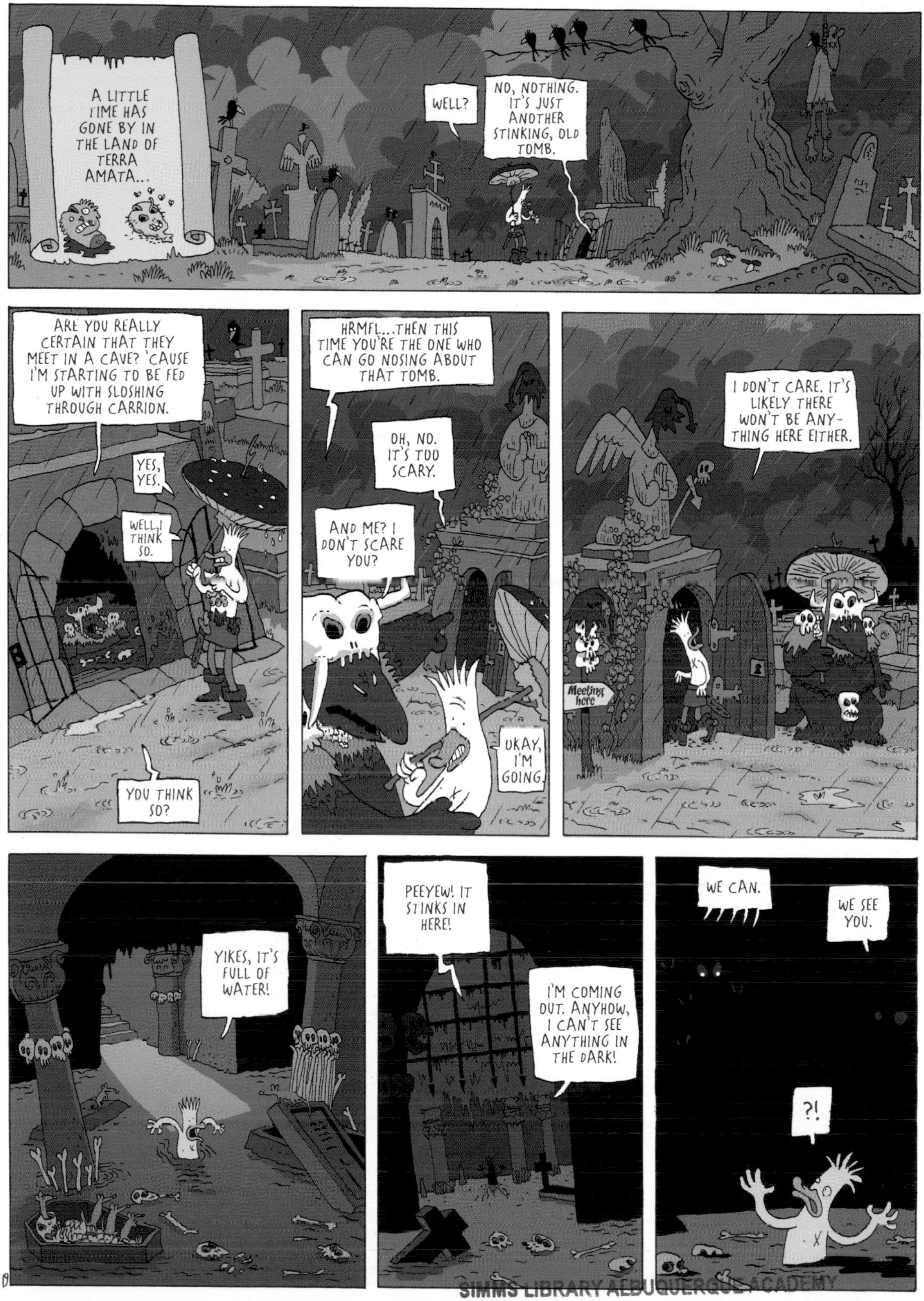
A LITTLE TIME HAS GONE BY IN THE LAND OF TERRA AMATA...
WELL?
NO, NOTHING. IT'S JUST ANOTHER STINKING, OLD TOMB.
ARE YOU REALLY CERTAIN THAT THEY MEET IN A CAVE? 'CAUSE I'M STARTING TO BE FED UP WITH SLOSHING THROUGH CARRION.
YES, YES.
WELL, I THINK SO.
YOU THINK SO?
HRMFL...THEN THIS TIME YOU'RE THE ONE WHO CAN GO NOSING ABOUT THAT TOMB.
OH, NO. IT'S TOO SCARY.
AND ME? I DON'T SCARE YOU?
OKAY, I'M GOING.
I DON'T CARE. IT'S LIKELY THERE WON'T BE ANYTHING HERE EITHER.
Meeting here
YIKES, IT'S FULL OF WATER!
PEEYEW! IT STINKS IN HERE!
I'M COMING OUT. ANYHOW, I CAN'T SEE ANYTHING IN THE DARK!
WE CAN.
WE SEE YOU.
?!

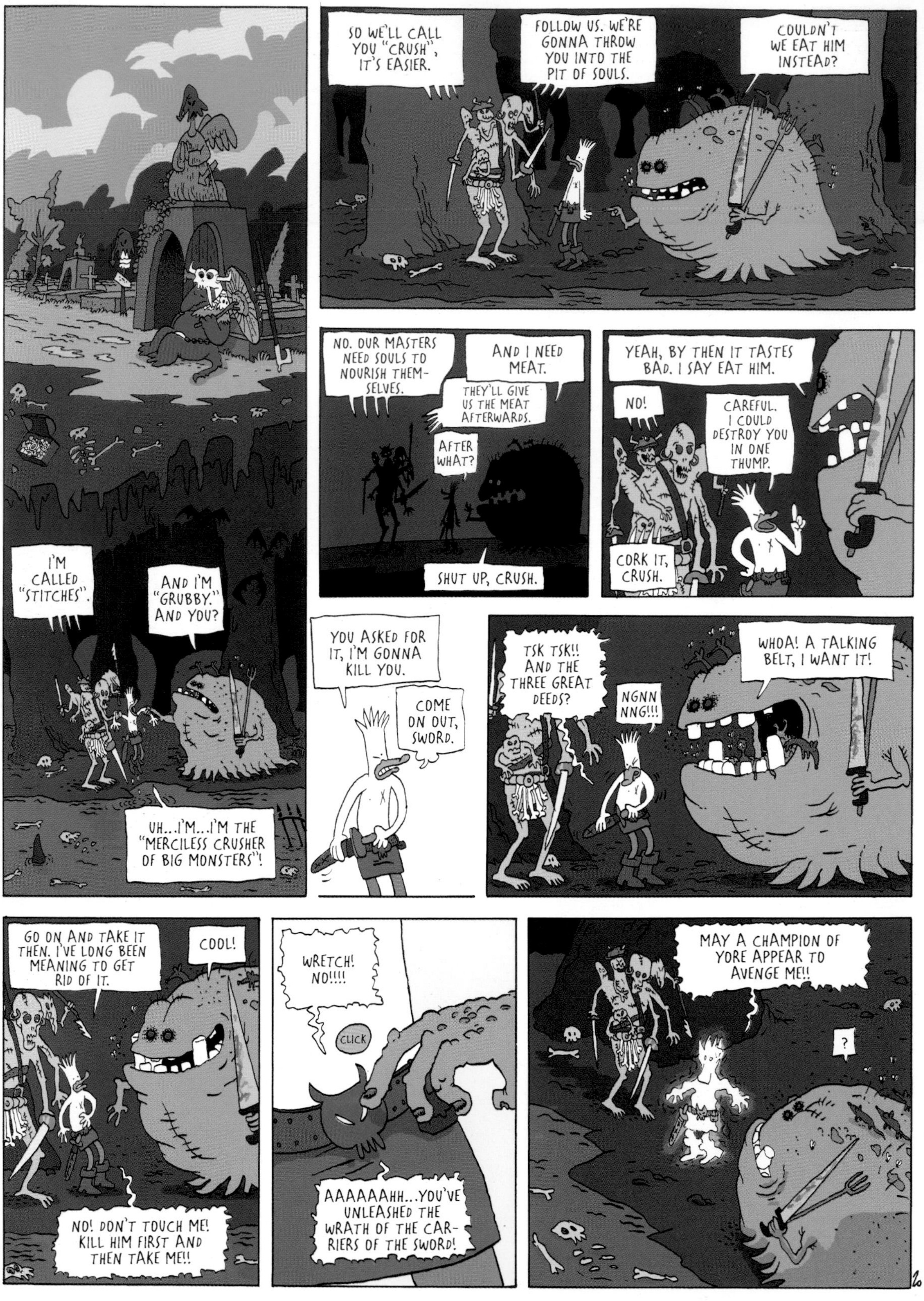
I'M CALLED "STITCHES".
AND I'M "GRUBBY." AND YOU?
UH...I'M...I'M THE "MERCILESS CRUSHER OF BIG MONSTERS"!
SO WE'LL CALL YOU "CRUSH", IT'S EASIER.
FOLLOW US. WE'RE GONNA THROW YOU INTO THE PIT OF SOULS.
COULDN'T WE EAT HIM INSTEAD?
NO. OUR MASTERS NEED SOULS TO NOURISH THEMSELVES.
AND I NEED MEAT.
THEY'LL GIVE US THE MEAT AFTERWARDS.
AFTER WHAT?
SHUT UP, CRUSH.
YEAH, BY THEN IT TASTES BAD. I SAY EAT HIM.
NO!
CAREFUL. I COULD DESTROY YOU IN ONE THUMP.
CORK IT, CRUSH.
YOU ASKED FOR IT, I'M GONNA KILL YOU.
COME ON OUT, SWORD.
TSK TSK!! AND THE THREE GREAT DEEDS?
NGNN NNG!!!
WHOA! A TALKING BELT, I WANT IT!
GO ON AND TAKE IT THEN. I'VE LONG BEEN MEANING TO GET RID OF IT.
COOL!
NO! DON'T TOUCH ME! KILL HIM FIRST AND THEN TAKE ME!!
WRETCH! NO!!!!
CLICK
AAAAAAHH...YOU'VE UNLEASHED THE WRATH OF THE CARRIERS OF THE SWORD!
MAY A CHAMPION OF YORE APPEAR TO AVENGE ME!!
?

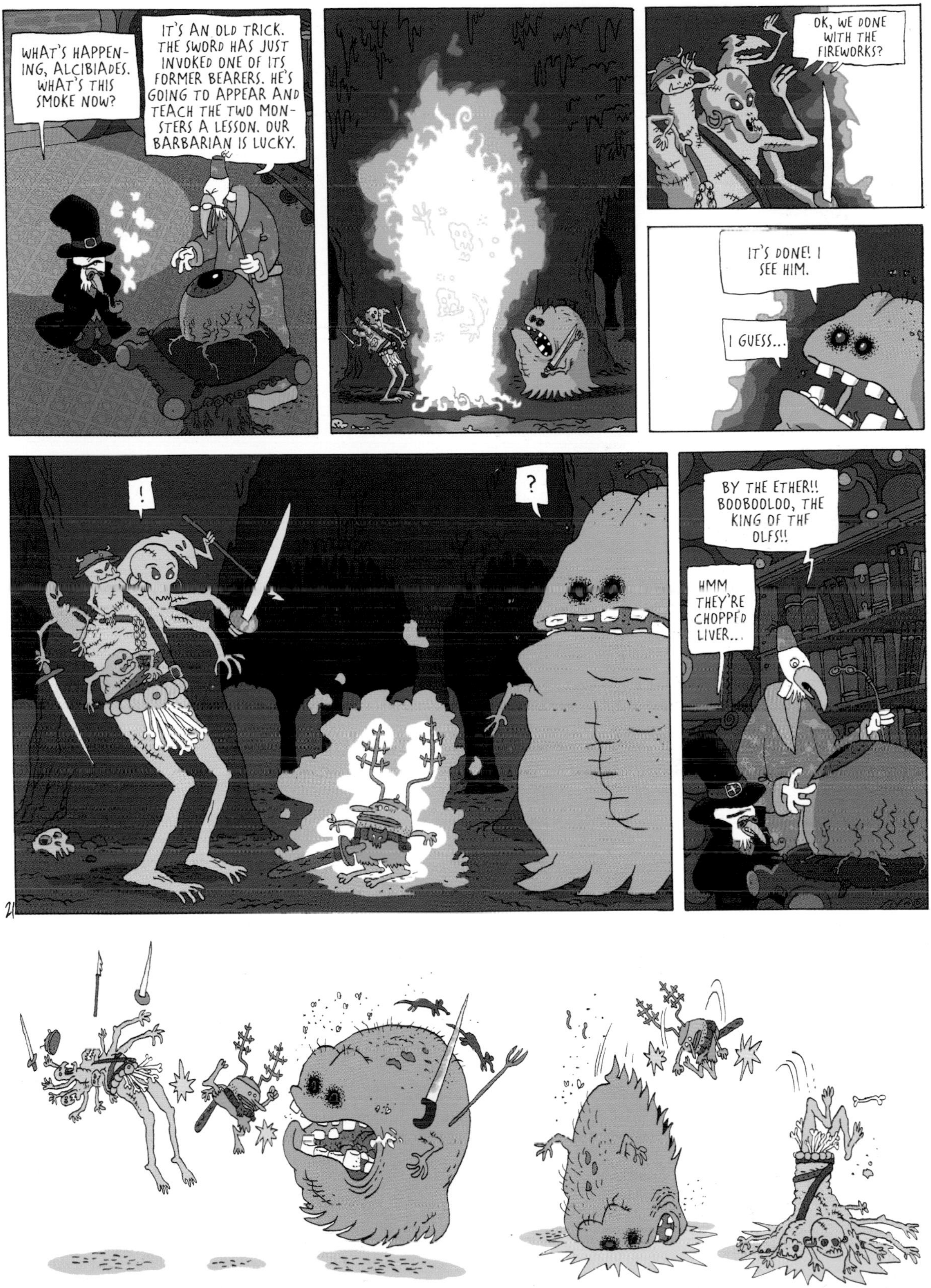
WHAT'S HAPPENING, ALCIBIADES. WHAT'S THIS SMOKE NOW?
IT'S AN OLD TRICK. THE SWORD HAS JUST INVOKED ONE OF ITS FORMER BEARERS. HE'S GOING TO APPEAR AND TEACH THE TWO MONSTERS A LESSON. OUR BARBARIAN IS LUCKY.
OK, WE DONE WITH THE FIREWORKS?
IT'S DONE! I SEE HIM.
I GUESS...
!
?
BY THE ETHER!! BOOBOOLOO, THE KING OF THE OLFS!!
HMM, THEY'RE CHOPPED LIVER...

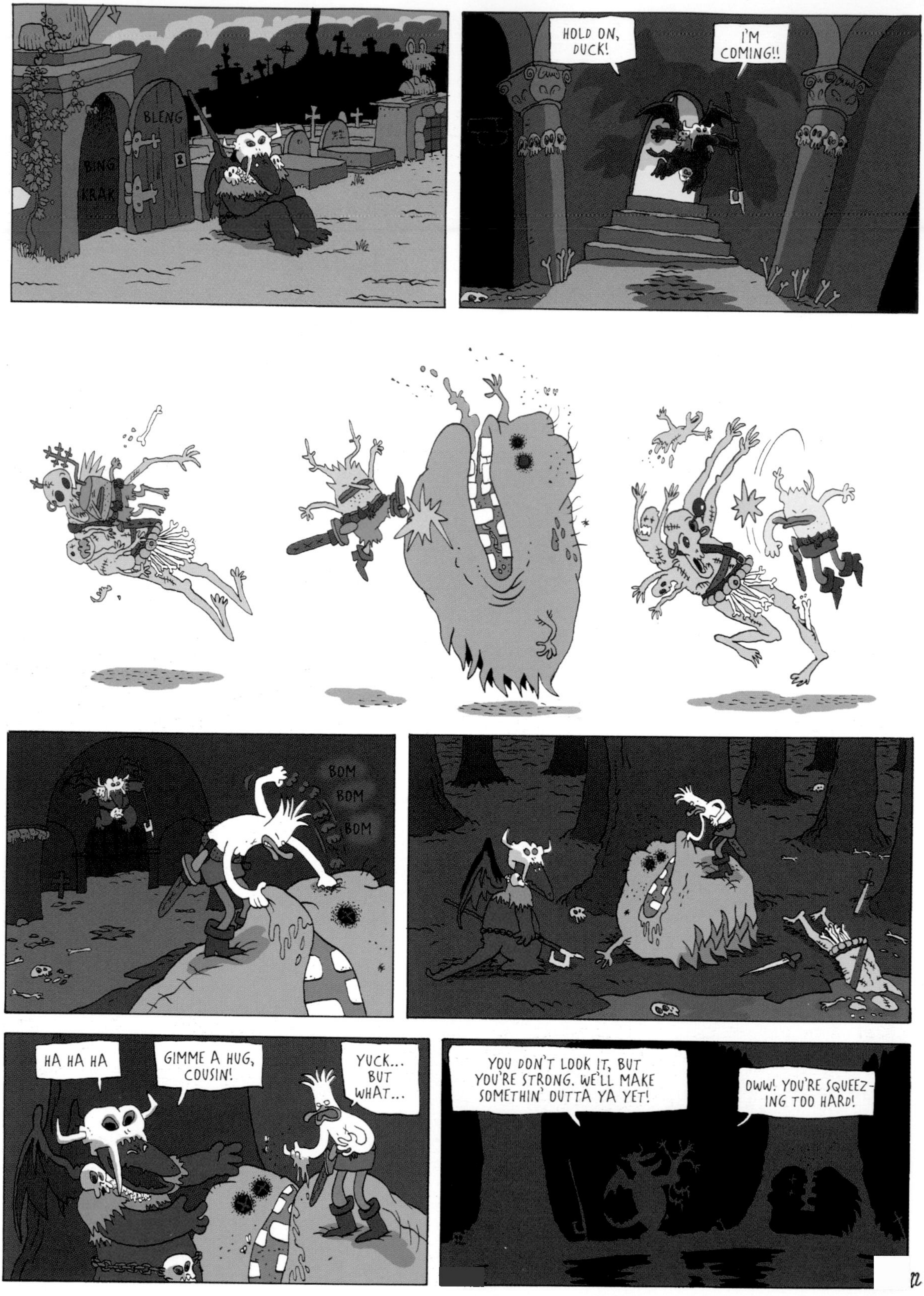
BLENG
BING
KRAK
HOLD ON, DUCK!
I'M COMING!!
BOM
BOM
BOM
HA HA HA
GIMME A HUG, COUSIN!
YUCK... BUT WHAT...
YOU DON'T LOOK IT, BUT YOU'RE STRONG. WE'LL MAKE SOMETHIN' OUTTA YA YET!
OWW! YOU'RE SQUEEZ-ING TOO HARD!

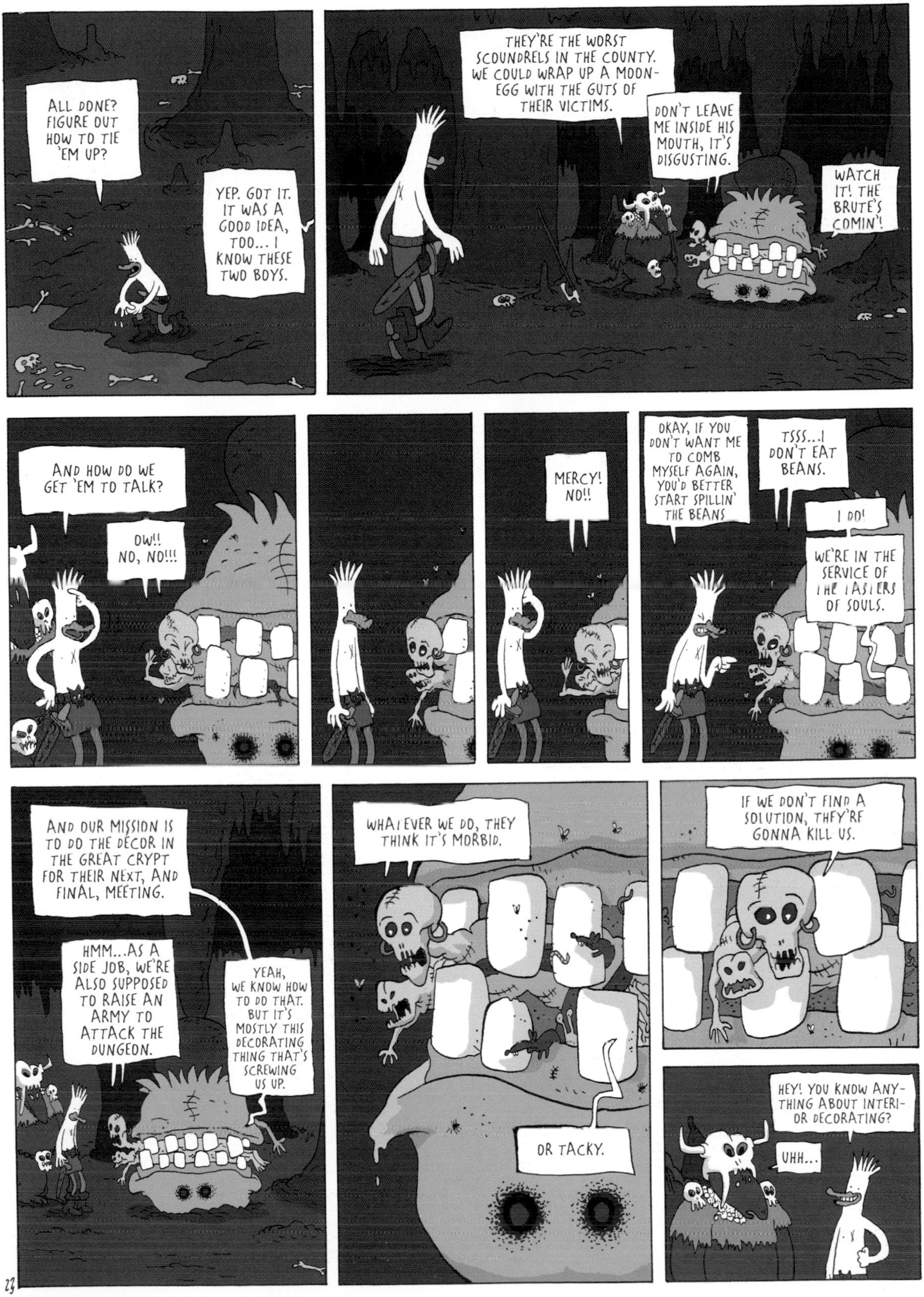
ALL DONE? FIGURE OUT HOW TO TIE 'EM UP?
YEP. GOT IT. IT WAS A GOOD IDEA, TOO... I KNOW THESE TWO BOYS.
THEY'RE THE WORST SCOUNDRELS IN THE COUNTY. WE COULD WRAP UP A MOON-EGG WITH THE GUTS OF THEIR VICTIMS.
DON'T LEAVE ME INSIDE HIS MOUTH, IT'S DISGUSTING.
WATCH IT! THE BRUTE'S COMIN'!
AND HOW DO WE GET 'EM TO TALK?
OW!! NO, NO!!!
MERCY! NO!!
OKAY, IF YOU DON'T WANT ME TO COMB MYSELF AGAIN, YOU'D BETTER START SPILLIN' THE BEANS
TSSS...I DON'T EAT BEANS.
I DO!
WE'RE IN THE SERVICE OF THE TASTERS OF SOULS.
AND OUR MISSION IS TO DO THE DECOR IN THE GREAT CRYPT FOR THEIR NEXT, AND FINAL, MEETING.
HMM...AS A SIDE JOB, WE'RE ALSO SUPPOSED TO RAISE AN ARMY TO ATTACK THE DUNGEON.
YEAH, WE KNOW HOW TO DO THAT. BUT IT'S MOSTLY THIS DECORATING THING THAT'S SCREWING US UP.
WHATEVER WE DO, THEY THINK IT'S MORBID.
OR TACKY.
IF WE DON'T FIND A SOLUTION, THEY'RE GONNA KILL US.
HEY! YOU KNOW ANYTHING ABOUT INTERIOR DECORATING?
UHH...

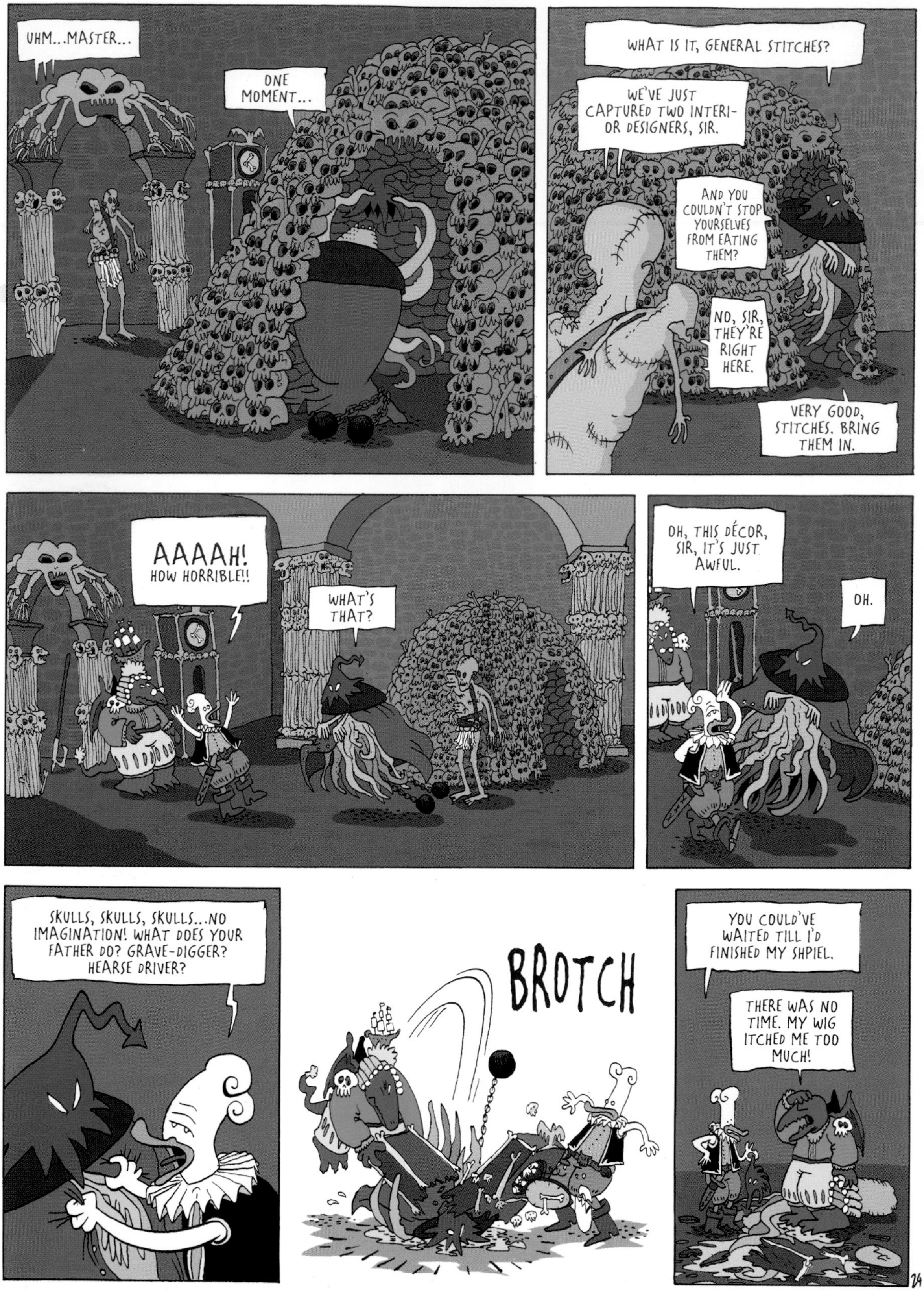

UHM...MASTER...
ONE MOMENT...
WHAT IS IT, GENERAL STITCHES?
WE'VE JUST CAPTURED TWO INTERI-OR DESIGNERS, SIR.
AND YOU COULDN'T STOP YOURSELVES FROM EATING THEM?
NO, SIR, THEY'RE RIGHT HERE.
VERY GOOD, STITCHES. BRING THEM IN.
AAAAH! HOW HORRIBLE!!
WHAT'S THAT?
OH, THIS DÉCOR, SIR, IT'S JUST AWFUL.
OH.
SKULLS, SKULLS, SKULLS...NO IMAGINATION! WHAT DOES YOUR FATHER DO? GRAVE-DIGGER? HEARSE DRIVER?
BROTCH
YOU COULD'VE WAITED TILL I'D FINISHED MY SHPIEL.
THERE WAS NO TIME. MY WIG ITCHED ME TOO MUCH!

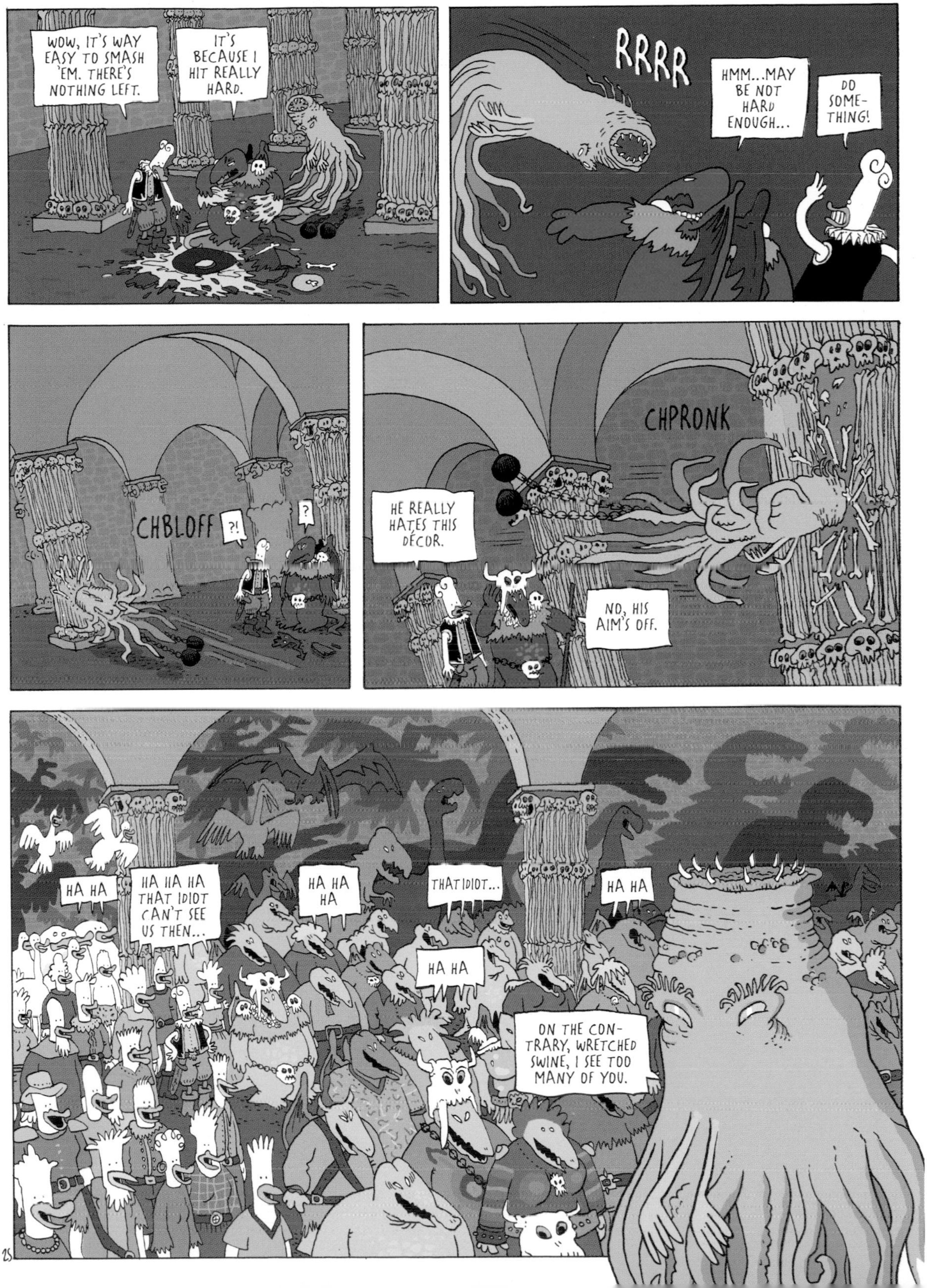
WOW, IT'S WAY EASY TO SMASH 'EM. THERE'S NOTHING LEFT.
IT'S BECAUSE I HIT REALLY HARD.
RRRR
HMM...MAY BE NOT HARD ENOUGH...
DO SOME-THING!
CHBLOFF
?!
?
CHPRONK
HE REALLY HATES THIS DÉCOR.
NO, HIS AIM'S OFF.
HA HA
HA HA HA THAT IDIOT CAN'T SEE US THEN...
HA HA HA
THAT IDIOT...
HA HA
HA HA
ON THE CON-TRARY, WRETCHED SWINE, I SEE TOO MANY OF YOU.

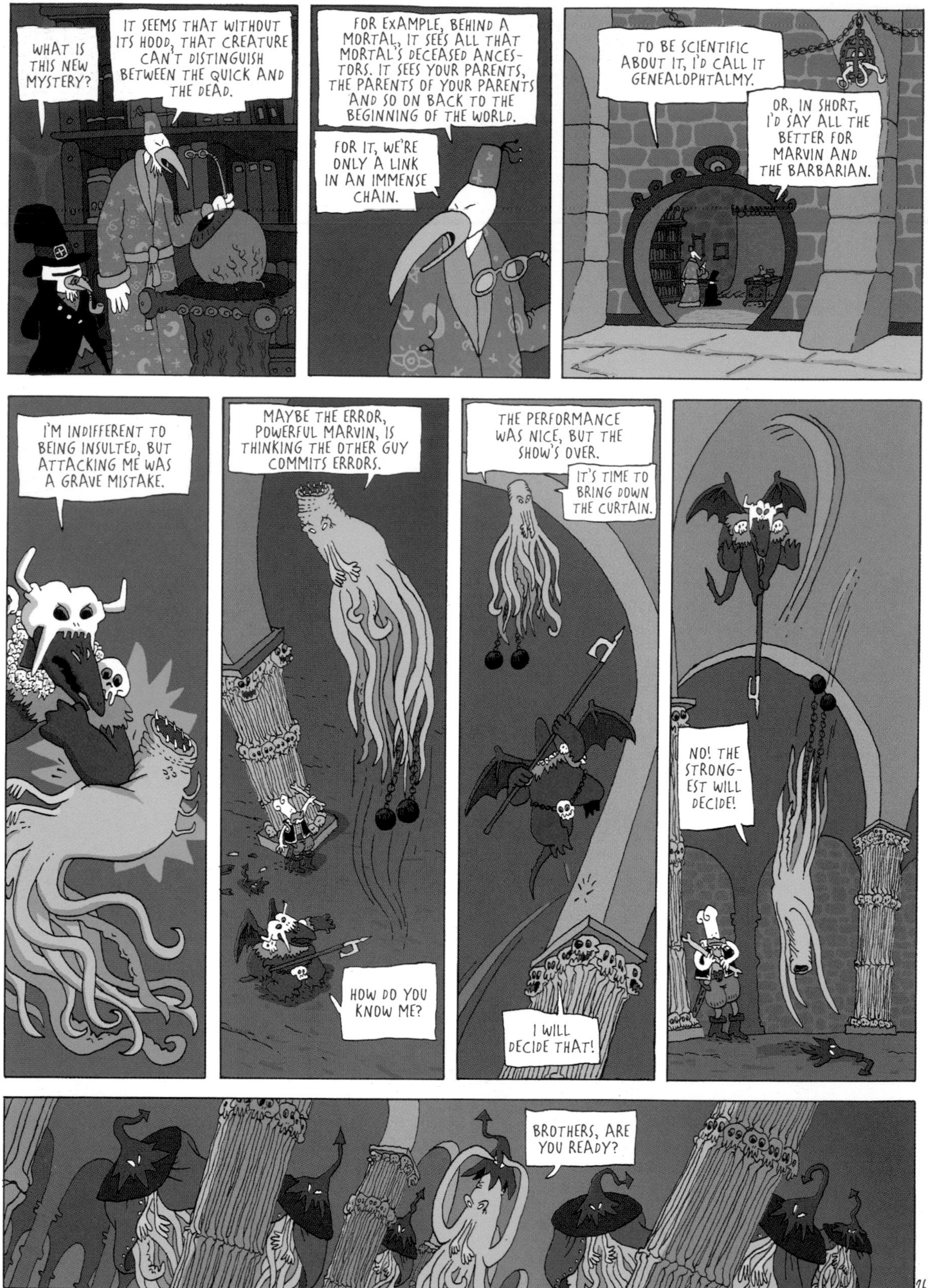

WHAT IS THIS NEW MYSTERY?
IT SEEMS THAT WITHOUT ITS HOOD, THAT CREATURE CAN'T DISTINGUISH BETWEEN THE QUICK AND THE DEAD.
FOR EXAMPLE, BEHIND A MORTAL, IT SEES ALL THAT MORTAL'S DECEASED ANCESTORS. IT SEES YOUR PARENTS, THE PARENTS OF YOUR PARENTS AND SO ON BACK TO THE BEGINNING OF THE WORLD.
FOR IT, WE'RE ONLY A LINK IN AN IMMENSE CHAIN.
TO BE SCIENTIFIC ABOUT IT, I'D CALL IT GENEALOPHTALMY.
OR, IN SHORT, I'D SAY ALL THE BETTER FOR MARVIN AND THE BARBARIAN.
I'M INDIFFERENT TO BEING INSULTED, BUT ATTACKING ME WAS A GRAVE MISTAKE.
MAYBE THE ERROR, POWERFUL MARVIN, IS THINKING THE OTHER GUY COMMITS ERRORS.
HOW DO YOU KNOW ME?
THE PERFORMANCE WAS NICE, BUT THE SHOW'S OVER.
IT'S TIME TO BRING DOWN THE CURTAIN.
I WILL DECIDE THAT!
NO! THE STRONGEST WILL DECIDE!
BROTHERS, ARE YOU READY?

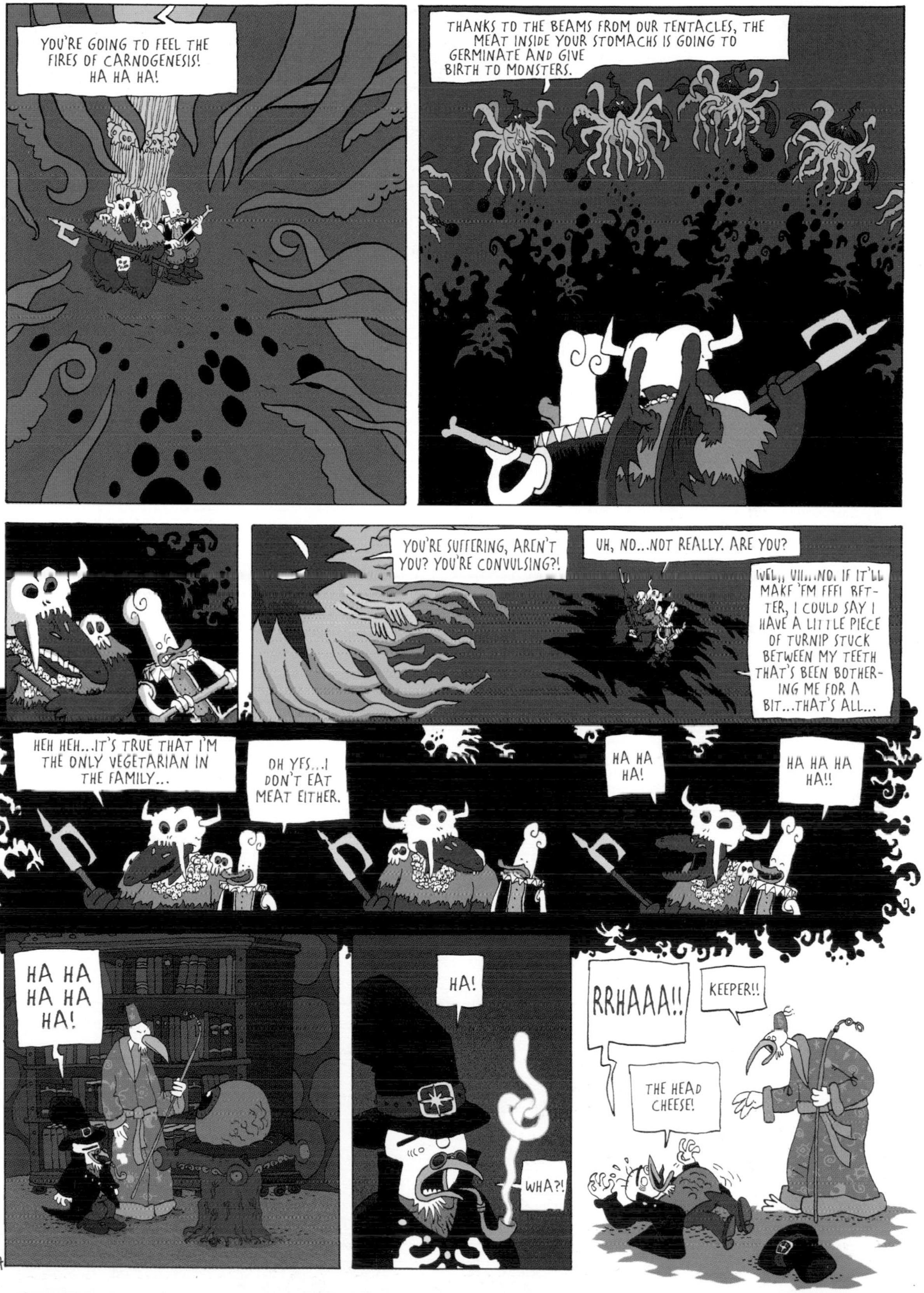
YOU'RE GOING TO FEEL THE FIRES OF CARNOGENESIS! HA HA HA!
THANKS TO THE BEAMS FROM OUR TENTACLES, THE MEAT INSIDE YOUR STOMACHS IS GOING TO GERMINATE AND GIVE BIRTH TO MONSTERS.
YOU'RE SUFFERING, AREN'T YOU? YOU'RE CONVULSING?!
UH, NO...NOT REALLY. ARE YOU?
WELL, UH...NO. IF IT'LL MAKE 'EM FEEL BETTER, I COULD SAY I HAVE A LITTLE PIECE OF TURNIP STUCK BETWEEN MY TEETH THAT'S BEEN BOTHERING ME FOR A BIT...THAT'S ALL...
HEH HEH...IT'S TRUE THAT I'M THE ONLY VEGETARIAN IN THE FAMILY...
OH YES...I DON'T EAT MEAT EITHER.
HA HA HA!
HA HA HA HA!!
HA HA HA HA HA!
HA!
WHA?!
RRHAAA!!
KEEPER!!
THE HEAD CHEESE!

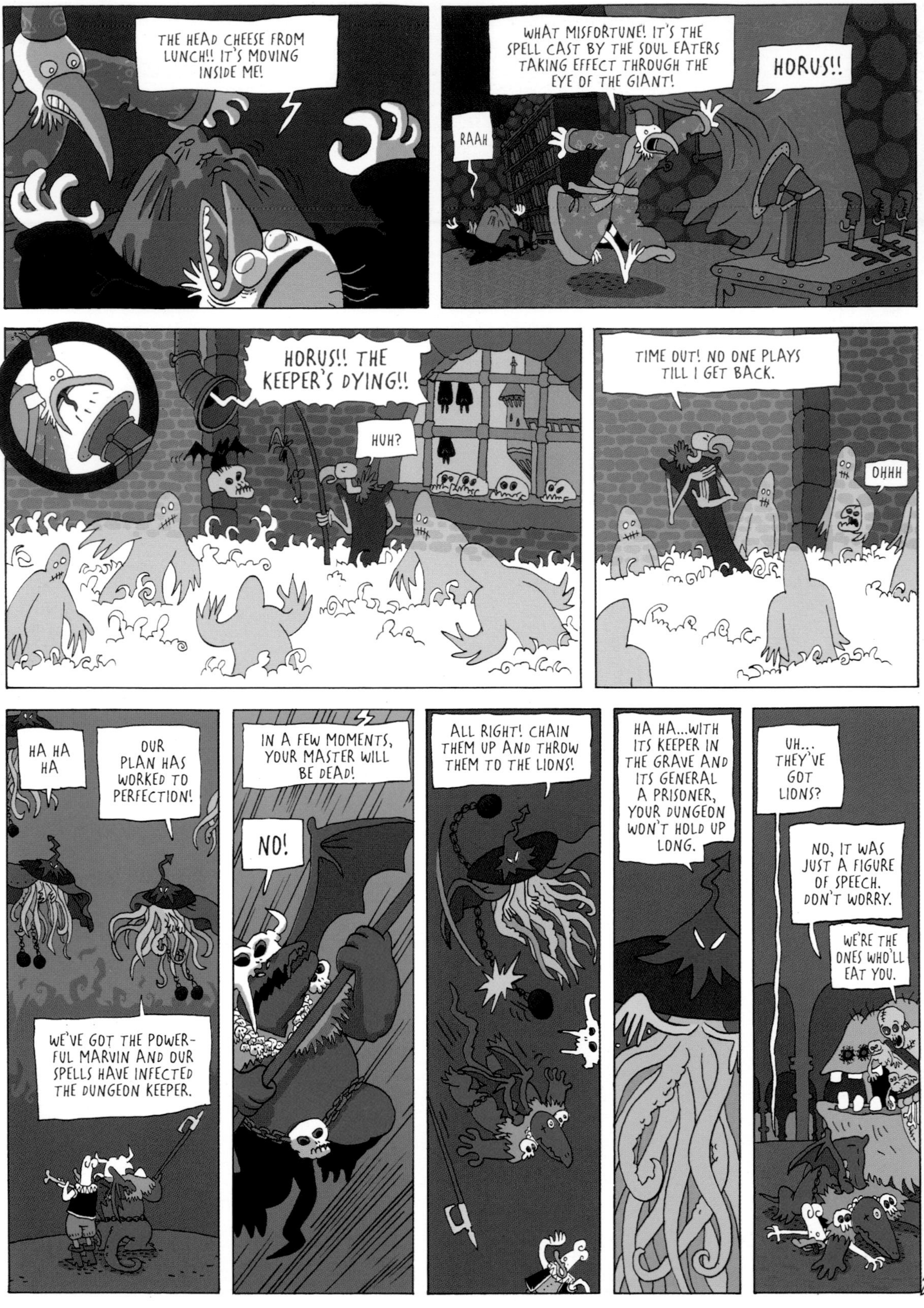
THE HEAD CHEESE FROM LUNCH!! IT'S MOVING INSIDE ME!
WHAT MISFORTUNE! IT'S THE SPELL CAST BY THE SOUL EATERS TAKING EFFECT THROUGH THE EYE OF THE GIANT!
RAAH
HORUS!!
HORUS!! THE KEEPER'S DYING!!
HUH?
TIME OUT! NO ONE PLAYS TILL I GET BACK.
OHHH
HA HA HA
OUR PLAN HAS WORKED TO PERFECTION!
WE'VE GOT THE POWERFUL MARVIN AND OUR SPELLS HAVE INFECTED THE DUNGEON KEEPER.
IN A FEW MOMENTS, YOUR MASTER WILL BE DEAD!
NO!
ALL RIGHT! CHAIN THEM UP AND THROW THEM TO THE LIONS!
HA HA...WITH ITS KEEPER IN THE GRAVE AND ITS GENERAL A PRISONER, YOUR DUNGEON WON'T HOLD UP LONG.
UH... THEY'VE GOT LIONS?
NO, IT WAS JUST A FIGURE OF SPEECH. DON'T WORRY.
WE'RE THE ONES WHO'LL EAT YOU.

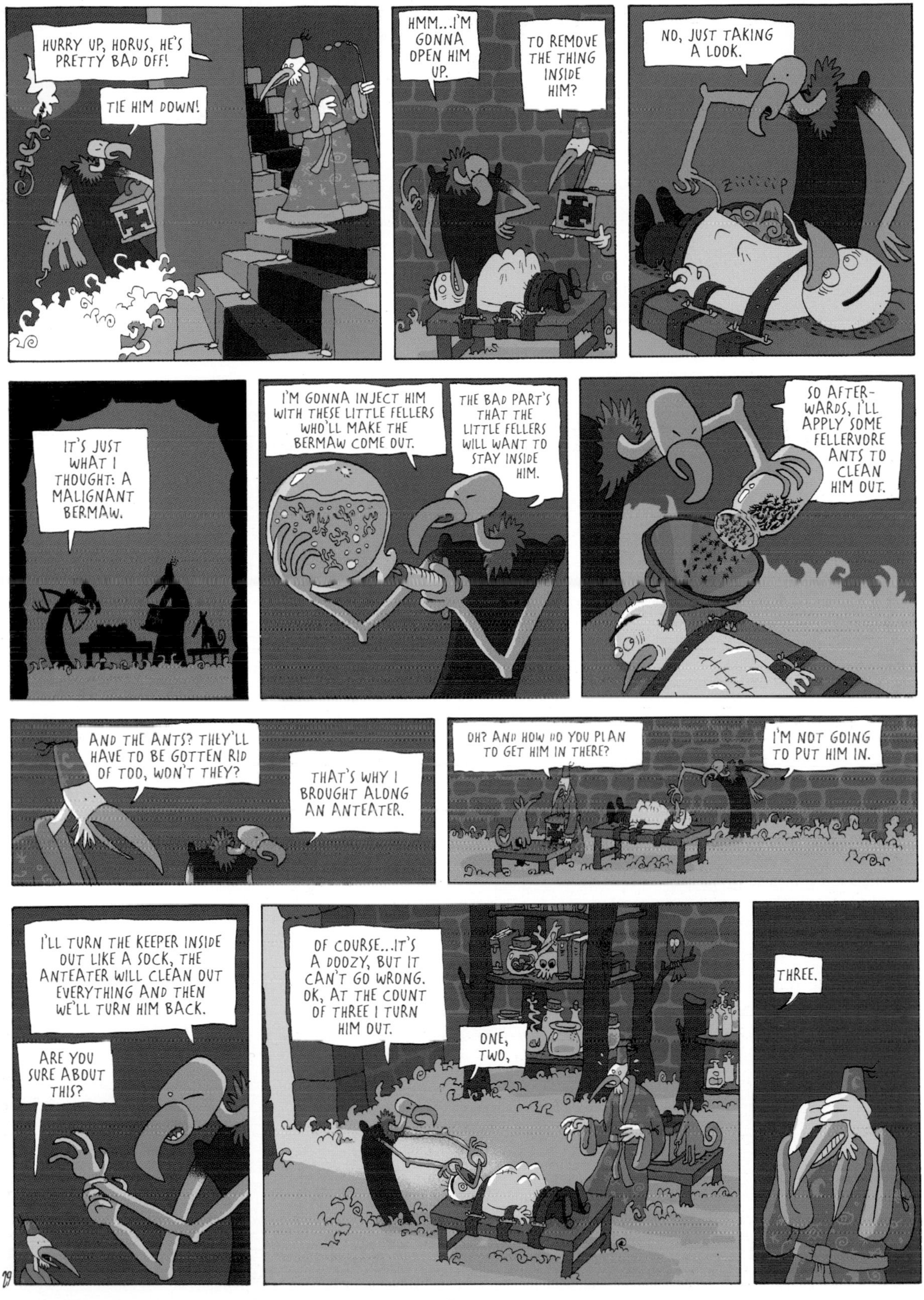

HURRY UP, HORUS, HE'S PRETTY BAD OFF!
TIE HIM DOWN!
HMM...I'M GONNA OPEN HIM UP.
TO REMOVE THE THING INSIDE HIM?
NO, JUST TAKING A LOOK.
ZIIIIIIP
IT'S JUST WHAT I THOUGHT: A MALIGNANT BERMAW.
I'M GONNA INJECT HIM WITH THESE LITTLE FELLERS WHO'LL MAKE THE BERMAW COME OUT.
THE BAD PART'S THAT THE LITTLE FELLERS WILL WANT TO STAY INSIDE HIM.
SO AFTERWARDS, I'LL APPLY SOME FELLERVORE ANTS TO CLEAN HIM OUT.
AND THE ANTS? THEY'LL HAVE TO BE GOTTEN RID OF TOO, WON'T THEY?
THAT'S WHY I BROUGHT ALONG AN ANTEATER.
OH? AND HOW DO YOU PLAN TO GET HIM IN THERE?
I'M NOT GOING TO PUT HIM IN.
I'LL TURN THE KEEPER INSIDE OUT LIKE A SOCK, THE ANTEATER WILL CLEAN OUT EVERYTHING AND THEN WE'LL TURN HIM BACK.
ARE YOU SURE ABOUT THIS?
OF COURSE...IT'S A DOOZY, BUT IT CAN'T GO WRONG. OK, AT THE COUNT OF THREE I TURN HIM OUT.
ONE, TWO,
THREE.

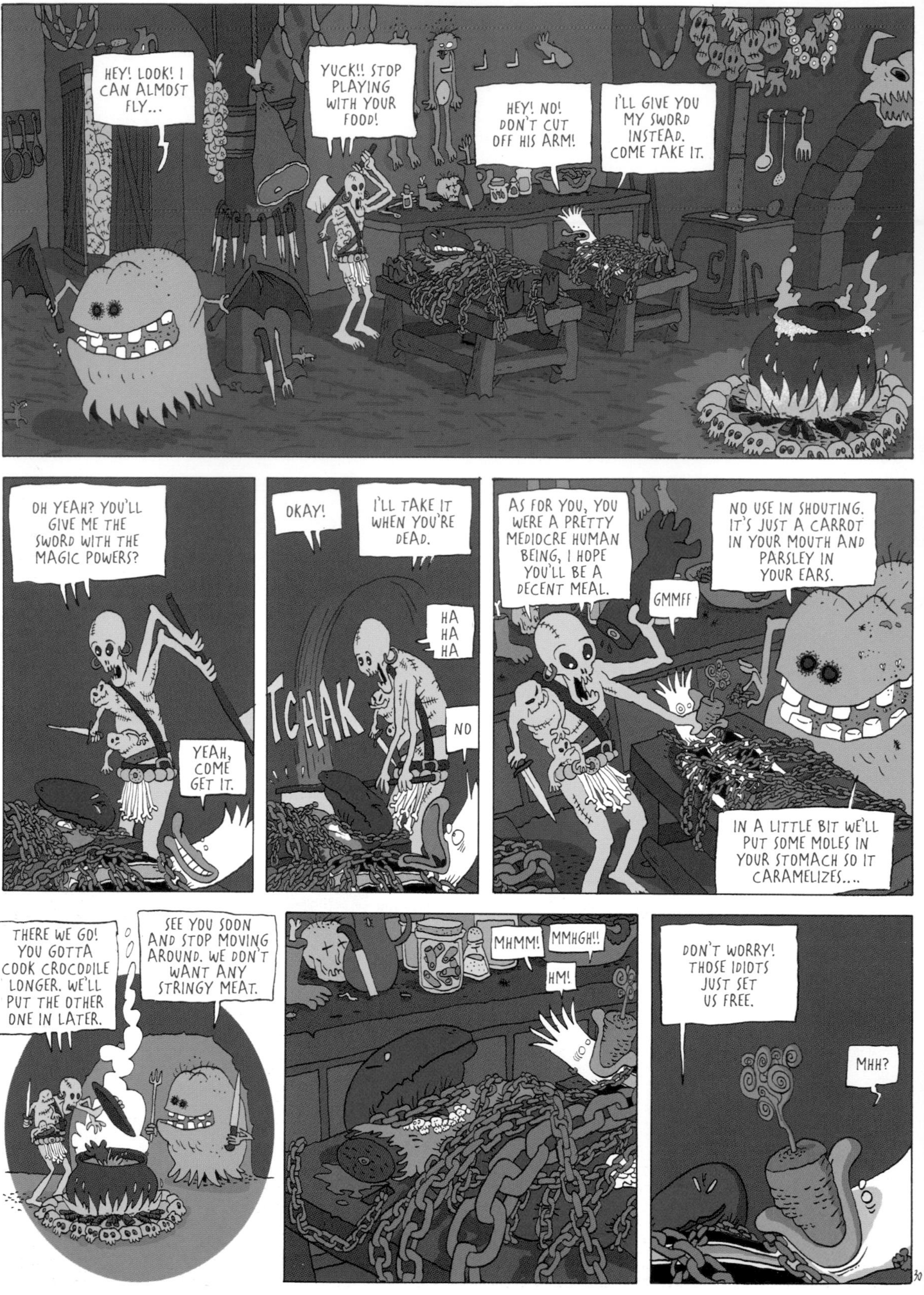
HEY! LOOK! I CAN ALMOST FLY...
YUCK!! STOP PLAYING WITH YOUR FOOD!
HEY! NO! DON'T CUT OFF HIS ARM!
I'LL GIVE YOU MY SWORD INSTEAD. COME TAKE IT.
OH YEAH? YOU'LL GIVE ME THE SWORD WITH THE MAGIC POWERS?
YEAH, COME GET IT.
OKAY!
I'LL TAKE IT WHEN YOU'RE DEAD.
HA HA HA
TCHAK
NO
AS FOR YOU, YOU WERE A PRETTY MEDIOCRE HUMAN BEING, I HOPE YOU'LL BE A DECENT MEAL.
GMMFF
NO USE IN SHOUTING. IT'S JUST A CARROT IN YOUR MOUTH AND PARSLEY IN YOUR EARS.
IN A LITTLE BIT WE'LL PUT SOME MOLES IN YOUR STOMACH SO IT CARAMELIZES....
THERE WE GO! YOU GOTTA COOK CROCODILE LONGER. WE'LL PUT THE OTHER ONE IN LATER.
SEE YOU SOON AND STOP MOVING AROUND. WE DON'T WANT ANY STRINGY MEAT.
MHMM!
MMHGH!!
HM!
DON'T WORRY! THOSE IDIOTS JUST SET US FREE.
MHH?

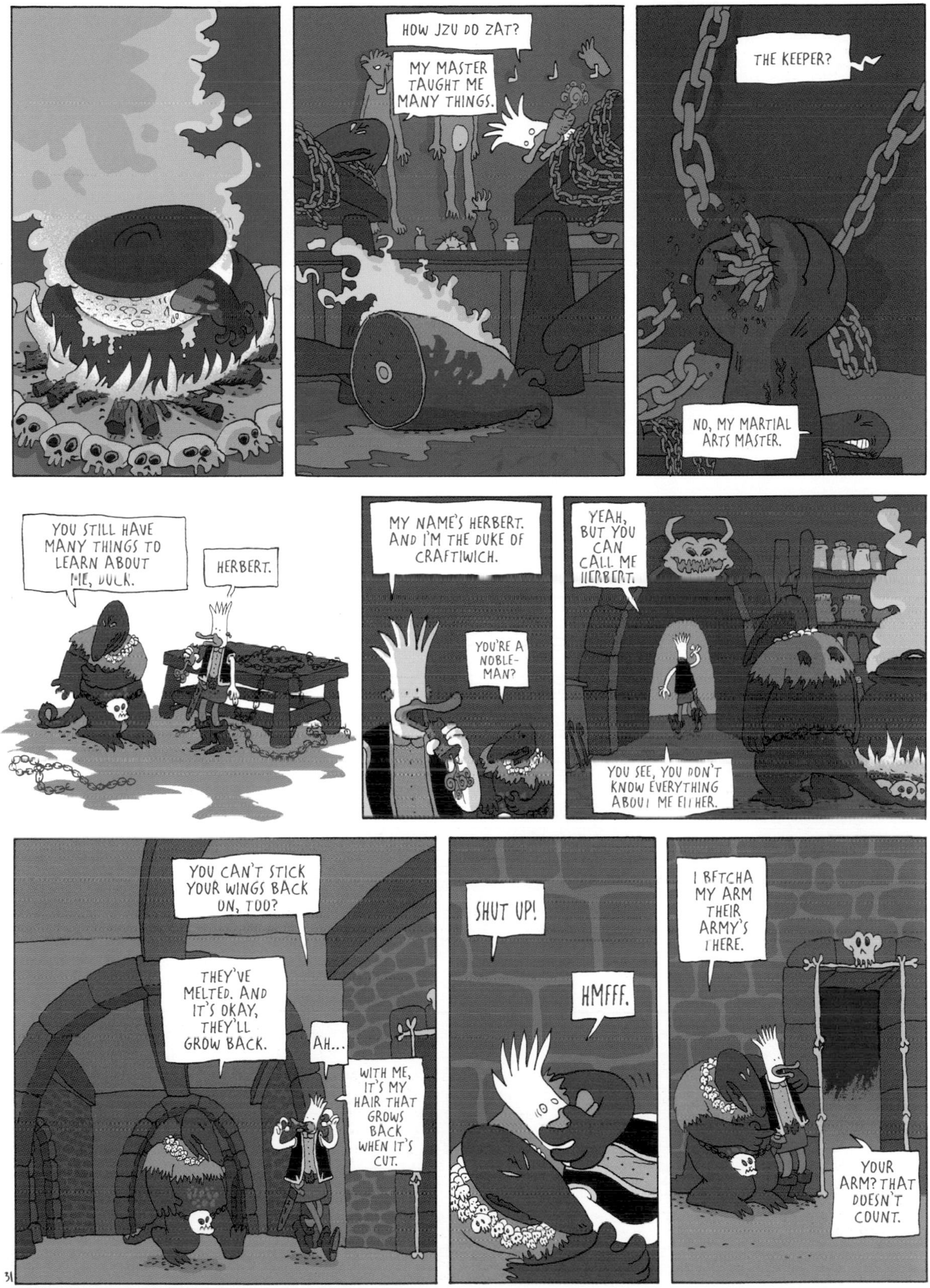

HOW JZU DO ZAT?
MY MASTER TAUGHT ME MANY THINGS.
THE KEEPER?
NO, MY MARTIAL ARTS MASTER.
YOU STILL HAVE MANY THINGS TO LEARN ABOUT ME, DUCK.
HERBERT.
MY NAME'S HERBERT. AND I'M THE DUKE OF CRAFTIWICH.
YOU'RE A NOBLE-MAN?
YEAH, BUT YOU CAN CALL ME HERBERT.
YOU SEE, YOU DON'T KNOW EVERYTHING ABOUT ME EITHER.
YOU CAN'T STICK YOUR WINGS BACK ON, TOO?
THEY'VE MELTED. AND IT'S OKAY, THEY'LL GROW BACK.
AH...
WITH ME, IT'S MY HAIR THAT GROWS BACK WHEN IT'S CUT.
SHUT UP!
HMFFF.
I BETCHA MY ARM THEIR ARMY'S THERE.
YOUR ARM? THAT DOESN'T COUNT.

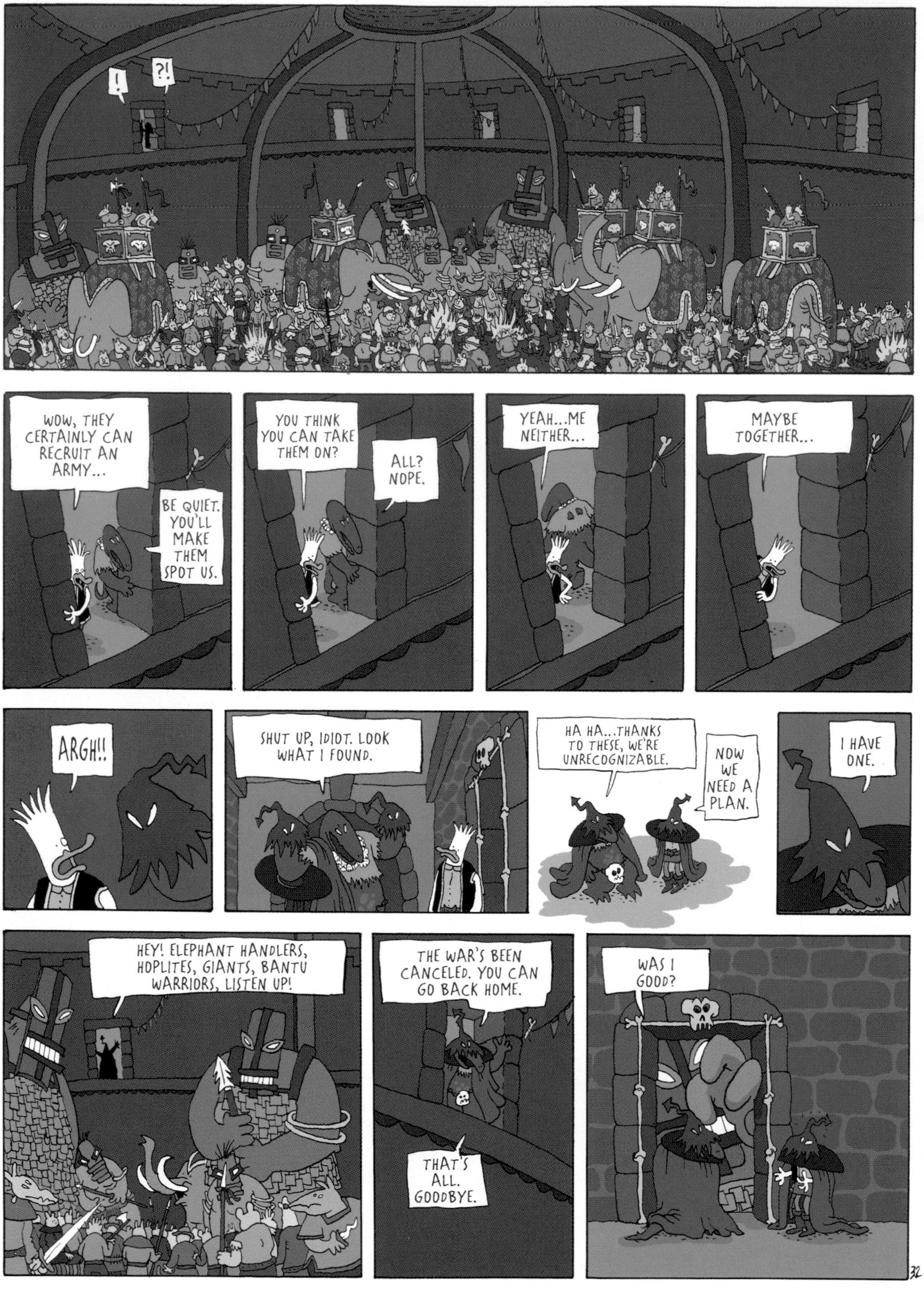
!
?!
WOW, THEY CERTAINLY CAN RECRUIT AN ARMY...
BE QUIET. YOU'LL MAKE THEM SPOT US.
YOU THINK YOU CAN TAKE THEM ON?
ALL? NOPE.
YEAH...ME NEITHER...
MAYBE TOGETHER...
ARGH!!
SHUT UP, IDIOT. LOOK WHAT I FOUND.
HA HA...THANKS TO THESE, WE'RE UNRECOGNIZABLE.
NOW WE NEED A PLAN.
I HAVE ONE.
HEY! ELEPHANT HANDLERS, HOPLITES, GIANTS, BANTU WARRIORS, LISTEN UP!
THE WAR'S BEEN CANCELED. YOU CAN GO BACK HOME.
THAT'S ALL. GOODBYE.
WAS I GOOD?

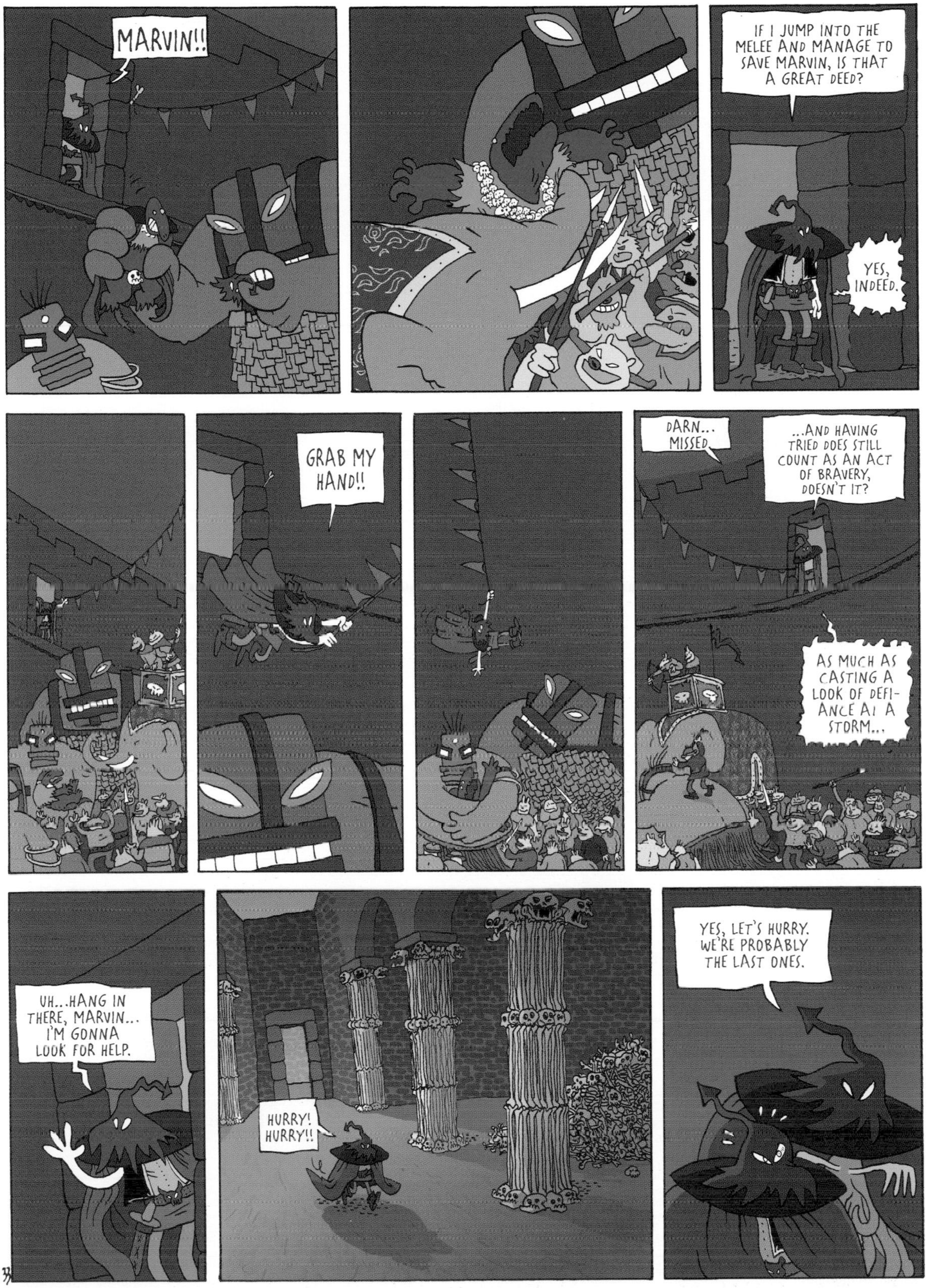
MARVIN!!
IF I JUMP INTO THE MELEE AND MANAGE TO SAVE MARVIN, IS THAT A GREAT DEED?
YES, INDEED.
GRAB MY HAND!!
DARN... MISSED.
...AND HAVING TRIED DOES STILL COUNT AS AN ACT OF BRAVERY, DOESN'T IT?
AS MUCH AS CASTING A LOOK OF DEFI-ANCE AT A STORM...
UH...HANG IN THERE, MARVIN... I'M GONNA LOOK FOR HELP.
HURRY! HURRY!!
YES, LET'S HURRY. WE'RE PROBABLY THE LAST ONES.

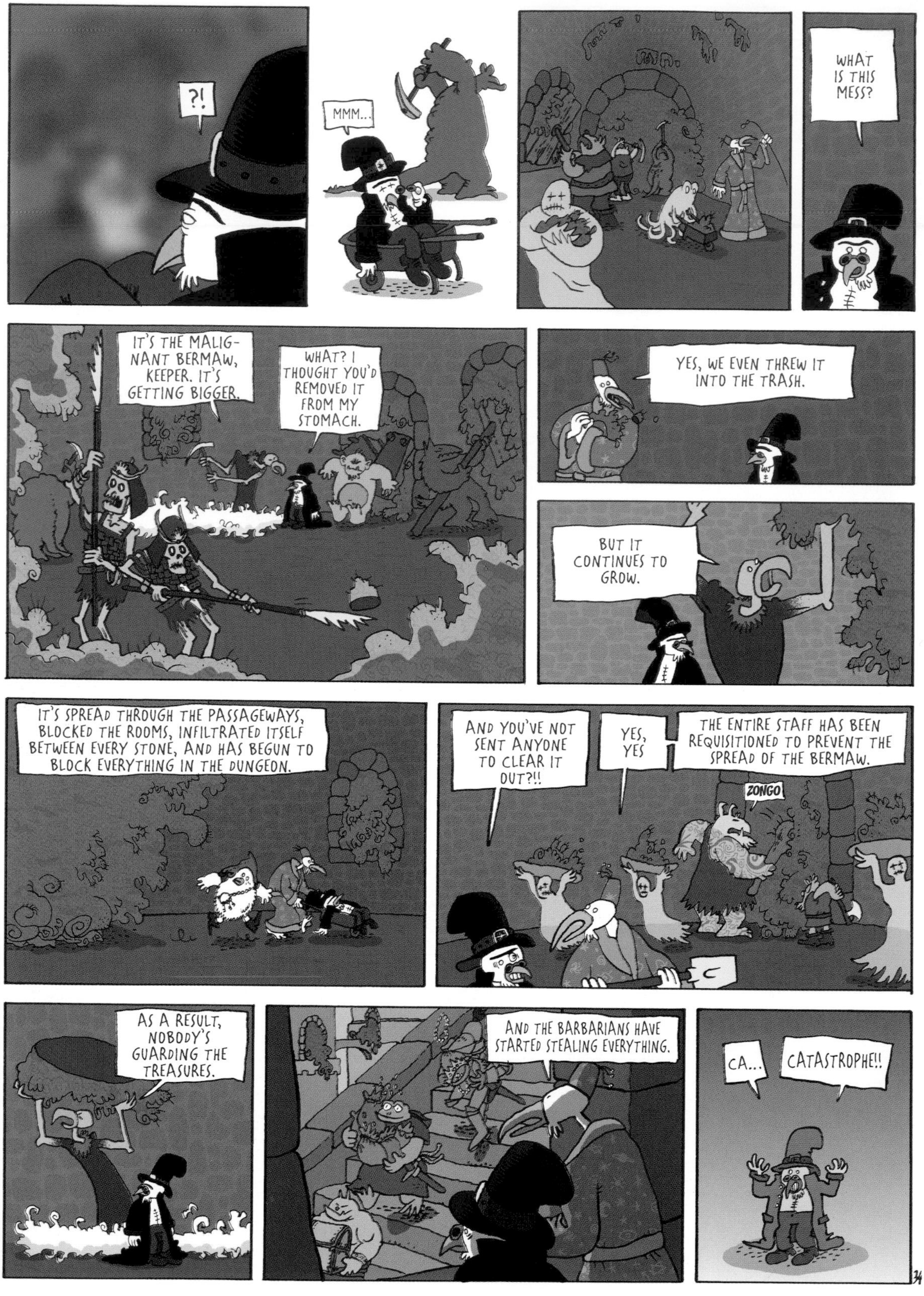
?!
MMM...
WHAT IS THIS MESS?
IT'S THE MALIGNANT BERMAW, KEEPER. IT'S GETTING BIGGER.
WHAT? I THOUGHT YOU'D REMOVED IT FROM MY STOMACH.
YES, WE EVEN THREW IT INTO THE TRASH.
BUT IT CONTINUES TO GROW.
IT'S SPREAD THROUGH THE PASSAGEWAYS, BLOCKED THE ROOMS, INFILTRATED ITSELF BETWEEN EVERY STONE, AND HAS BEGUN TO BLOCK EVERYTHING IN THE DUNGEON.
AND YOU'VE NOT SENT ANYONE TO CLEAR IT OUT?!!
YES, YES
THE ENTIRE STAFF HAS BEEN REQUISITIONED TO PREVENT THE SPREAD OF THE BERMAW.
ZONGO
AS A RESULT, NOBODY'S GUARDING THE TREASURES.
AND THE BARBARIANS HAVE STARTED STEALING EVERYTHING.
CA...
CATASTROPHE!!

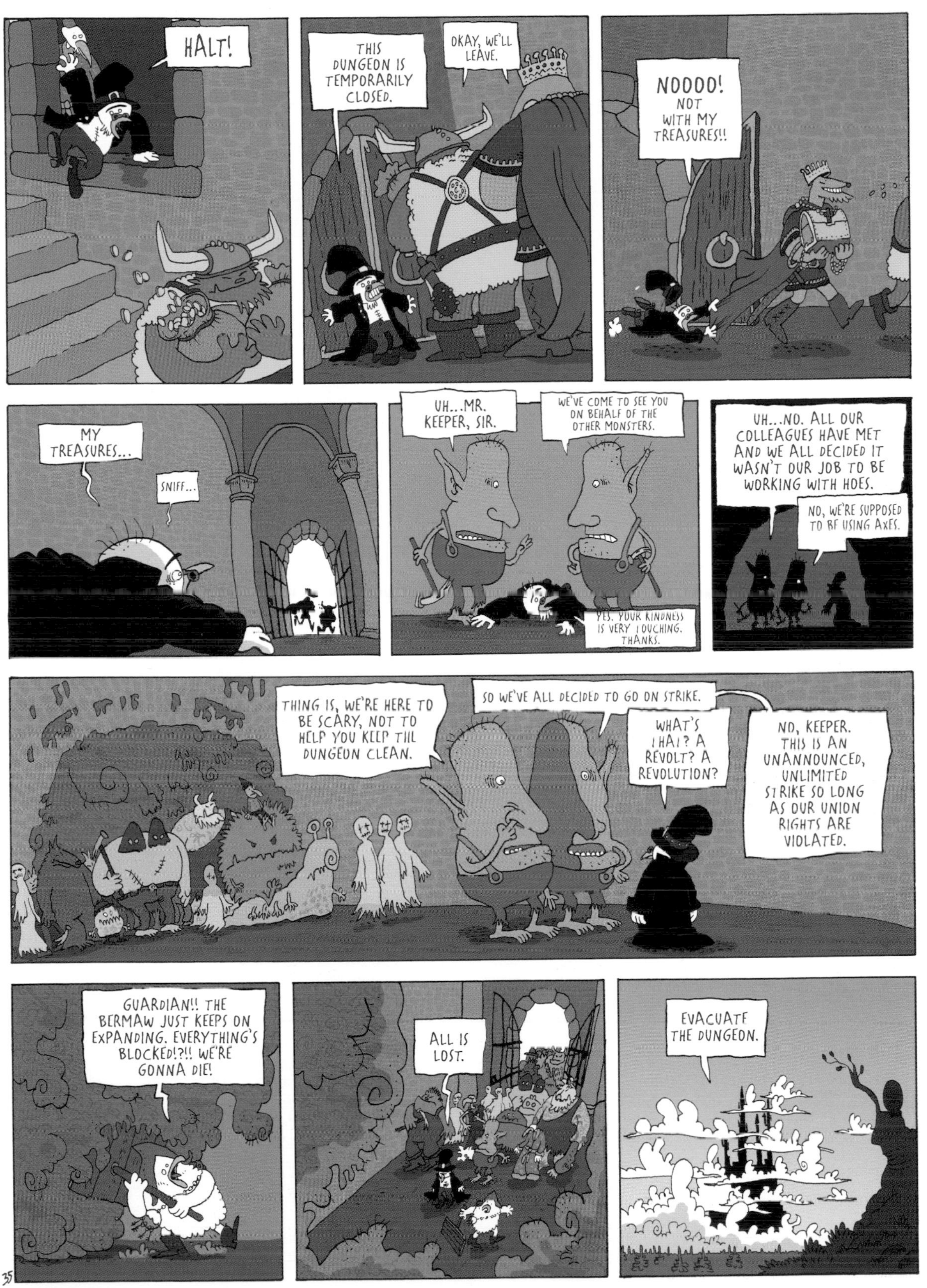
HALT!
THIS DUNGEON IS TEMPORARILY CLOSED.
OKAY, WE'LL LEAVE.
NOOOO! NOT WITH MY TREASURES!!
MY TREASURES...
SNIFF...
UH...MR. KEEPER, SIR.
WE'VE COME TO SEE YOU ON BEHALF OF THE OTHER MONSTERS.
YES. YOUR KINDNESS IS VERY TOUCHING. THANKS.
UH...NO. ALL OUR COLLEAGUES HAVE MET AND WE ALL DECIDED IT WASN'T OUR JOB TO BE WORKING WITH HOES.
NO, WE'RE SUPPOSED TO BE USING AXES.
THING IS, WE'RE HERE TO BE SCARY, NOT TO HELP YOU KEEP THE DUNGEON CLEAN.
SO WE'VE ALL DECIDED TO GO ON STRIKE.
WHAT'S THAT? A REVOLT? A REVOLUTION?
NO, KEEPER. THIS IS AN UNANNOUNCED, UNLIMITED STRIKE SO LONG AS OUR UNION RIGHTS ARE VIOLATED.
GUARDIAN!! THE BERMAW JUST KEEPS ON EXPANDING. EVERYTHING'S BLOCKED!?!! WE'RE GONNA DIE!
ALL IS LOST.
EVACUATE THE DUNGEON.

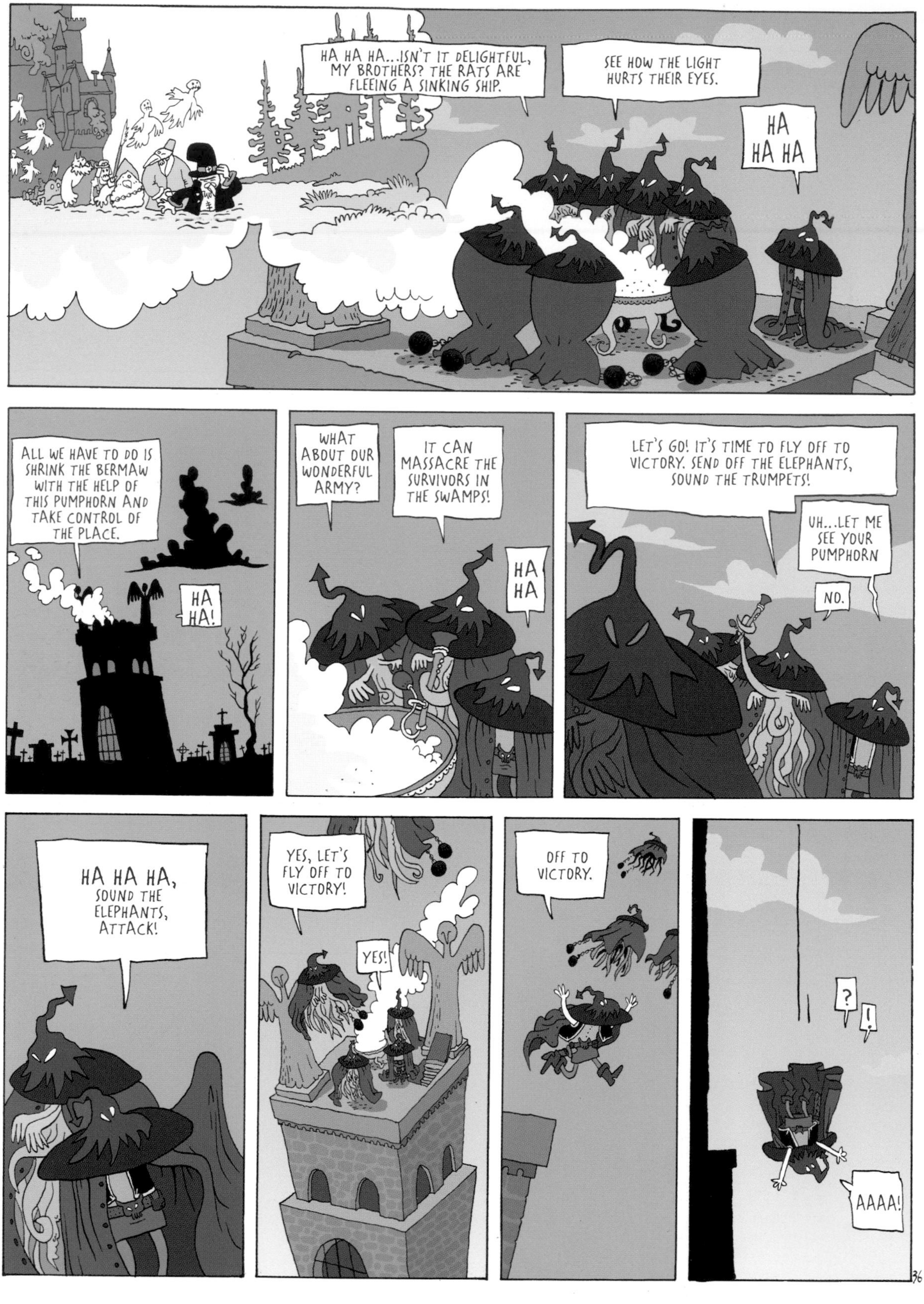
HA HA HA...ISN'T IT DELIGHTFUL, MY BROTHERS? THE RATS ARE FLEEING A SINKING SHIP.
SEE HOW THE LIGHT HURTS THEIR EYES.
HA HA HA
ALL WE HAVE TO DO IS SHRINK THE BERMAW WITH THE HELP OF THIS PUMPHORN AND TAKE CONTROL OF THE PLACE.
HA HA!
WHAT ABOUT OUR WONDERFUL ARMY?
IT CAN MASSACRE THE SURVIVORS IN THE SWAMPS!
HA HA
LET'S GO! IT'S TIME TO FLY OFF TO VICTORY. SEND OFF THE ELEPHANTS, SOUND THE TRUMPETS!
UH...LET ME SEE YOUR PUMPHORN
NO.
HA HA HA, SOUND THE ELEPHANTS, ATTACK!
YES, LET'S FLY OFF TO VICTORY!
YES!
OFF TO VICTORY.
?
!
AAAA!

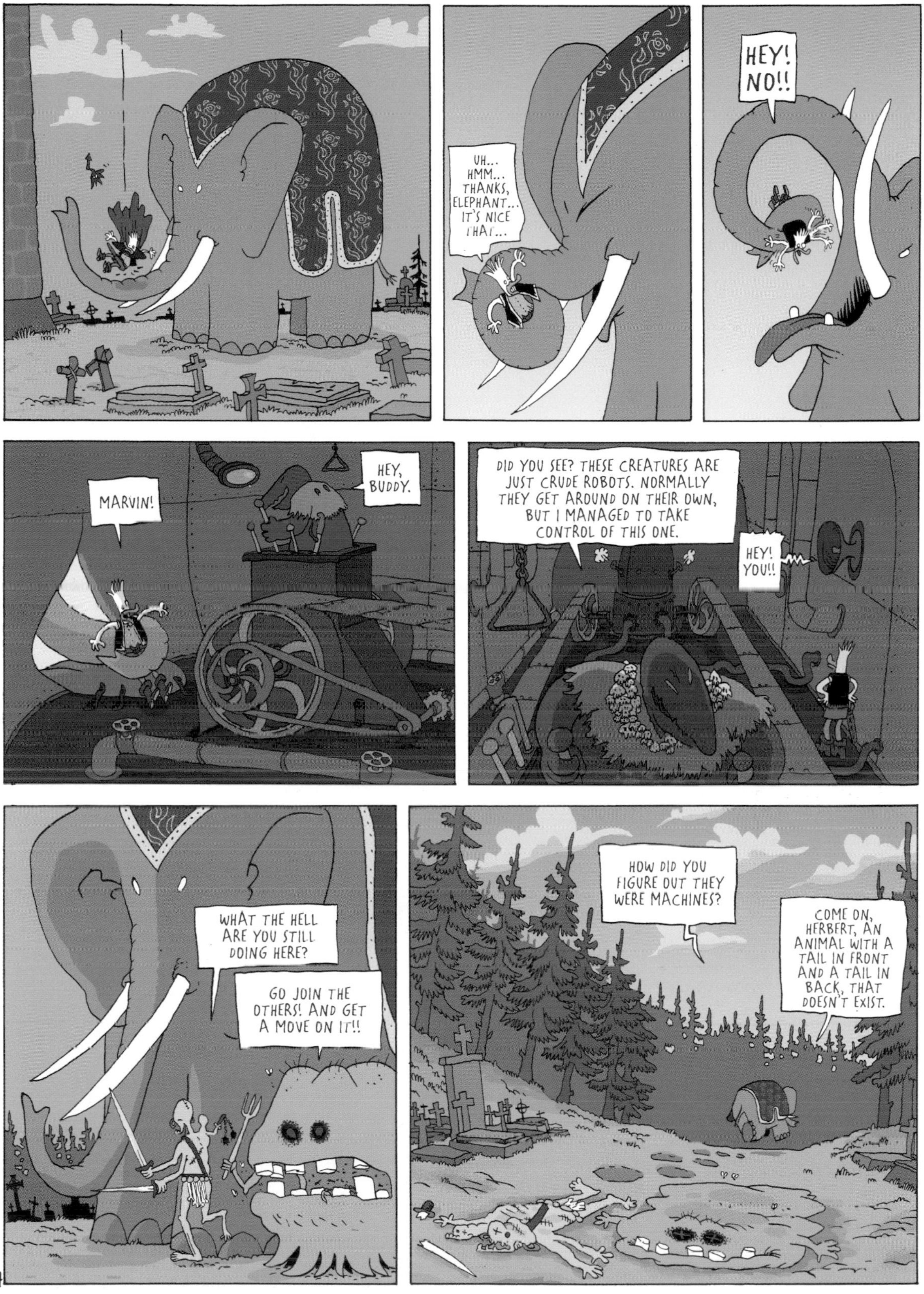
UH... HMM... THANKS, ELEPHANT... IT'S NICE THAT...
HEY! NO!!
MARVIN!
HEY, BUDDY.
DID YOU SEE? THESE CREATURES ARE JUST CRUDE ROBOTS. NORMALLY THEY GET AROUND ON THEIR OWN, BUT I MANAGED TO TAKE CONTROL OF THIS ONE.
HEY! YOU!!
WHAT THE HELL ARE YOU STILL DOING HERE?
GO JOIN THE OTHERS! AND GET A MOVE ON IT!!
HOW DID YOU FIGURE OUT THEY WERE MACHINES?
COME ON, HERBERT, AN ANIMAL WITH A TAIL IN FRONT AND A TAIL IN BACK, THAT DOESN'T EXIST.

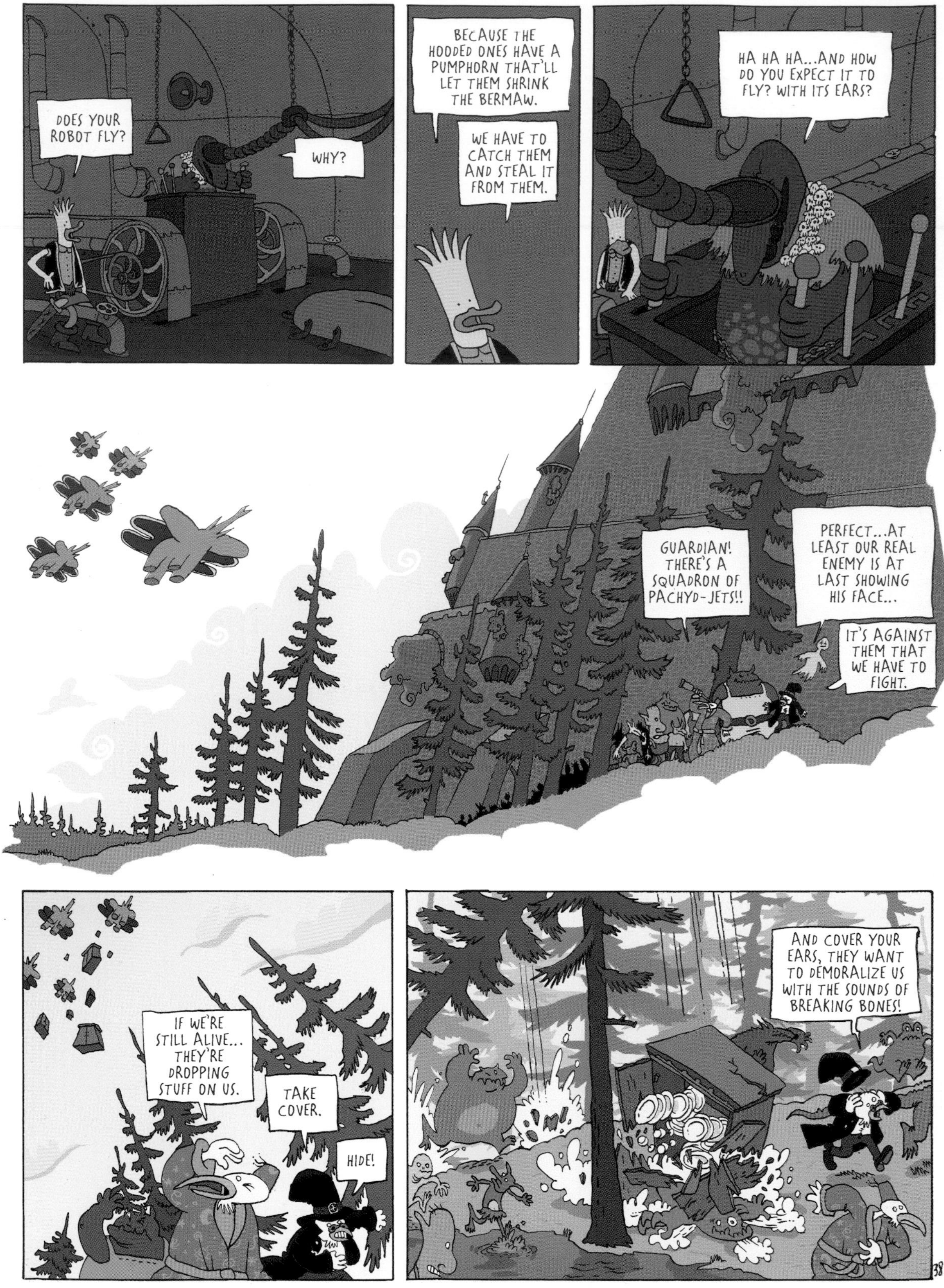
DOES YOUR ROBOT FLY?
WHY?
BECAUSE THE HOODED ONES HAVE A PUMPHORN THAT'LL LET THEM SHRINK THE BERMAW.
WE HAVE TO CATCH THEM AND STEAL IT FROM THEM.
HA HA HA...AND HOW DO YOU EXPECT IT TO FLY? WITH ITS EARS?
GUARDIAN! THERE'S A SQUADRON OF PACHYD-JETS!!
PERFECT...AT LEAST OUR REAL ENEMY IS AT LAST SHOWING HIS FACE...
IT'S AGAINST THEM THAT WE HAVE TO FIGHT.
IF WE'RE STILL ALIVE... THEY'RE DROPPING STUFF ON US.
TAKE COVER.
HIDE!
AND COVER YOUR EARS, THEY WANT TO DEMORALIZE US WITH THE SOUNDS OF BREAKING BONES!

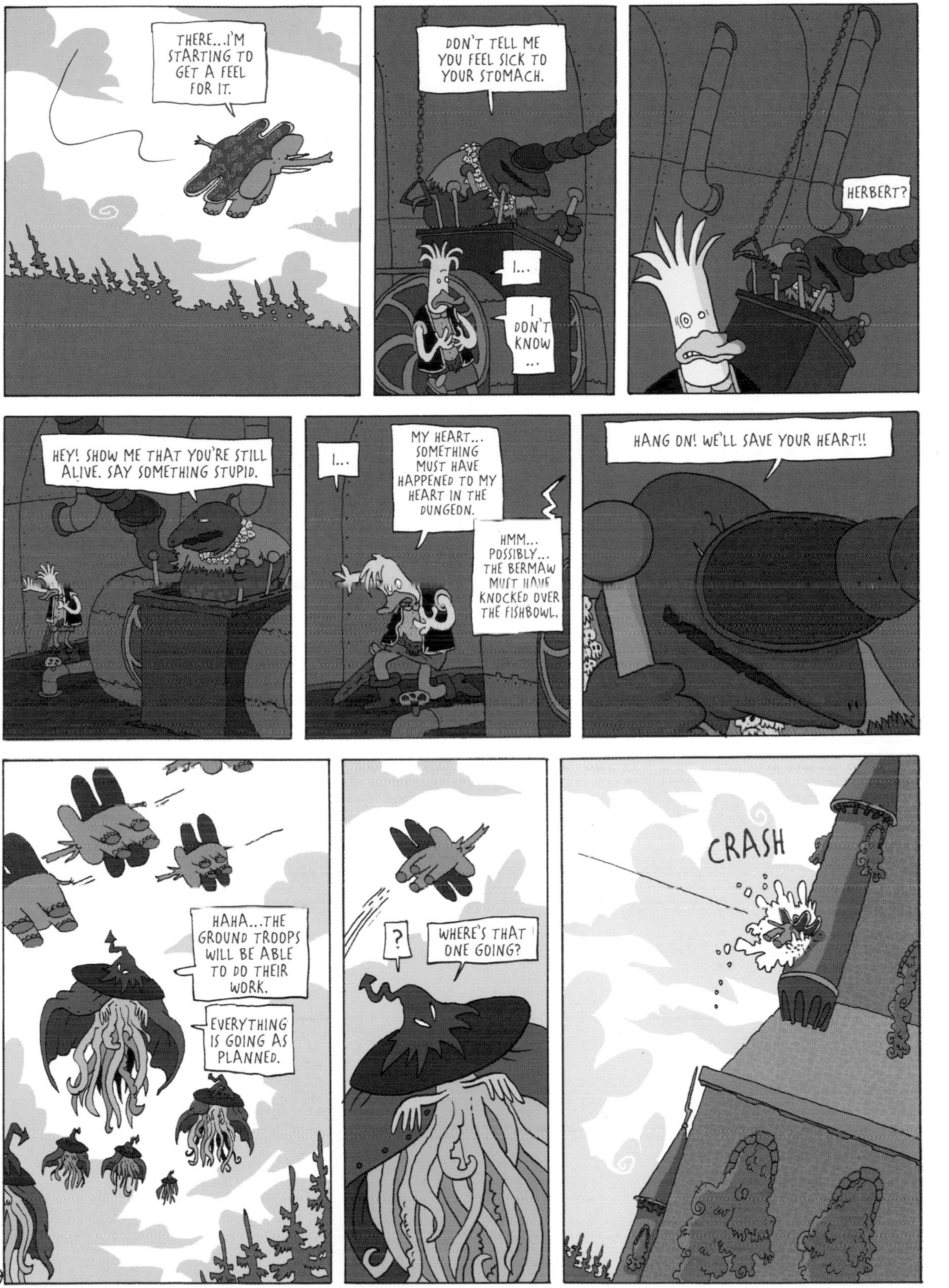
THERE...I'M STARTING TO GET A FEEL FOR IT.
DON'T TELL ME YOU FEEL SICK TO YOUR STOMACH.
I...
I DON'T KNOW ...
HERBERT?
HEY! SHOW ME THAT YOU'RE STILL ALIVE. SAY SOMETHING STUPID.
I...
MY HEART... SOMETHING MUST HAVE HAPPENED TO MY HEART IN THE DUNGEON.
HMM... POSSIBLY... THE BERMAW MUST HAVE KNOCKED OVER THE FISHBOWL.
HANG ON! WE'LL SAVE YOUR HEART!!
HAHA...THE GROUND TROOPS WILL BE ABLE TO DO THEIR WORK.
EVERYTHING IS GOING AS PLANNED.
?
WHERE'S THAT ONE GOING?
CRASH

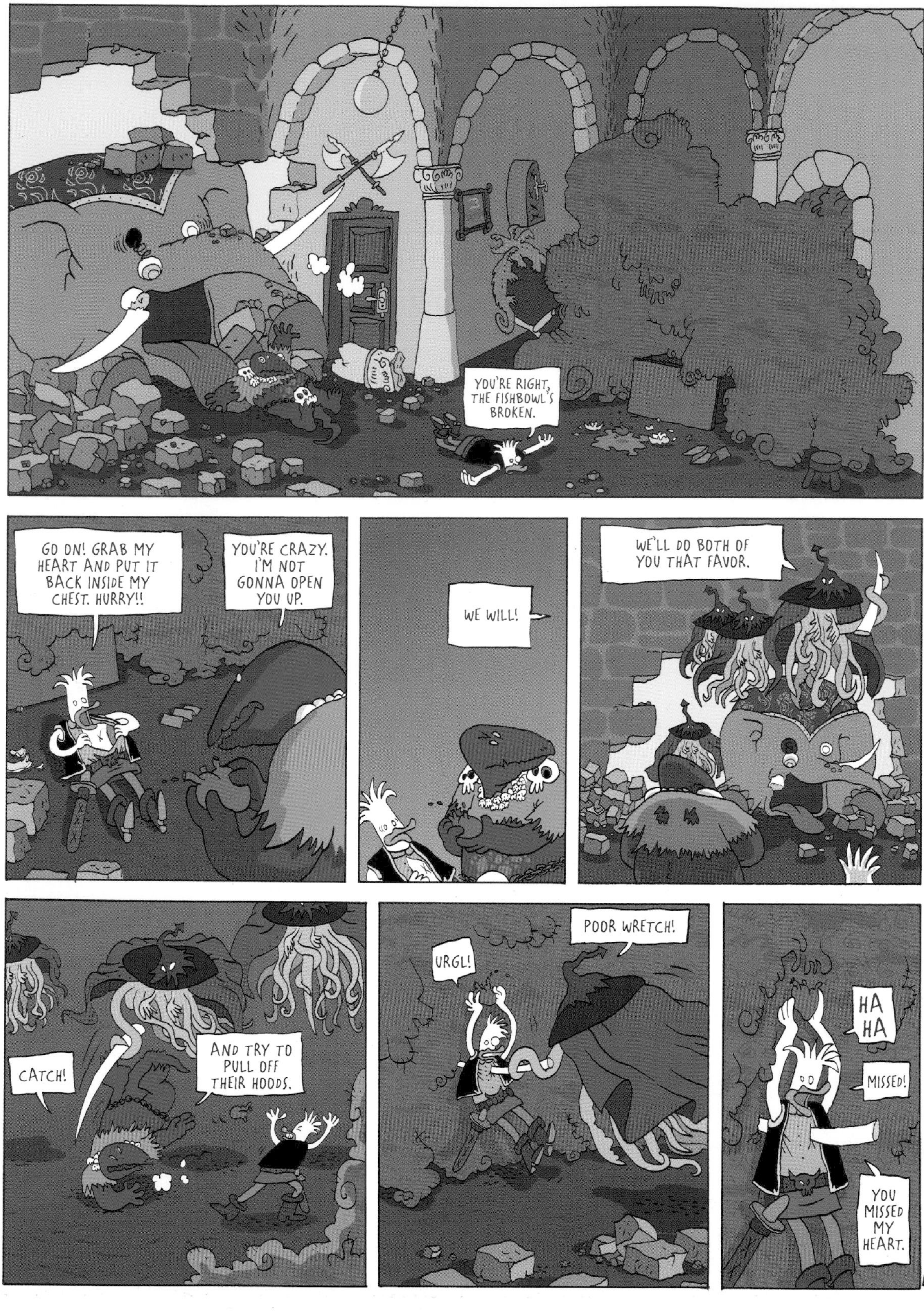
YOU'RE RIGHT, THE FISHBOWL'S BROKEN.
GO ON! GRAB MY HEART AND PUT IT BACK INSIDE MY CHEST. HURRY!!
YOU'RE CRAZY. I'M NOT GONNA OPEN YOU UP.
WE WILL!
WE'LL DO BOTH OF YOU THAT FAVOR.
CATCH!
AND TRY TO PULL OFF THEIR HOODS.
URGL!
POOR WRETCH!
HA HA
MISSED!
YOU MISSED MY HEART.

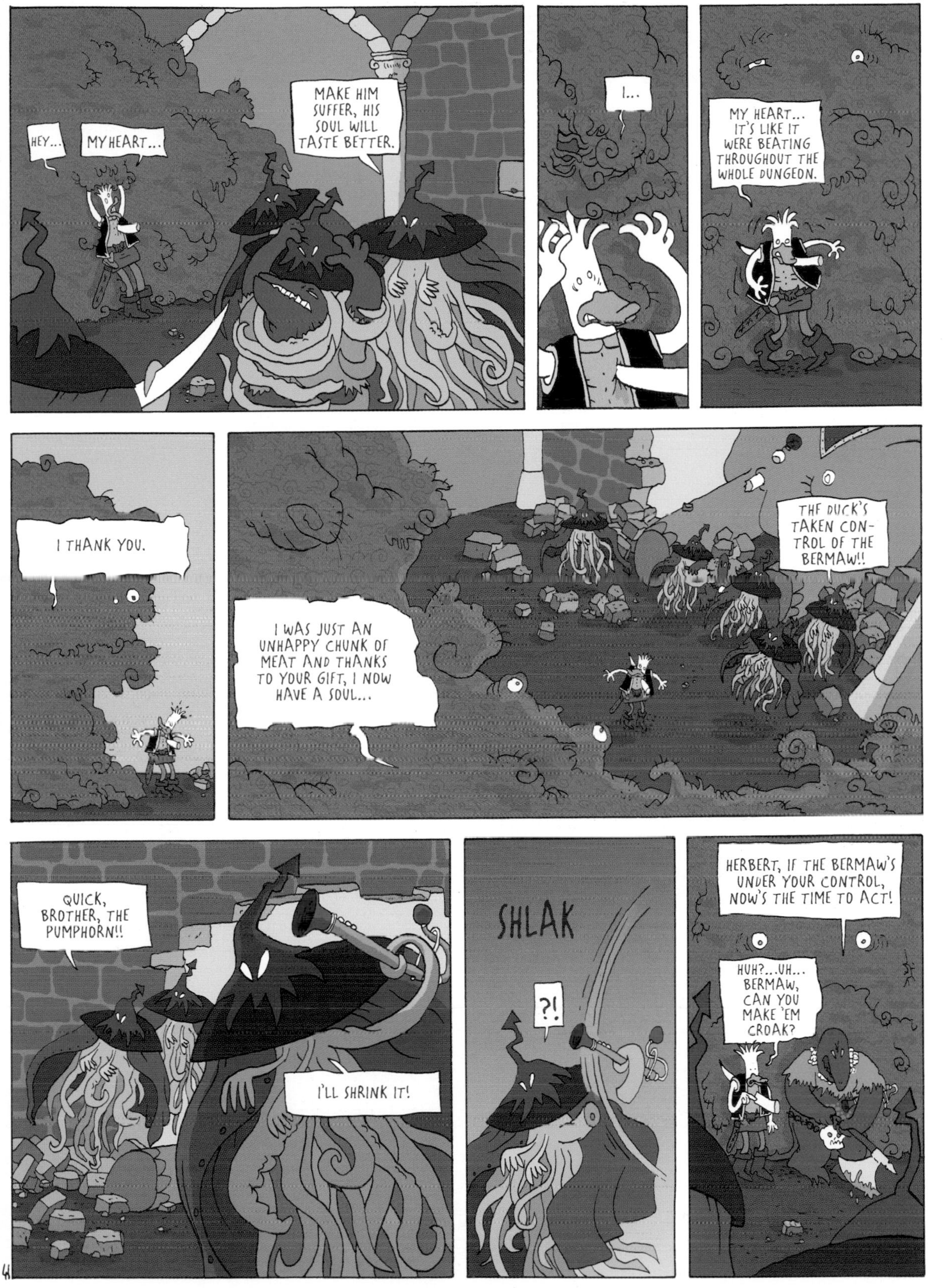
HEY...
MY HEART...
MAKE HIM SUFFER, HIS SOUL WILL TASTE BETTER.
I...
MY HEART... IT'S LIKE IT WERE BEATING THROUGHOUT THE WHOLE DUNGEON.
I THANK YOU.
I WAS JUST AN UNHAPPY CHUNK OF MEAT AND THANKS TO YOUR GIFT, I NOW HAVE A SOUL...
THE DUCK'S TAKEN CONTROL OF THE BERMAW!!
QUICK, BROTHER, THE PUMPHORN!!
I'LL SHRINK IT!
SHLAK
?!
HERBERT, IF THE BERMAW'S UNDER YOUR CONTROL, NOW'S THE TIME TO ACT!
HUH?...UH... BERMAW, CAN YOU MAKE 'EM CROAK?

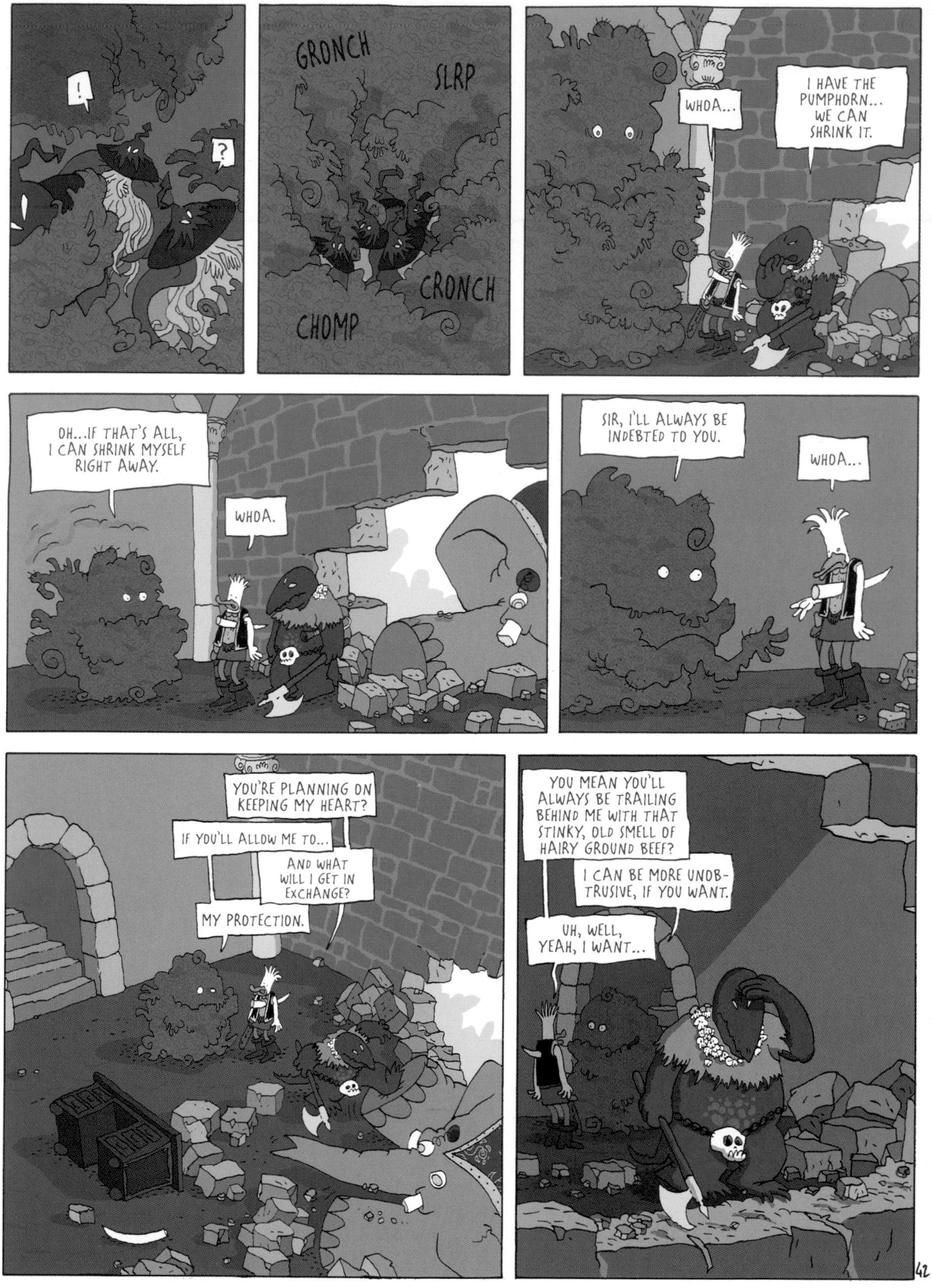
!
?
GRONCH
SLRP
CRONCH
CHOMP
WHOA...
I HAVE THE PUMPHORN... WE CAN SHRINK IT.
OH...IF THAT'S ALL, I CAN SHRINK MYSELF RIGHT AWAY.
WHOA.
SIR, I'LL ALWAYS BE INDEBTED TO YOU.
WHOA...
YOU'RE PLANNING ON KEEPING MY HEART?
IF YOU'LL ALLOW ME TO...
AND WHAT WILL I GET IN EXCHANGE?
MY PROTECTION.
YOU MEAN YOU'LL ALWAYS BE TRAILING BEHIND ME WITH THAT STINKY, OLD SMELL OF HAIRY GROUND BEEF?
I CAN BE MORE UNOB-TRUSIVE, IF YOU WANT.
UH, WELL, YEAH, I WANT...

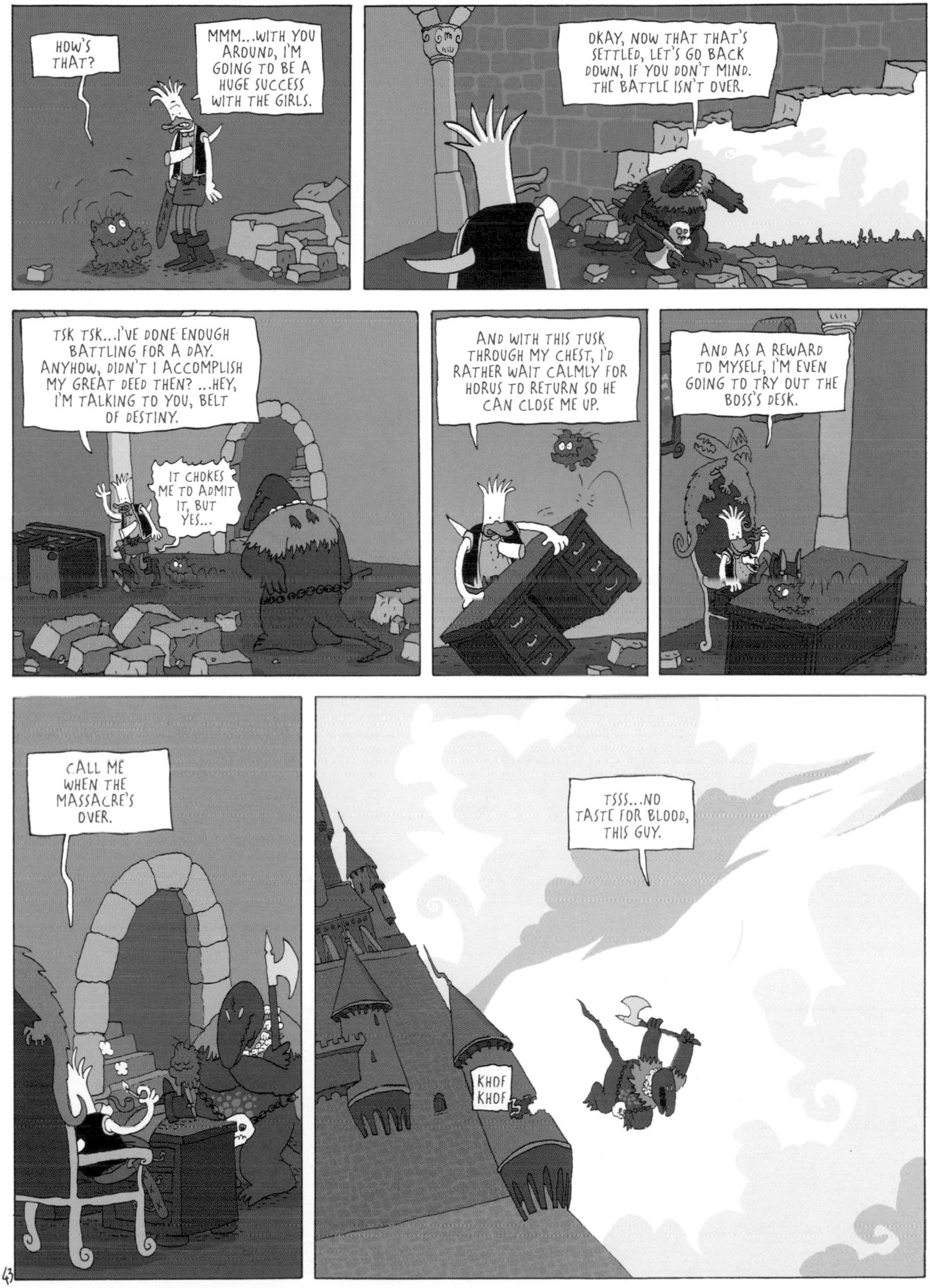

HOW'S THAT?
MMM...WITH YOU AROUND, I'M GOING TO BE A HUGE SUCCESS WITH THE GIRLS.
OKAY, NOW THAT THAT'S SETTLED, LET'S GO BACK DOWN, IF YOU DON'T MIND. THE BATTLE ISN'T OVER.
TSK TSK...I'VE DONE ENOUGH BATTLING FOR A DAY. ANYHOW, DIDN'T I ACCOMPLISH MY GREAT DEED THEN? ...HEY, I'M TALKING TO YOU, BELT OF DESTINY.
IT CHOKES ME TO ADMIT IT, BUT YES...
AND WITH THIS TUSK THROUGH MY CHEST, I'D RATHER WAIT CALMLY FOR HORUS TO RETURN SO HE CAN CLOSE ME UP.
AND AS A REWARD TO MYSELF, I'M EVEN GOING TO TRY OUT THE BOSS'S DESK.
CALL ME WHEN THE MASSACRE'S OVER.
TSSS...NO TASTE FOR BLOOD, THIS GUY.
KHOF KHOF

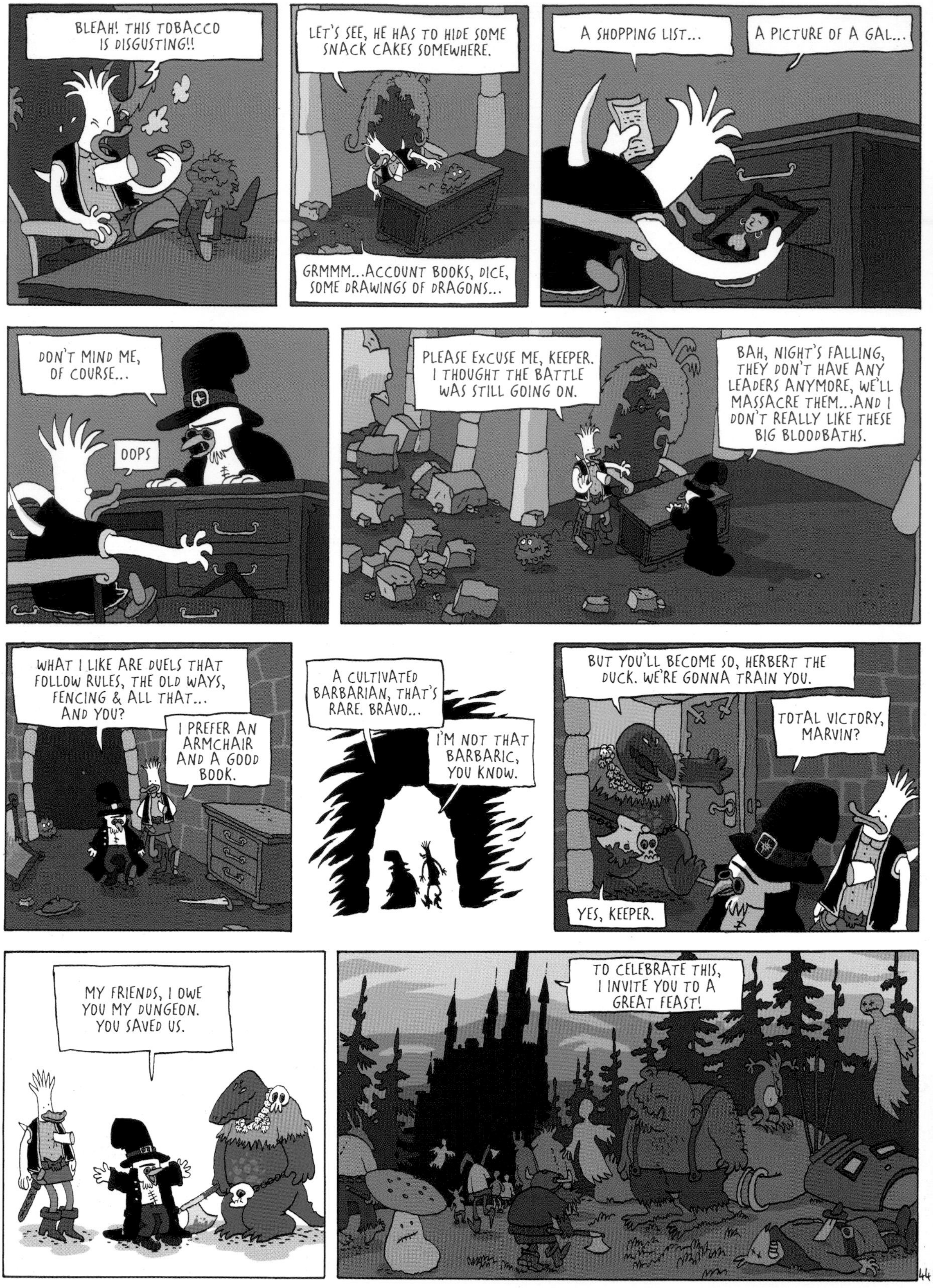
BLEAH! THIS TOBACCO IS DISGUSTING!!
LET'S SEE, HE HAS TO HIDE SOME SNACK CAKES SOMEWHERE.
GRMMM...ACCOUNT BOOKS, DICE, SOME DRAWINGS OF DRAGONS...
A SHOPPING LIST...
A PICTURE OF A GAL...
DON'T MIND ME, OF COURSE...
OOPS
PLEASE EXCUSE ME, KEEPER. I THOUGHT THE BATTLE WAS STILL GOING ON.
BAH, NIGHT'S FALLING, THEY DON'T HAVE ANY LEADERS ANYMORE, WE'LL MASSACRE THEM...AND I DON'T REALLY LIKE THESE BIG BLOODBATHS.
WHAT I LIKE ARE DUELS THAT FOLLOW RULES, THE OLD WAYS, FENCING & ALL THAT... AND YOU?
I PREFER AN ARMCHAIR AND A GOOD BOOK.
A CULTIVATED BARBARIAN, THAT'S RARE. BRAVO...
I'M NOT THAT BARBARIC, YOU KNOW.
BUT YOU'LL BECOME SO, HERBERT THE DUCK. WE'RE GONNA TRAIN YOU.
TOTAL VICTORY, MARVIN?
YES, KEEPER.
MY FRIENDS, I OWE YOU MY DUNGEON. YOU SAVED US.
TO CELEBRATE THIS, I INVITE YOU TO A GREAT FEAST!

Panel 1:
THERE'S JUST US FOR THE FEAST?

WHAT DID YOU EXPECT?

Panel 2:
I DON'T KNOW...EVERYONE GATHERED AROUND A FIRE, A BARD, ROASTING GAME...

HE'S A BIT STINGY, YOU KNOW.

Panel 3:
HANG IN THERE, MY FRIENDS, HERE'S OUR LITTLE MEAL PLATTER.

THANKS, BOSS.

SHOULDN'T HAVE.

Panel 4:
IT SMELLS GOOD. WHAT IS IT?

A HOODED ONE.

Panel 5:
THERE WERE TWO SURVIVORS. WE STUCK ONE IN A CAGE FOR THE BARBARIANS AND WE'RE EATING THE OTHER ONE.

OH...IT'S JUST THAT I DON'T EAT MEAT. BUT THE VEGGIES WILL BE ENOUGH.

Panel 6:
OTHERWISE, HOW'S IT GOING? DID YOU LOSE MUCH MONEY DURING ALL THIS?

BAH...IT'S GOOD FOR PUBLICITY. THE BARBARIANS WILL THINK THE DUNGEON'S VULNERABLE AND THERE'LL BE EVEN MORE OF THEM COMING TO GET MASSACRED.

Panel 7:
LATER THAT NIGHT.

COOKOO!

HEY! OUR HEROES!

Panel 8:
SORRY, BUT WE'RE A LITTLE HUNGRY.

THAT SMELLS GOOD, WHAT IS IT?

A HOODED ONE.

Panel 9:
WE WERE SUPPOSED TO STICK HIM IN A CAGE, BUT HE WOULDN'T LET US. HE BLEW UP TWO TROLLS SO WE KILLED HIM.

Panel 10:
HMM...AND THAT SMELLS GOOD, TOO. IS IT SQUASH?

NO, I SNEEZED.

Panel 11:
DID YOU HAVE TIME TO SPEAK TO THE KEEPER ABOUT THAT SMALL, SPECIAL BONUS?

YUP.

AND HE SAID...?

NO.

49

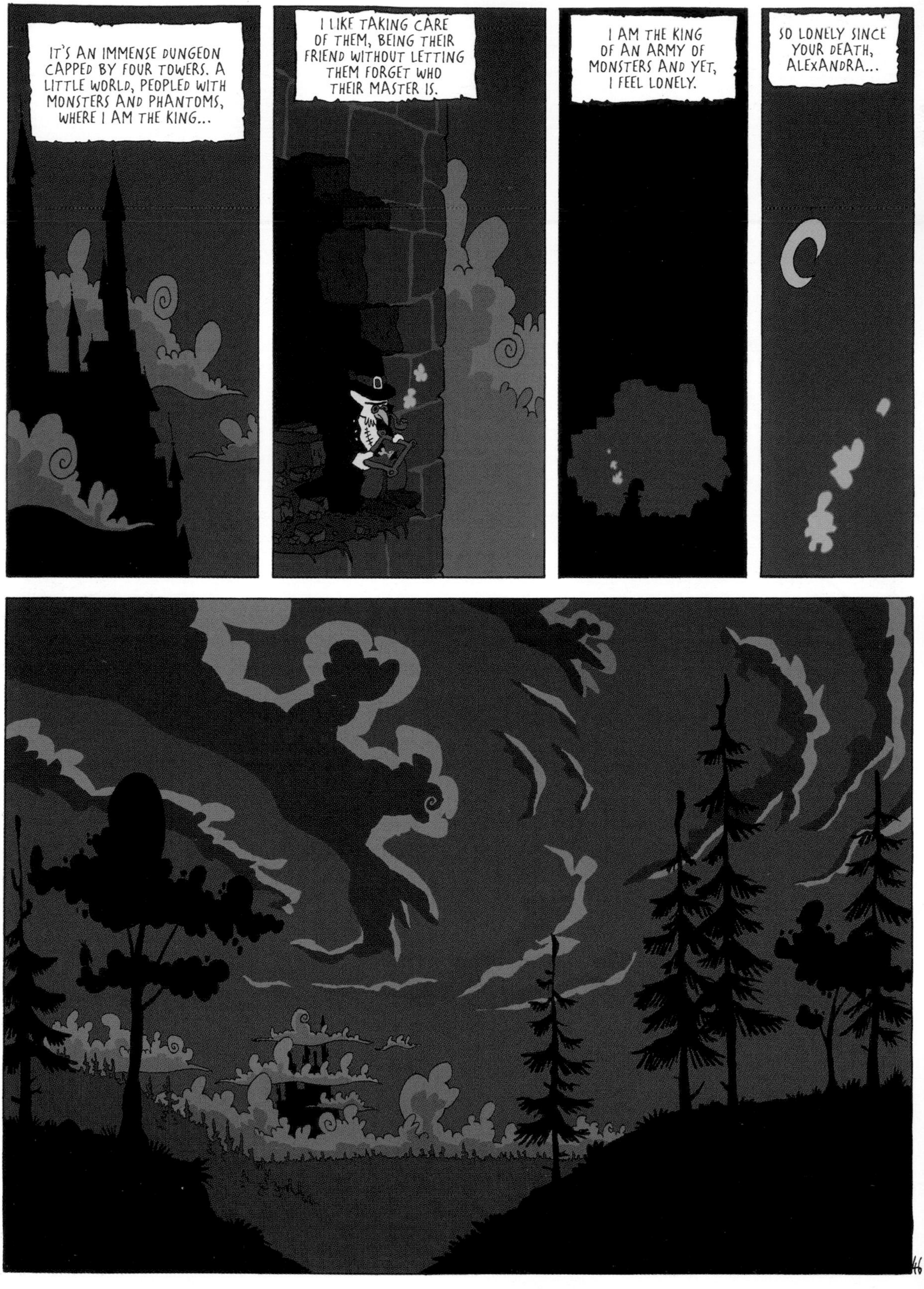
IT'S AN IMMENSE DUNGEON CAPPED BY FOUR TOWERS. A LITTLE WORLD, PEOPLED WITH MONSTERS AND PHANTOMS, WHERE I AM THE KING...
I LIKE TAKING CARE OF THEM, BEING THEIR FRIEND WITHOUT LETTING THEM FORGET WHO THEIR MASTER IS.
I AM THE KING OF AN ARMY OF MONSTERS AND YET, I FEEL LONELY.
SO LONELY SINCE YOUR DEATH, ALEXANDRA...

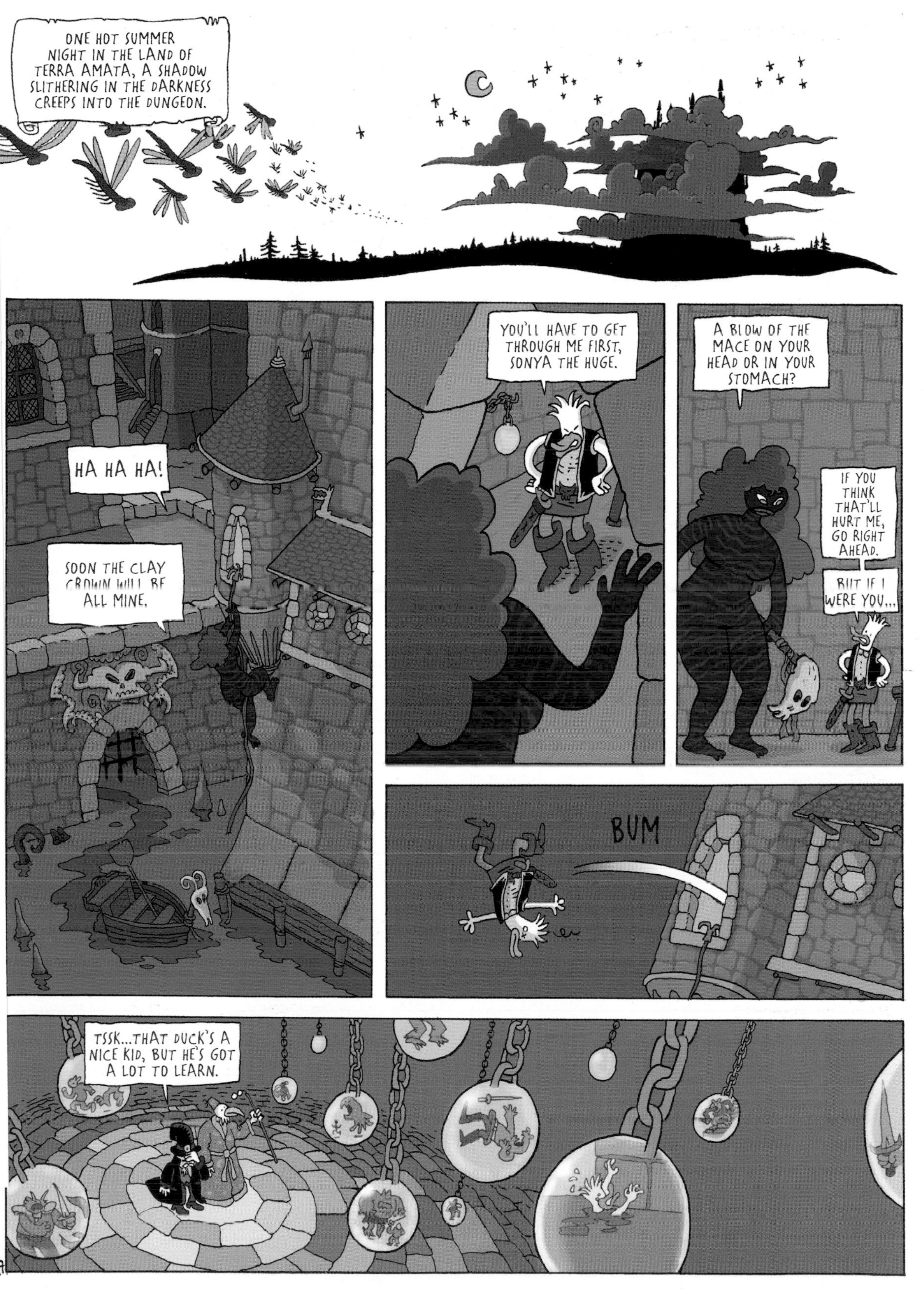
ONE HOT SUMMER NIGHT IN THE LAND OF TERRA AMATA, A SHADOW SLITHERING IN THE DARKNESS CREEPS INTO THE DUNGEON.
HA HA HA!
SOON THE CLAY CROWN WILL BE ALL MINE.
YOU'LL HAVE TO GET THROUGH ME FIRST, SONYA THE HUGE.
A BLOW OF THE MACE ON YOUR HEAD OR IN YOUR STOMACH?
IF YOU THINK THAT'LL HURT ME, GO RIGHT AHEAD.
BUT IF I WERE YOU...
BUM
TSSK...THAT DUCK'S A NICE KID, BUT HE'S GOT A LOT TO LEARN.

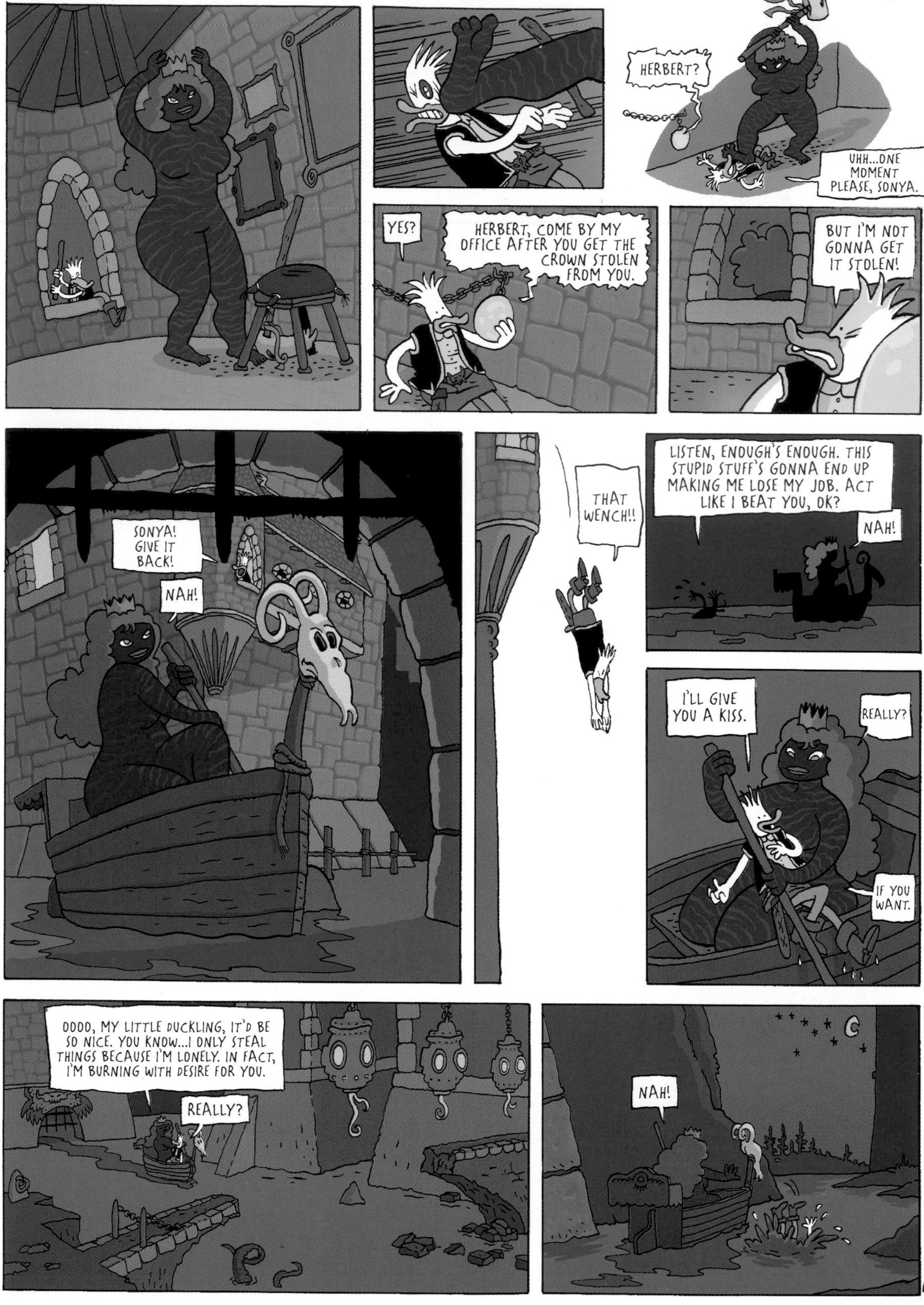
HERBERT?
UHH...ONE MOMENT PLEASE, SONYA.
YES?
HERBERT, COME BY MY OFFICE AFTER YOU GET THE CROWN STOLEN FROM YOU.
BUT I'M NOT GONNA GET IT STOLEN!
SONYA! GIVE IT BACK!
NAH!
THAT WENCH!!
LISTEN, ENOUGH'S ENOUGH. THIS STUPID STUFF'S GONNA END UP MAKING ME LOSE MY JOB. ACT LIKE I BEAT YOU, OK?
NAH!
I'LL GIVE YOU A KISS.
REALLY?
IF YOU WANT.
OOOO, MY LITTLE DUCKLING, IT'D BE SO NICE. YOU KNOW...I ONLY STEAL THINGS BECAUSE I'M LONELY. IN FACT, I'M BURNING WITH DESIRE FOR YOU.
REALLY?
NAH!

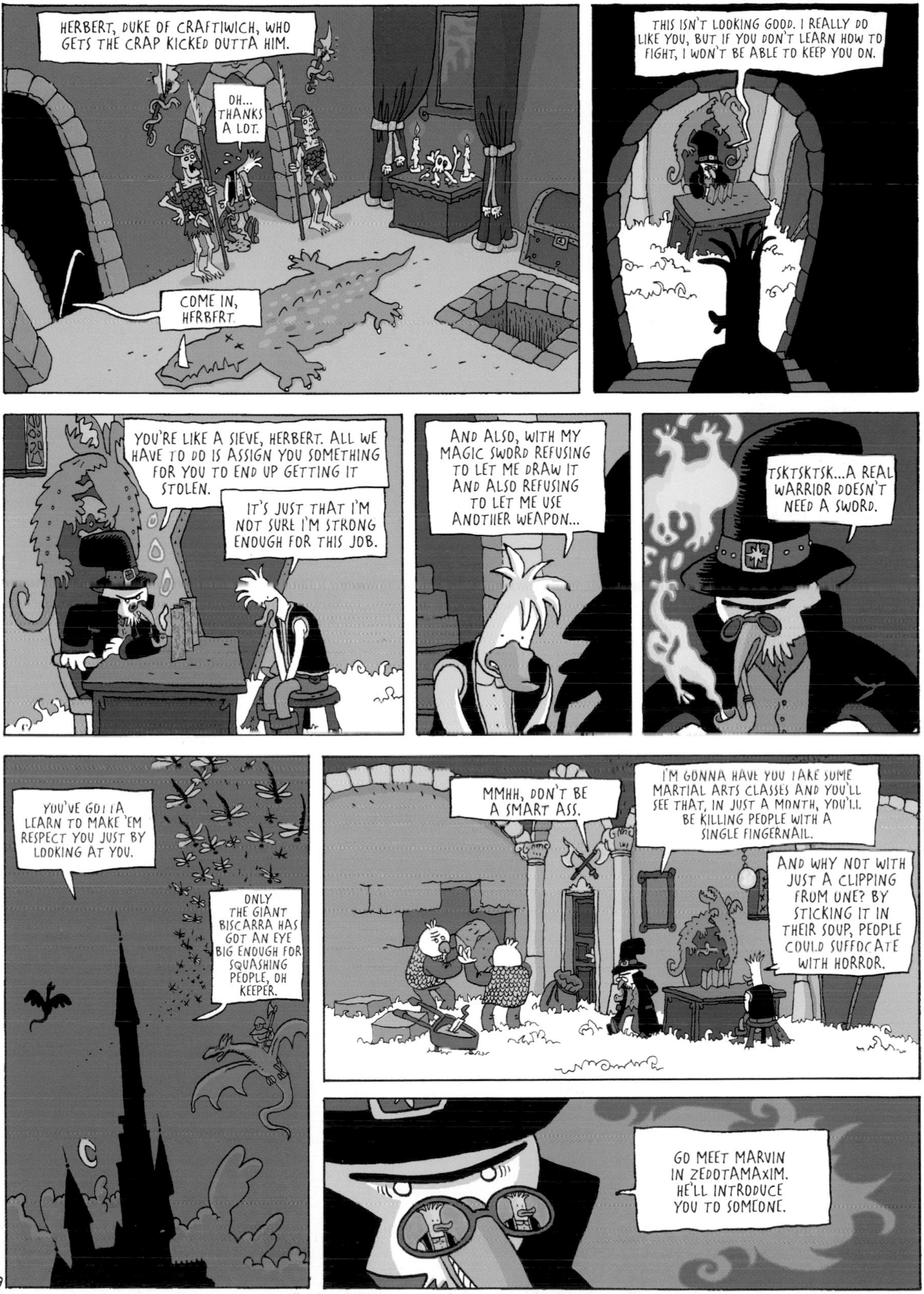
HERBERT, DUKE OF CRAFTIWICH, WHO GETS THE CRAP KICKED OUTTA HIM.
OH... THANKS A LOT.
COME IN, HERBERT.
THIS ISN'T LOOKING GOOD. I REALLY DO LIKE YOU, BUT IF YOU DON'T LEARN HOW TO FIGHT, I WON'T BE ABLE TO KEEP YOU ON.
YOU'RE LIKE A SIEVE, HERBERT. ALL WE HAVE TO DO IS ASSIGN YOU SOMETHING FOR YOU TO END UP GETTING IT STOLEN.
IT'S JUST THAT I'M NOT SURE I'M STRONG ENOUGH FOR THIS JOB.
AND ALSO, WITH MY MAGIC SWORD REFUSING TO LET ME DRAW IT AND ALSO REFUSING TO LET ME USE ANOTHER WEAPON...
TSKTSKTSK...A REAL WARRIOR DOESN'T NEED A SWORD.
YOU'VE GOTTA LEARN TO MAKE 'EM RESPECT YOU JUST BY LOOKING AT YOU.
ONLY THE GIANT BISCARRA HAS GOT AN EYE BIG ENOUGH FOR SQUASHING PEOPLE, OH KEEPER.
MMHH, DON'T BE A SMART ASS.
I'M GONNA HAVE YOU TAKE SOME MARTIAL ARTS CLASSES AND YOU'LL SEE THAT, IN JUST A MONTH, YOU'LL BE KILLING PEOPLE WITH A SINGLE FINGERNAIL.
AND WHY NOT WITH JUST A CLIPPING FROM ONE? BY STICKING IT IN THEIR SOUP, PEOPLE COULD SUFFOCATE WITH HORROR.
GO MEET MARVIN IN ZEDOTAMAXIM. HE'LL INTRODUCE YOU TO SOMEONE.

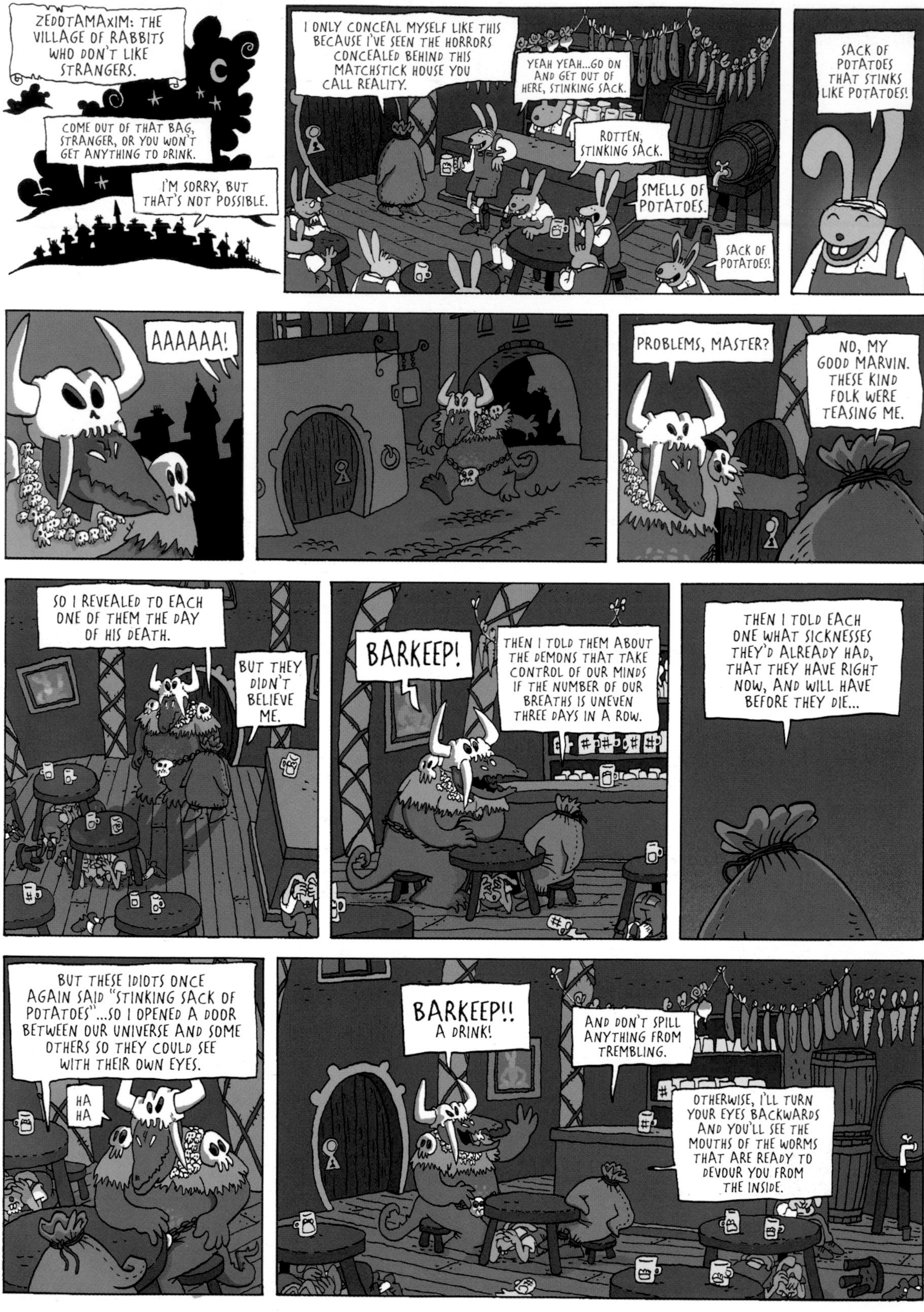

ZEDOTAMAXIM: THE VILLAGE OF RABBITS WHO DON'T LIKE STRANGERS.
COME OUT OF THAT BAG, STRANGER, OR YOU WON'T GET ANYTHING TO DRINK.
I'M SORRY, BUT THAT'S NOT POSSIBLE.
I ONLY CONCEAL MYSELF LIKE THIS BECAUSE I'VE SEEN THE HORRORS CONCEALED BEHIND THIS MATCHSTICK HOUSE YOU CALL REALITY.
YEAH YEAH...GO ON AND GET OUT OF HERE, STINKING SACK.
ROTTEN, STINKING SACK.
SMELLS OF POTATOES.
SACK OF POTATOES!
SACK OF POTATOES THAT STINKS LIKE POTATOES!
AAAAAA!
PROBLEMS, MASTER?
NO, MY GOOD MARVIN. THESE KIND FOLK WERE TEASING ME.
SO I REVEALED TO EACH ONE OF THEM THE DAY OF HIS DEATH.
BUT THEY DIDN'T BELIEVE ME.
BARKEEP!
THEN I TOLD THEM ABOUT THE DEMONS THAT TAKE CONTROL OF OUR MINDS IF THE NUMBER OF OUR BREATHS IS UNEVEN THREE DAYS IN A ROW.
THEN I TOLD EACH ONE WHAT SICKNESSES THEY'D ALREADY HAD, THAT THEY HAVE RIGHT NOW, AND WILL HAVE BEFORE THEY DIE...
BUT THESE IDIOTS ONCE AGAIN SAID "STINKING SACK OF POTATOES"...SO I OPENED A DOOR BETWEEN OUR UNIVERSE AND SOME OTHERS SO THEY COULD SEE WITH THEIR OWN EYES.
HA HA
BARKEEP!! A DRINK!
AND DON'T SPILL ANYTHING FROM TREMBLING.
OTHERWISE, I'LL TURN YOUR EYES BACKWARDS AND YOU'LL SEE THE MOUTHS OF THE WORMS THAT ARE READY TO DEVOUR YOU FROM THE INSIDE.

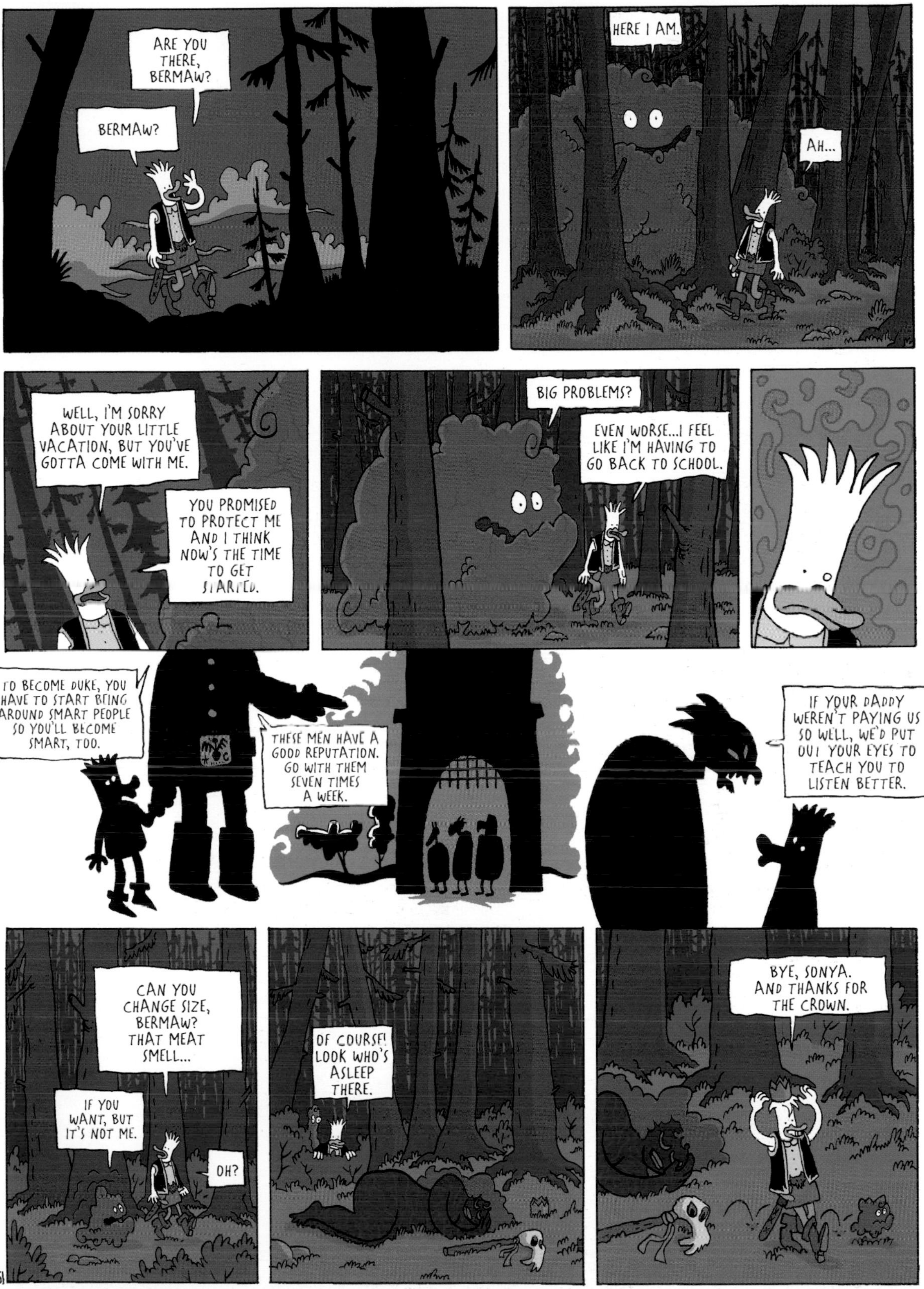
ARE YOU THERE, BERMAW?
BERMAW?
HERE I AM.
AH...
WELL, I'M SORRY ABOUT YOUR LITTLE VACATION, BUT YOU'VE GOTTA COME WITH ME.
YOU PROMISED TO PROTECT ME AND I THINK NOW'S THE TIME TO GET STARTED.
BIG PROBLEMS?
EVEN WORSE...I FEEL LIKE I'M HAVING TO GO BACK TO SCHOOL.
TO BECOME DUKE, YOU HAVE TO START BEING AROUND SMART PEOPLE SO YOU'LL BECOME SMART, TOO.
THESE MEN HAVE A GOOD REPUTATION. GO WITH THEM SEVEN TIMES A WEEK.
IF YOUR DADDY WEREN'T PAYING US SO WELL, WE'D PUT OUT YOUR EYES TO TEACH YOU TO LISTEN BETTER.
CAN YOU CHANGE SIZE, BERMAW? THAT MEAT SMELL...
IF YOU WANT, BUT IT'S NOT ME.
OH?
OF COURSE! LOOK WHO'S ASLEEP THERE.
BYE, SONYA. AND THANKS FOR THE CROWN.

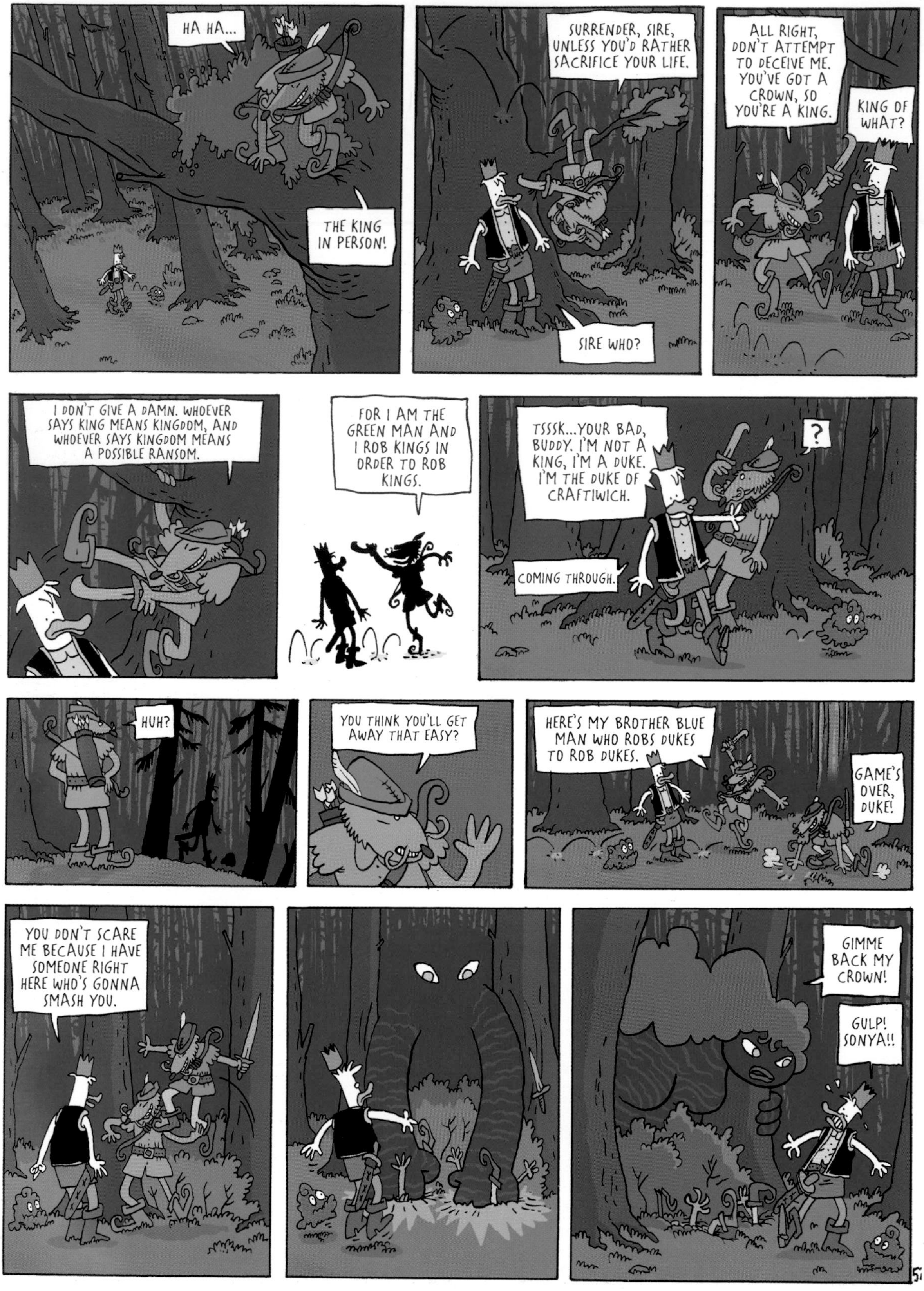
HA HA...
THE KING IN PERSON!
SURRENDER, SIRE, UNLESS YOU'D RATHER SACRIFICE YOUR LIFE.
SIRE WHO?
ALL RIGHT, DON'T ATTEMPT TO DECEIVE ME. YOU'VE GOT A CROWN, SO YOU'RE A KING.
KING OF WHAT?
I DON'T GIVE A DAMN. WHOEVER SAYS KING MEANS KINGDOM, AND WHOEVER SAYS KINGDOM MEANS A POSSIBLE RANSOM.
FOR I AM THE GREEN MAN AND I ROB KINGS IN ORDER TO ROB KINGS.
TSSSK...YOUR BAD, BUDDY. I'M NOT A KING, I'M A DUKE. I'M THE DUKE OF CRAFTIWICH.
?
COMING THROUGH.
HUH?
YOU THINK YOU'LL GET AWAY THAT EASY?
HERE'S MY BROTHER BLUE MAN WHO ROBS DUKES TO ROB DUKES.
GAME'S OVER, DUKE!
YOU DON'T SCARE ME BECAUSE I HAVE SOMEONE RIGHT HERE WHO'S GONNA SMASH YOU.
GIMME BACK MY CROWN!
GULP! SONYA!!

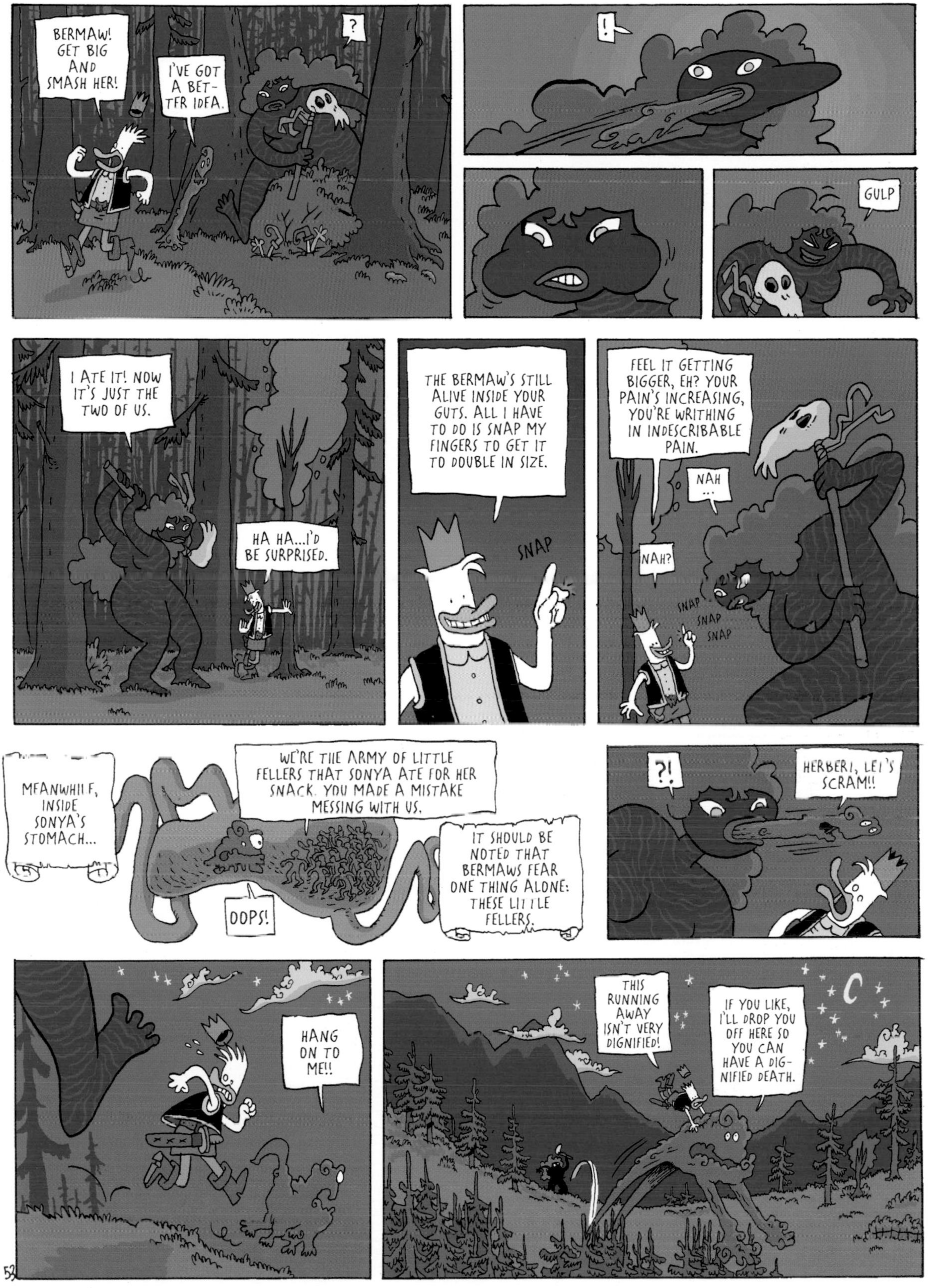
BERMAW! GET BIG AND SMASH HER!
?
I'VE GOT A BETTER IDEA.
!
GULP
I ATE IT! NOW IT'S JUST THE TWO OF US.
HA HA...I'D BE SURPRISED.
THE BERMAW'S STILL ALIVE INSIDE YOUR GUTS. ALL I HAVE TO DO IS SNAP MY FINGERS TO GET IT TO DOUBLE IN SIZE.
SNAP
FEEL IT GETTING BIGGER, EH? YOUR PAIN'S INCREASING, YOU'RE WRITHING IN INDESCRIBABLE PAIN.
NAH ...
NAH?
SNAP SNAP SNAP
MEANWHILE, INSIDE SONYA'S STOMACH...
WE'RE THE ARMY OF LITTLE FELLERS THAT SONYA ATE FOR HER SNACK. YOU MADE A MISTAKE MESSING WITH US.
OOPS!
IT SHOULD BE NOTED THAT BERMAWS FEAR ONE THING ALONE: THESE LITTLE FELLERS.
?!
HERBERT, LET'S SCRAM!!
HANG ON TO ME!!
THIS RUNNING AWAY ISN'T VERY DIGNIFIED!
IF YOU LIKE, I'LL DROP YOU OFF HERE SO YOU CAN HAVE A DIGNIFIED DEATH.

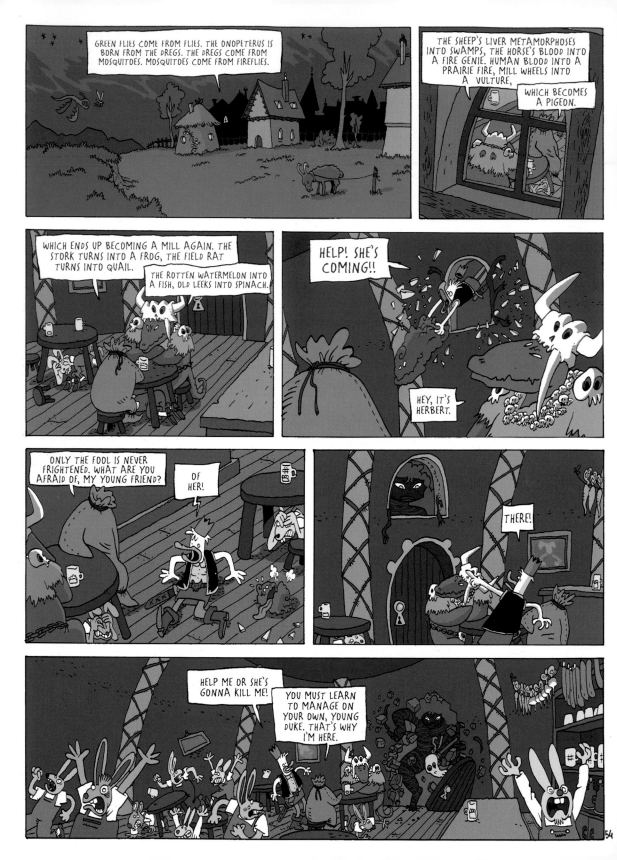

GREEN FLIES COME FROM FLIES. THE ONOPETERUS IS BORN FROM THE DREGS. THE DREGS COME FROM MOSQUITOES. MOSQUITOES COME FROM FIREFLIES.

THE SHEEP'S LIVER METAMORPHOSES INTO SWAMPS, THE HORSE'S BLOOD INTO A FIRE GENIE. HUMAN BLOOD INTO A PRAIRIE FIRE, MILL WHEELS INTO A VULTURE, WHICH BECOMES A PIGEON.

WHICH ENDS UP BECOMING A MILL AGAIN. THE STORK TURNS INTO A FROG, THE FIELD RAT TURNS INTO QUAIL.

THE ROTTEN WATERMELON INTO A FISH, OLD LEEKS INTO SPINACH.

HELP! SHE'S COMING!!

HEY, IT'S HERBERT.

ONLY THE FOOL IS NEVER FRIGHTENED. WHAT ARE YOU AFRAID OF, MY YOUNG FRIEND?

OF HER!

THERE!

HELP ME OR SHE'S GONNA KILL ME!

YOU MUST LEARN TO MANAGE ON YOUR OWN, YOUNG DUKE. THAT'S WHY I'M HERE.

54

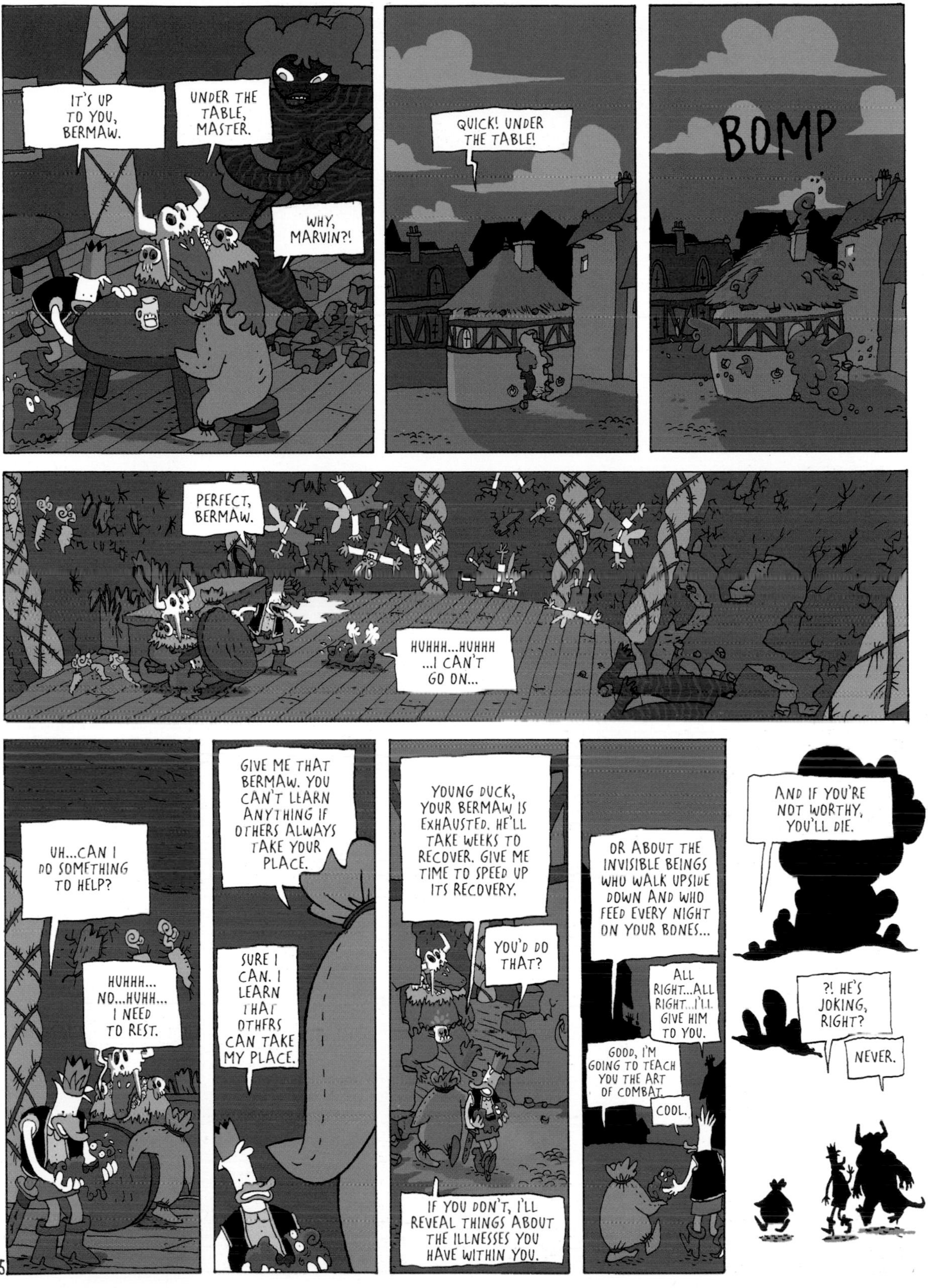

IT'S UP TO YOU, BERMAW.
UNDER THE TABLE, MASTER.
WHY, MARVIN?!
QUICK! UNDER THE TABLE!
BOMP
PERFECT, BERMAW.
HUHHH...HUHHH ...I CAN'T GO ON...
UH...CAN I DO SOMETHING TO HELP?
HUHHH... NO...HUHH... I NEED TO REST.
GIVE ME THAT BERMAW. YOU CAN'T LEARN ANYTHING IF OTHERS ALWAYS TAKE YOUR PLACE.
SURE I CAN. I LEARN THAT OTHERS CAN TAKE MY PLACE.
YOUNG DUCK, YOUR BERMAW IS EXHAUSTED. HE'LL TAKE WEEKS TO RECOVER. GIVE ME TIME TO SPEED UP ITS RECOVERY.
YOU'D DO THAT?
IF YOU DON'T, I'LL REVEAL THINGS ABOUT THE ILLNESSES YOU HAVE WITHIN YOU.
OR ABOUT THE INVISIBLE BEINGS WHO WALK UPSIDE DOWN AND WHO FEED EVERY NIGHT ON YOUR BONES...
ALL RIGHT...ALL RIGHT...I'LL GIVE HIM TO YOU.
GOOD, I'M GOING TO TEACH YOU THE ART OF COMBAT.
COOL.
AND IF YOU'RE NOT WORTHY, YOU'LL DIE.
?! HE'S JOKING, RIGHT?
NEVER.

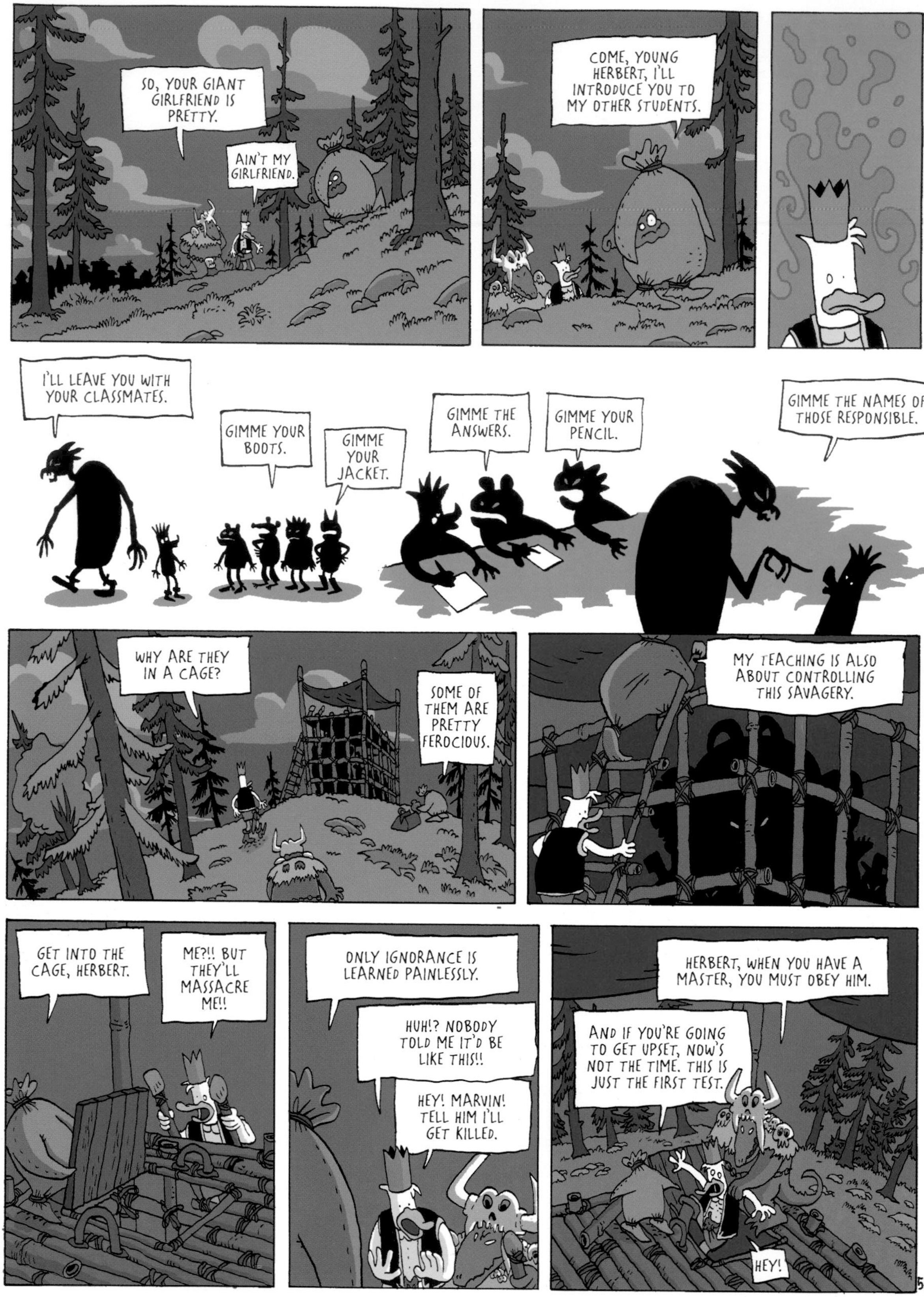
SO, YOUR GIANT GIRLFRIEND IS PRETTY.
AIN'T MY GIRLFRIEND.
COME, YOUNG HERBERT, I'LL INTRODUCE YOU TO MY OTHER STUDENTS.
I'LL LEAVE YOU WITH YOUR CLASSMATES.
GIMME YOUR BOOTS.
GIMME YOUR JACKET.
GIMME THE ANSWERS.
GIMME YOUR PENCIL.
GIMME THE NAMES OF THOSE RESPONSIBLE.
WHY ARE THEY IN A CAGE?
SOME OF THEM ARE PRETTY FEROCIOUS.
MY TEACHING IS ALSO ABOUT CONTROLLING THIS SAVAGERY.
GET INTO THE CAGE, HERBERT.
ME?!! BUT THEY'LL MASSACRE ME!!
ONLY IGNORANCE IS LEARNED PAINLESSLY.
HUH!? NOBODY TOLD ME IT'D BE LIKE THIS!!
HEY! MARVIN! TELL HIM I'LL GET KILLED.
HERBERT, WHEN YOU HAVE A MASTER, YOU MUST OBEY HIM.
AND IF YOU'RE GOING TO GET UPSET, NOW'S NOT THE TIME. THIS IS JUST THE FIRST TEST.
HEY!

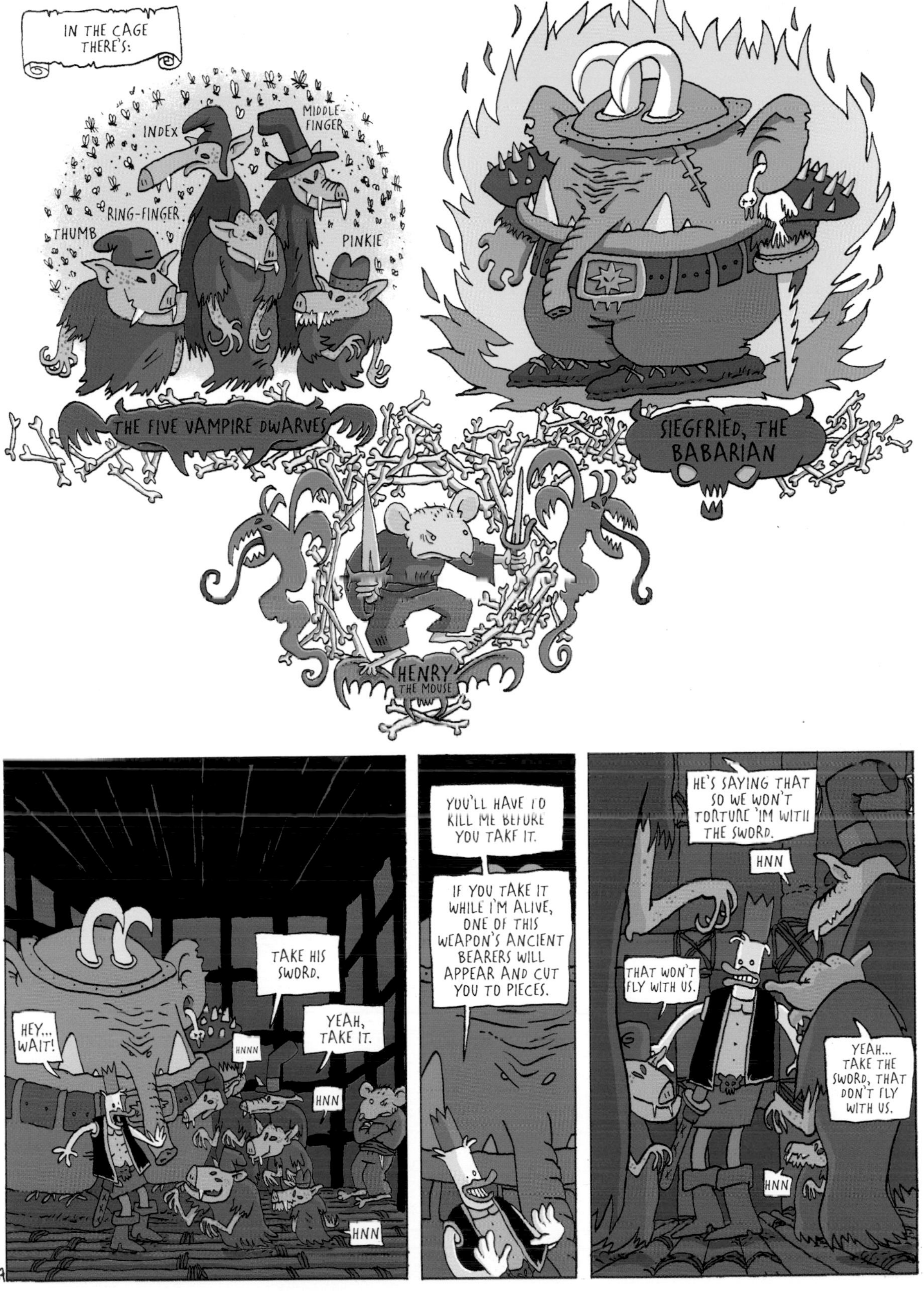
IN THE CAGE THERE'S:
INDEX
MIDDLE-FINGER
RING-FINGER
THUMB
PINKIE
THE FIVE VAMPIRE DWARVES
SIEGFRIED, THE BABARIAN
HENRY THE MOUSE
HEY... WAIT!
TAKE HIS SWORD.
HNNN
YEAH, TAKE IT.
HNN
HNN
YOU'LL HAVE TO KILL ME BEFORE YOU TAKE IT.
IF YOU TAKE IT WHILE I'M ALIVE, ONE OF THIS WEAPON'S ANCIENT BEARERS WILL APPEAR AND CUT YOU TO PIECES.
HE'S SAYING THAT SO WE WON'T TORTURE 'IM WITH THE SWORD.
HNN
THAT WON'T FLY WITH US.
YEAH... TAKE THE SWORD, THAT DON'T FLY WITH US.
HNN

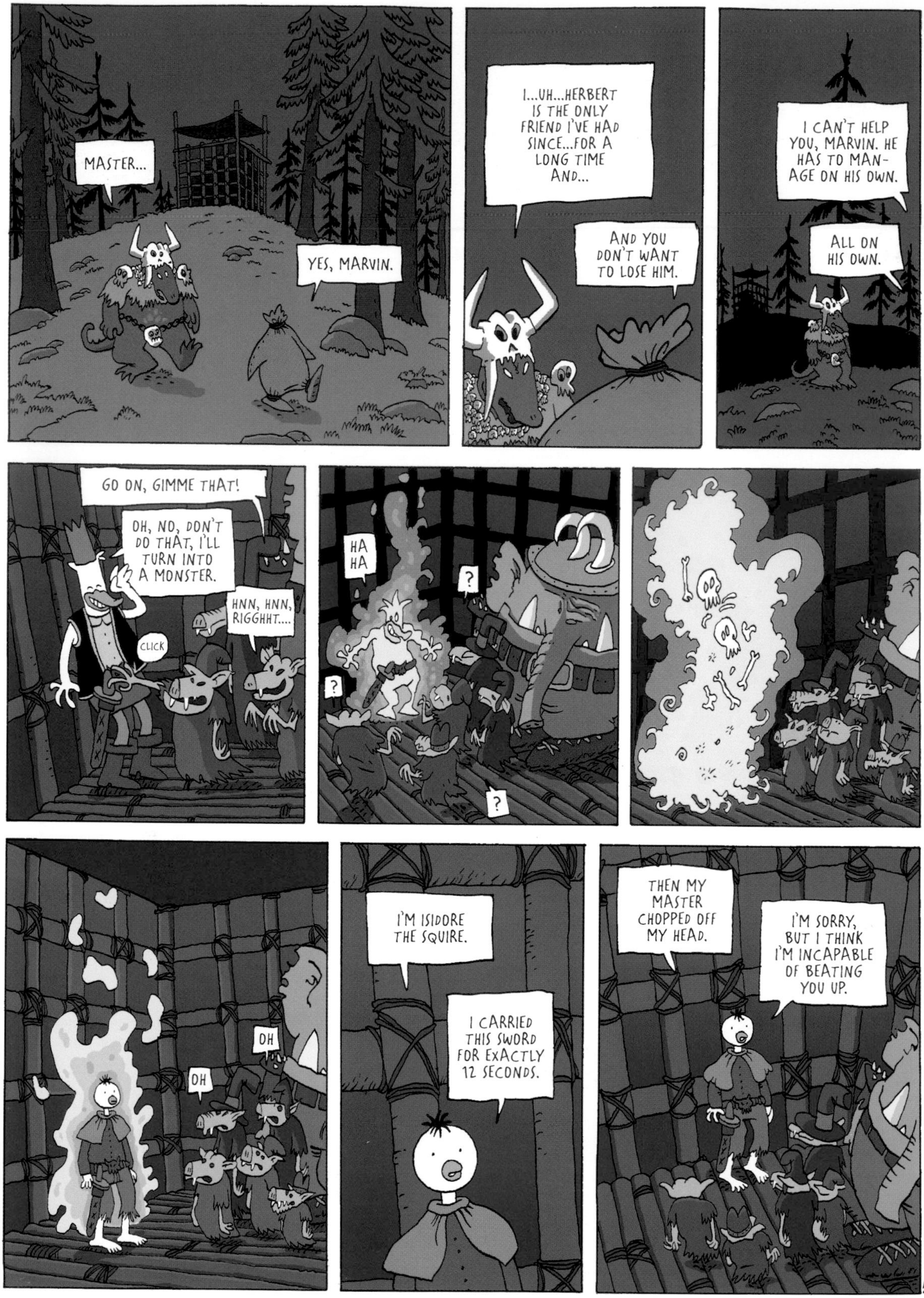
MASTER...
YES, MARVIN.
I...UH...HERBERT IS THE ONLY FRIEND I'VE HAD SINCE...FOR A LONG TIME AND...
AND YOU DON'T WANT TO LOSE HIM.
I CAN'T HELP YOU, MARVIN. HE HAS TO MAN-AGE ON HIS OWN.
ALL ON HIS OWN.
GO ON, GIMME THAT!
OH, NO, DON'T DO THAT, I'LL TURN INTO A MONSTER.
CLICK
HNN, HNN, RIGGHHT....
HA HA
?
?
?
OH
OH
I'M ISIDORE THE SQUIRE.
I CARRIED THIS SWORD FOR EXACTLY 12 SECONDS.
THEN MY MASTER CHOPPED OFF MY HEAD.
I'M SORRY, BUT I THINK I'M INCAPABLE OF BEATING YOU UP.

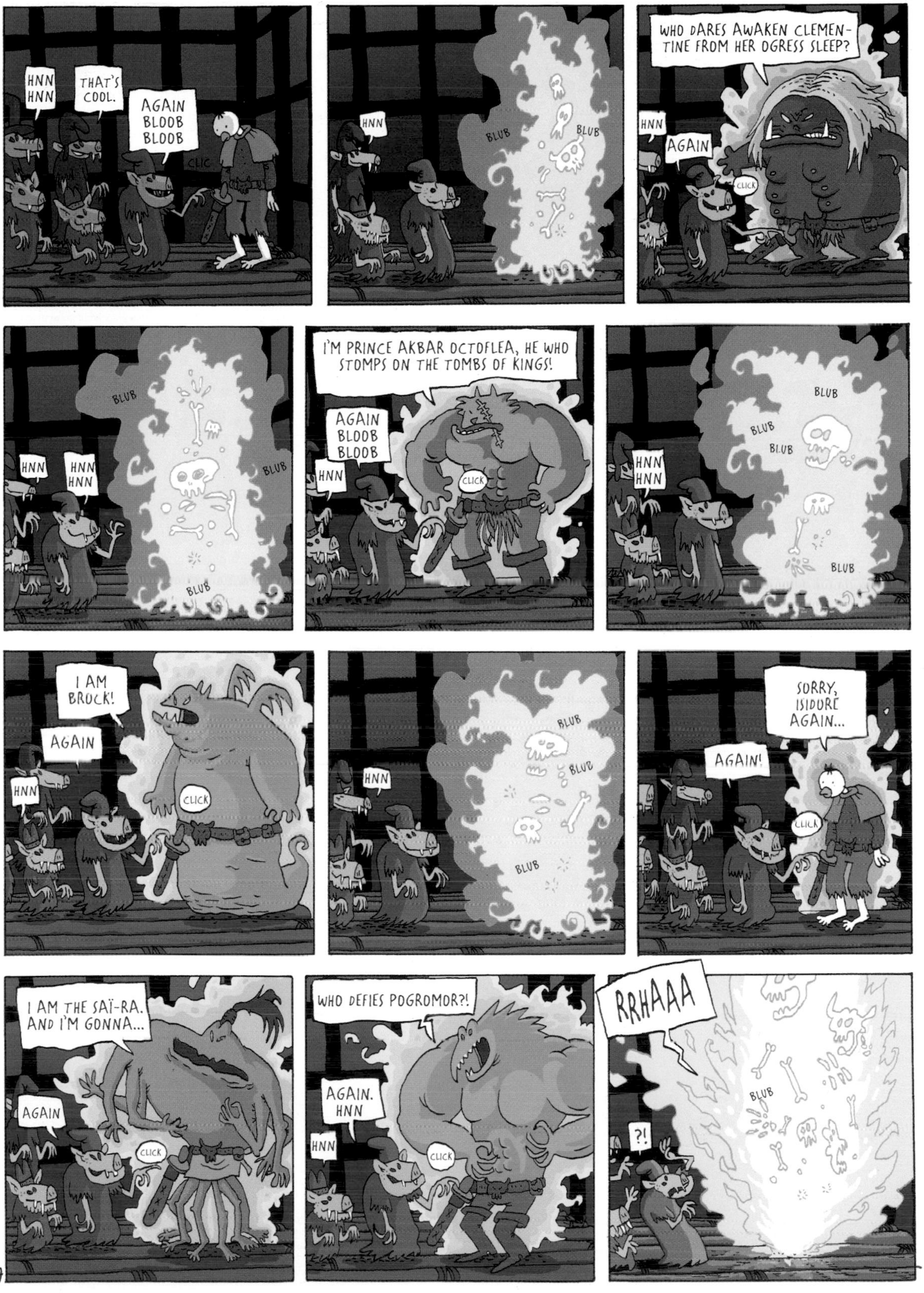
HNN HNN
THAT'S COOL.
AGAIN BLOOB BLOOB
CLIC
HNN
BLUB
BLUB
WHO DARES AWAKEN CLEMENTINE FROM HER OGRESS SLEEP?
HNN
AGAIN
CLICK
BLUB
HNN
HNN HNN
BLUB
BLUB
I'M PRINCE AKBAR OCTOFLEA, HE WHO STOMPS ON THE TOMBS OF KINGS!
AGAIN BLOOB BLOOB
HNN
CLICK
BLUB
BLUB
BLUB
HNN HNN
BLUB
I AM BROCK!
AGAIN
HNN
CLICK
HNN
BLUB
BLUB
BLUB
SORRY, ISIDORE AGAIN...
AGAIN!
CLICK
I AM THE SAÏ-RA. AND I'M GONNA...
AGAIN
CLICK
WHO DEFIES POGROMOR?!
AGAIN. HNN
HNN
CLICK
RRHAAA
BLUB
?!

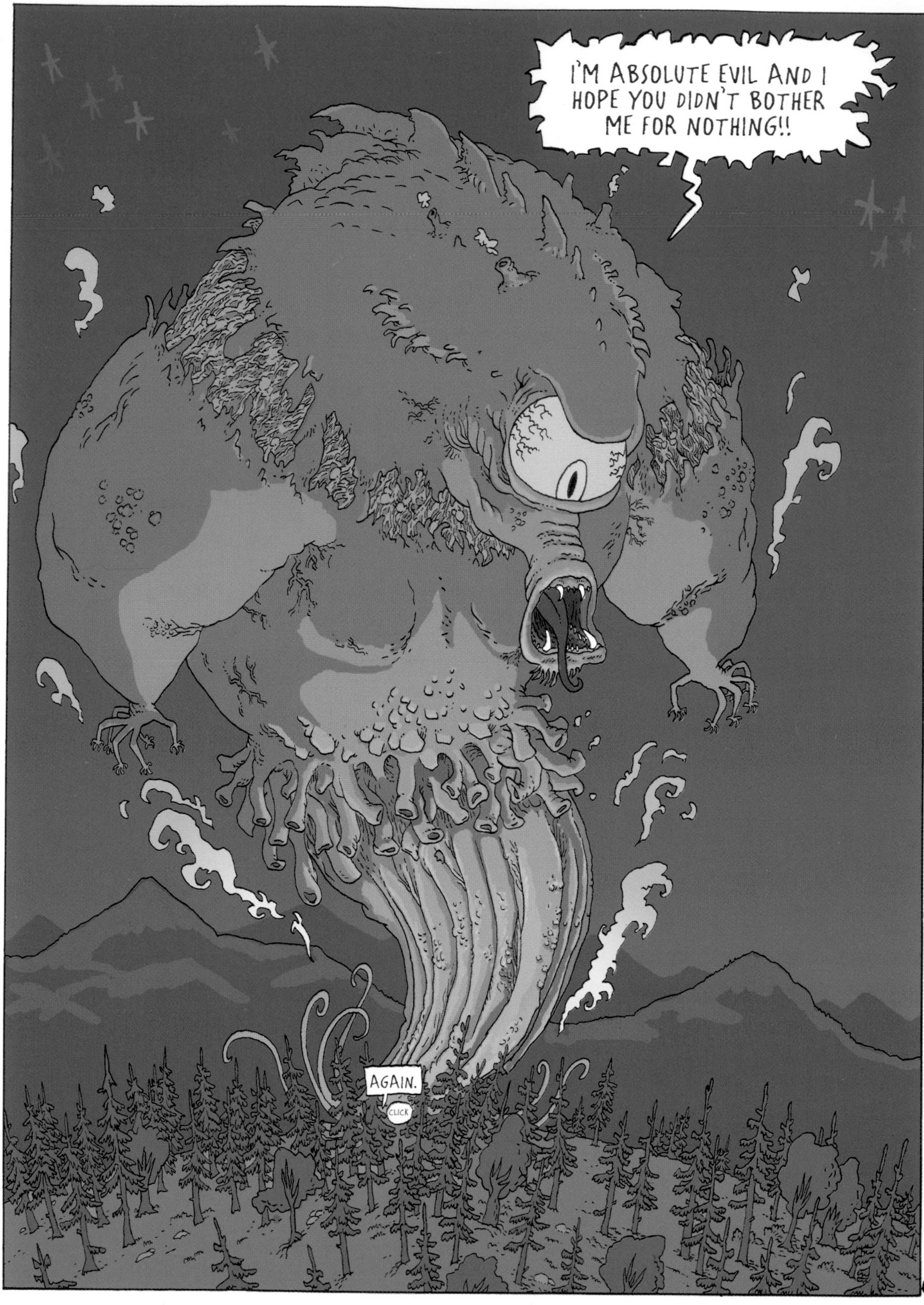
I'M ABSOLUTE EVIL AND I HOPE YOU DIDN'T BOTHER ME FOR NOTHING!!
AGAIN.
CLICK

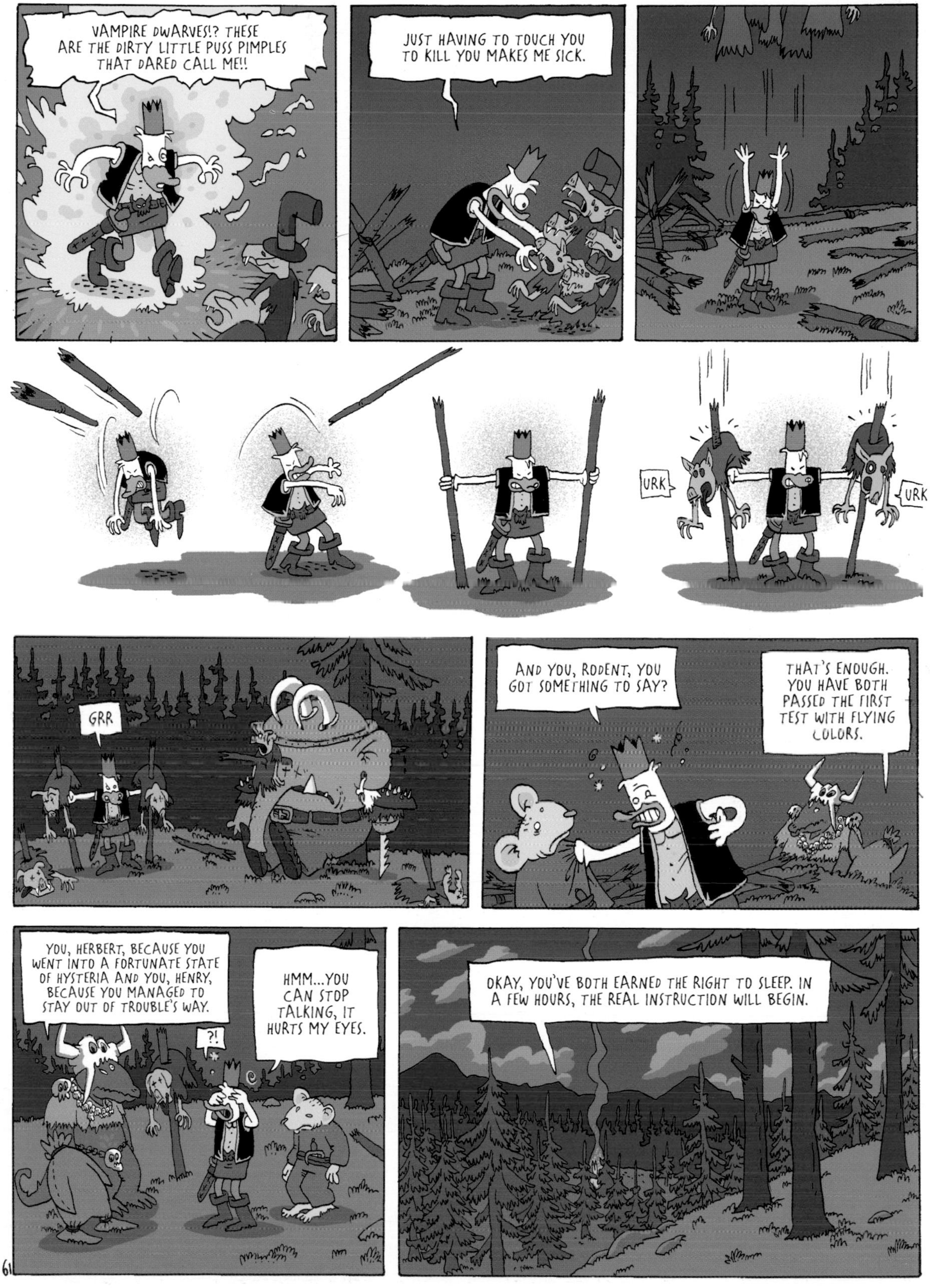
VAMPIRE DWARVES!? THESE ARE THE DIRTY LITTLE PUSS PIMPLES THAT DARED CALL ME!!
JUST HAVING TO TOUCH YOU TO KILL YOU MAKES ME SICK.
URK
URK
GRR
AND YOU, RODENT, YOU GOT SOMETHING TO SAY?
THAT'S ENOUGH. YOU HAVE BOTH PASSED THE FIRST TEST WITH FLYING COLORS.
YOU, HERBERT, BECAUSE YOU WENT INTO A FORTUNATE STATE OF HYSTERIA AND YOU, HENRY, BECAUSE YOU MANAGED TO STAY OUT OF TROUBLE'S WAY.
HMM...YOU CAN STOP TALKING, IT HURTS MY EYES.
?!
OKAY, YOU'VE BOTH EARNED THE RIGHT TO SLEEP. IN A FEW HOURS, THE REAL INSTRUCTION WILL BEGIN.

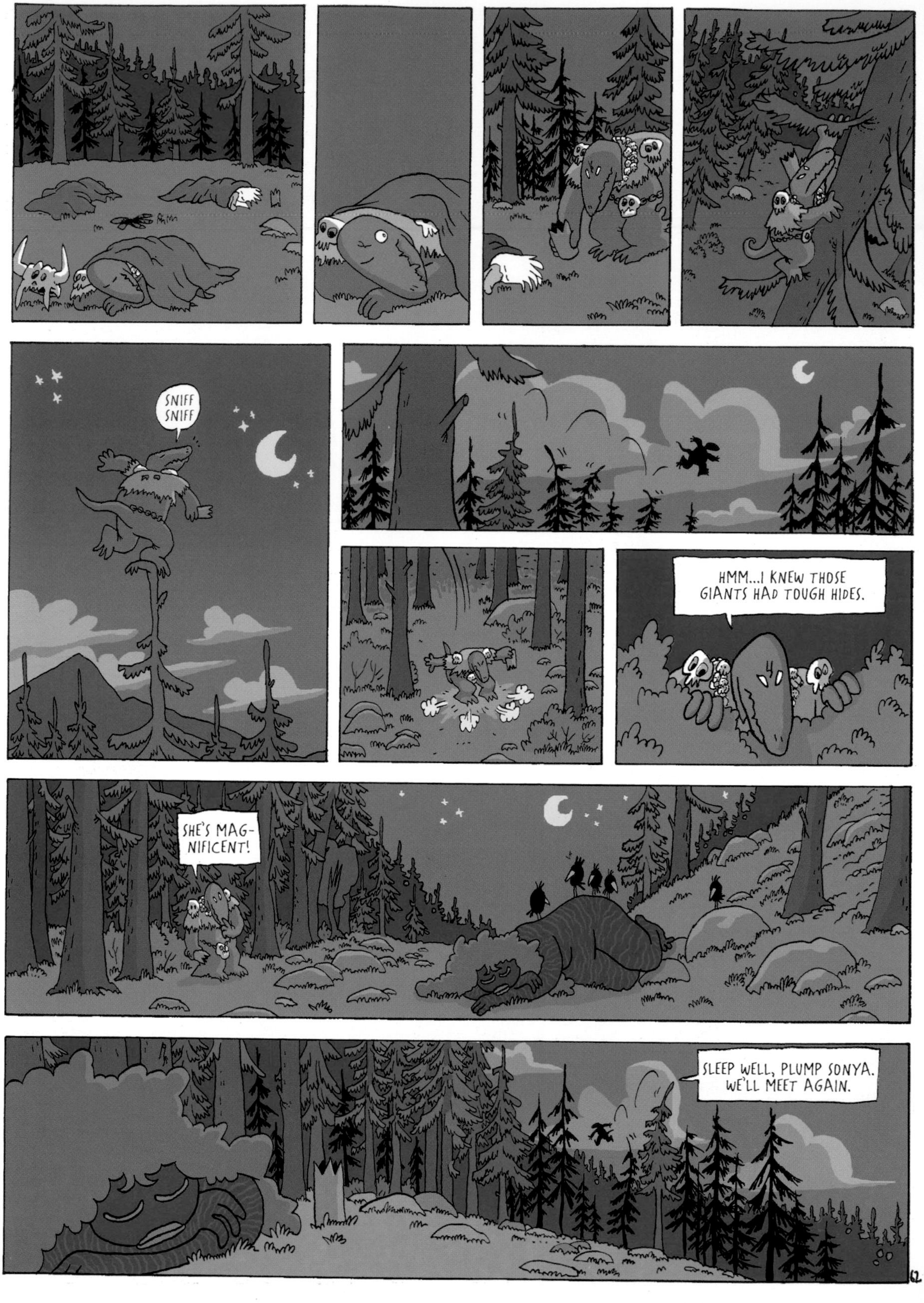
SNIFF SNIFF
HMM...I KNEW THOSE GIANTS HAD TOUGH HIDES.
SHE'S MAG-NIFICENT!
SLEEP WELL, PLUMP SONYA. WE'LL MEET AGAIN.

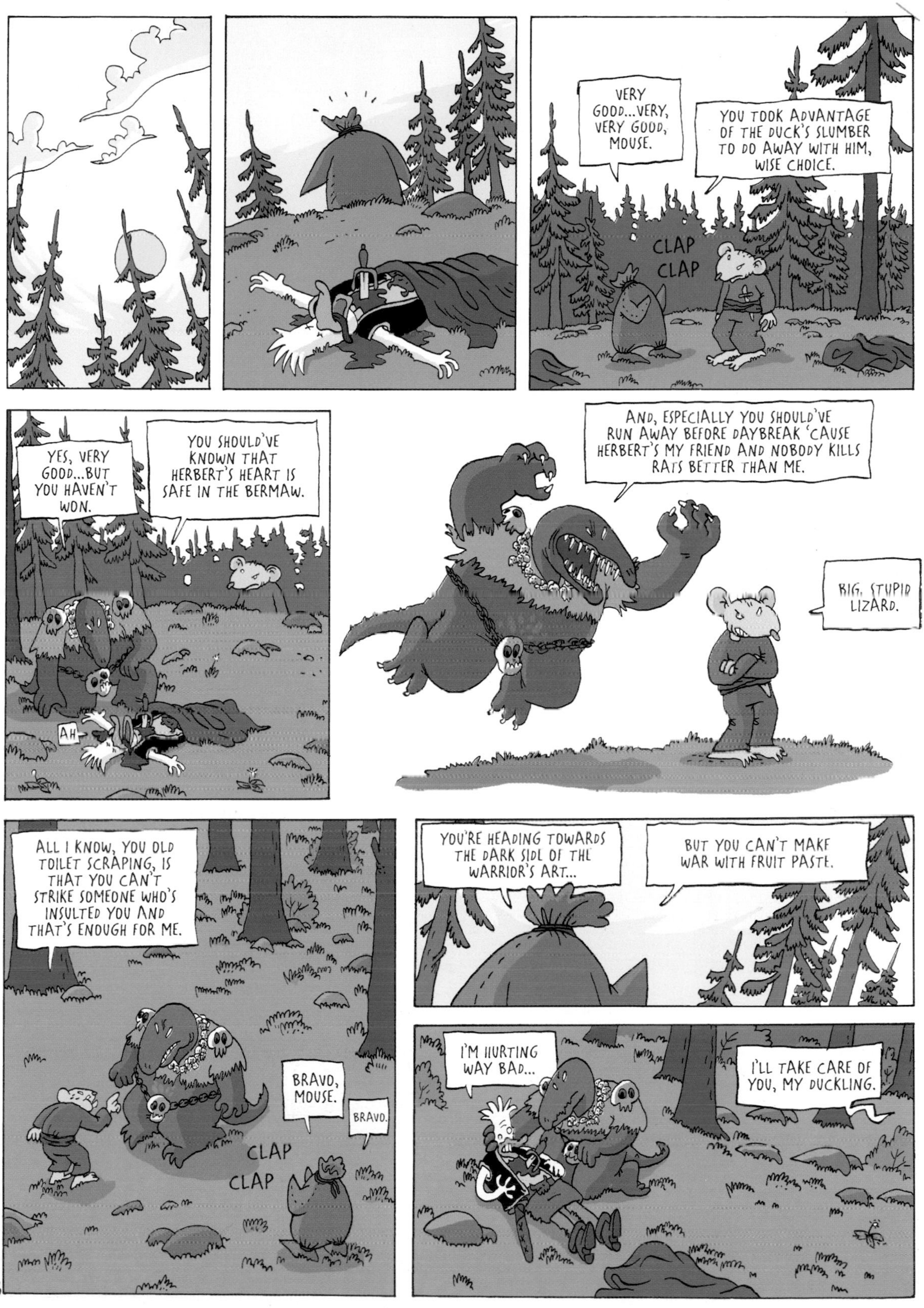

VERY GOOD...VERY, VERY GOOD, MOUSE.
YOU TOOK ADVANTAGE OF THE DUCK'S SLUMBER TO DO AWAY WITH HIM, WISE CHOICE.
CLAP CLAP
YES, VERY GOOD...BUT YOU HAVEN'T WON.
YOU SHOULD'VE KNOWN THAT HERBERT'S HEART IS SAFE IN THE BERMAW.
AH
AND, ESPECIALLY YOU SHOULD'VE RUN AWAY BEFORE DAYBREAK 'CAUSE HERBERT'S MY FRIEND AND NOBODY KILLS RATS BETTER THAN ME.
BIG, STUPID LIZARD.
ALL I KNOW, YOU OLD TOILET SCRAPING, IS THAT YOU CAN'T STRIKE SOMEONE WHO'S INSULTED YOU AND THAT'S ENOUGH FOR ME.
BRAVO, MOUSE.
BRAVO.
CLAP
CLAP
YOU'RE HEADING TOWARDS THE DARK SIDE OF THE WARRIOR'S ART...
BUT YOU CAN'T MAKE WAR WITH FRUIT PASTE.
I'M HURTING WAY BAD...
I'LL TAKE CARE OF YOU, MY DUCKLING.

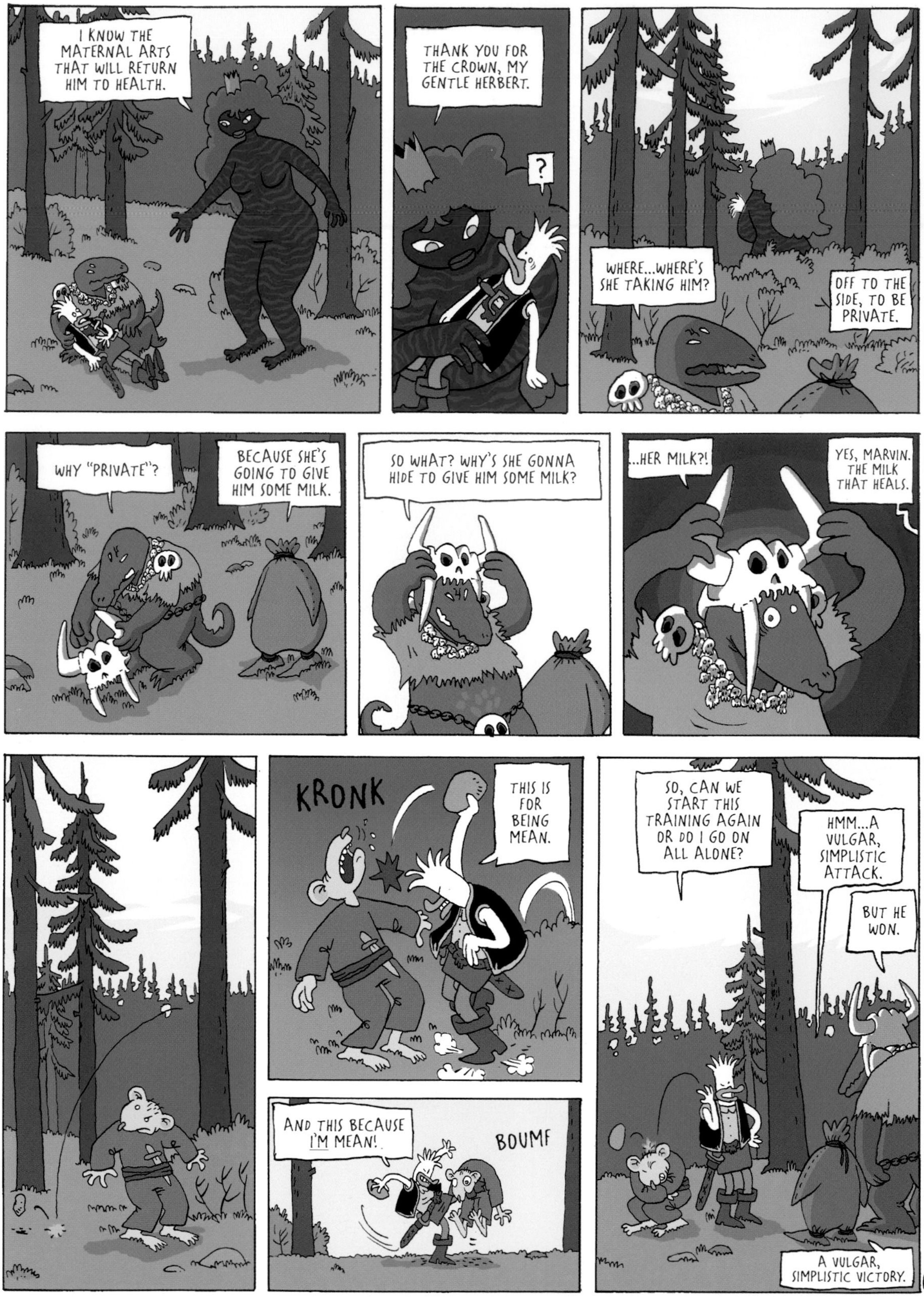

I KNOW THE MATERNAL ARTS THAT WILL RETURN HIM TO HEALTH.
THANK YOU FOR THE CROWN, MY GENTLE HERBERT.
?
WHERE...WHERE'S SHE TAKING HIM?
OFF TO THE SIDE, TO BE PRIVATE.
WHY "PRIVATE"?
BECAUSE SHE'S GOING TO GIVE HIM SOME MILK.
SO WHAT? WHY'S SHE GONNA HIDE TO GIVE HIM SOME MILK?
...HER MILK?!
YES, MARVIN. THE MILK THAT HEALS.
KRONK
THIS IS FOR BEING MEAN.
AND THIS BECAUSE I'M MEAN!
BOUMF
SO, CAN WE START THIS TRAINING AGAIN OR DO I GO ON ALL ALONE?
HMM...A VULGAR, SIMPLISTIC ATTACK.
BUT HE WON.
A VULGAR, SIMPLISTIC VICTORY.

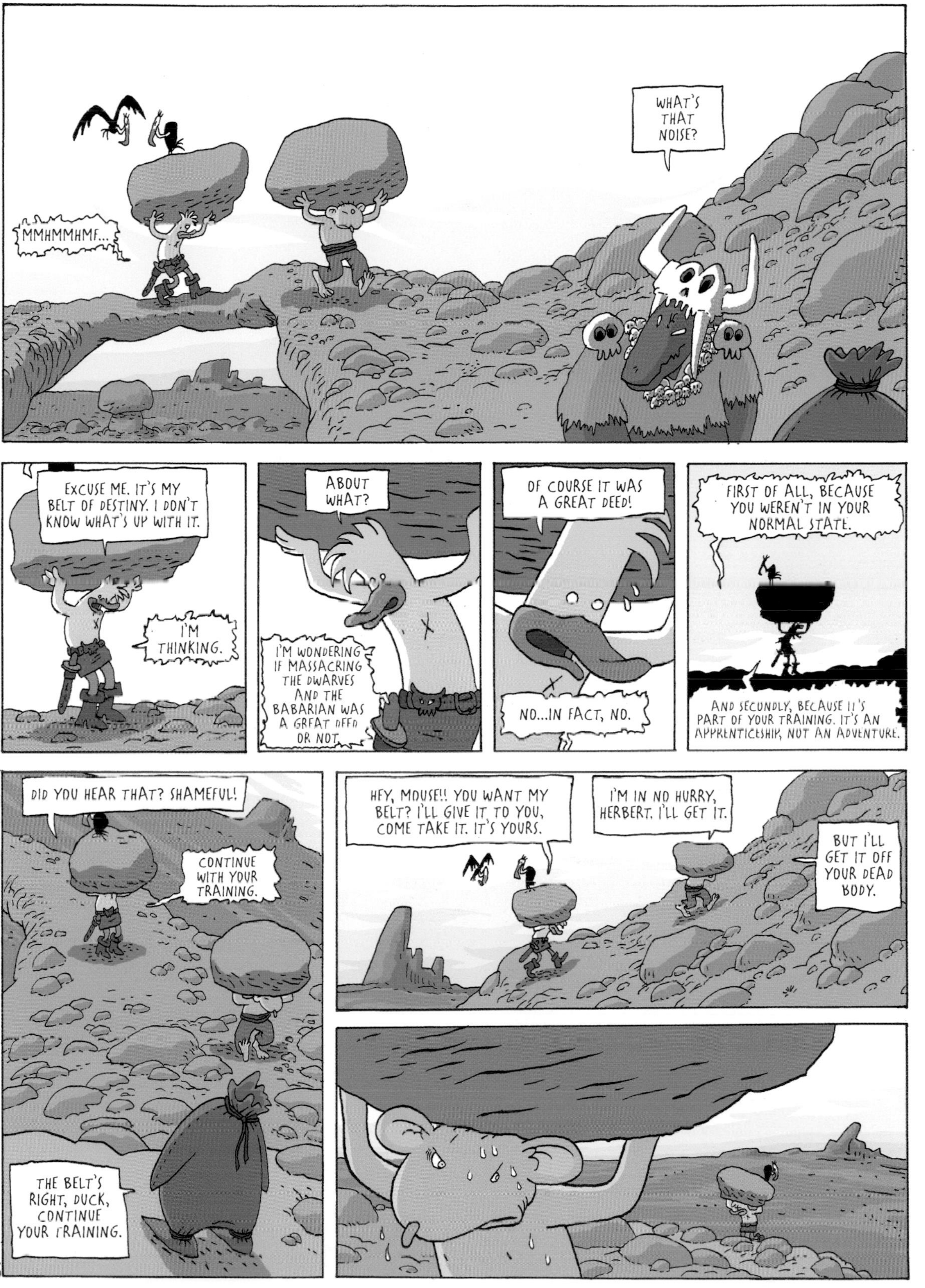
MMHMMHMF...
WHAT'S THAT NOISE?
EXCUSE ME. IT'S MY BELT OF DESTINY. I DON'T KNOW WHAT'S UP WITH IT.
I'M THINKING.
ABOUT WHAT?
I'M WONDERING IF MASSACRING THE DWARVES AND THE BABARIAN WAS A GREAT DEED OR NOT.
OF COURSE IT WAS A GREAT DEED!
NO...IN FACT, NO.
FIRST OF ALL, BECAUSE YOU WEREN'T IN YOUR NORMAL STATE.
AND SECONDLY, BECAUSE IT'S PART OF YOUR TRAINING. IT'S AN APPRENTICESHIP, NOT AN ADVENTURE.
DID YOU HEAR THAT? SHAMEFUL!
CONTINUE WITH YOUR TRAINING.
THE BELT'S RIGHT, DUCK, CONTINUE YOUR TRAINING.
HEY, MOUSE!! YOU WANT MY BELT? I'LL GIVE IT TO YOU, COME TAKE IT. IT'S YOURS.
I'M IN NO HURRY, HERBERT. I'LL GET IT.
BUT I'LL GET IT OFF YOUR DEAD BODY.

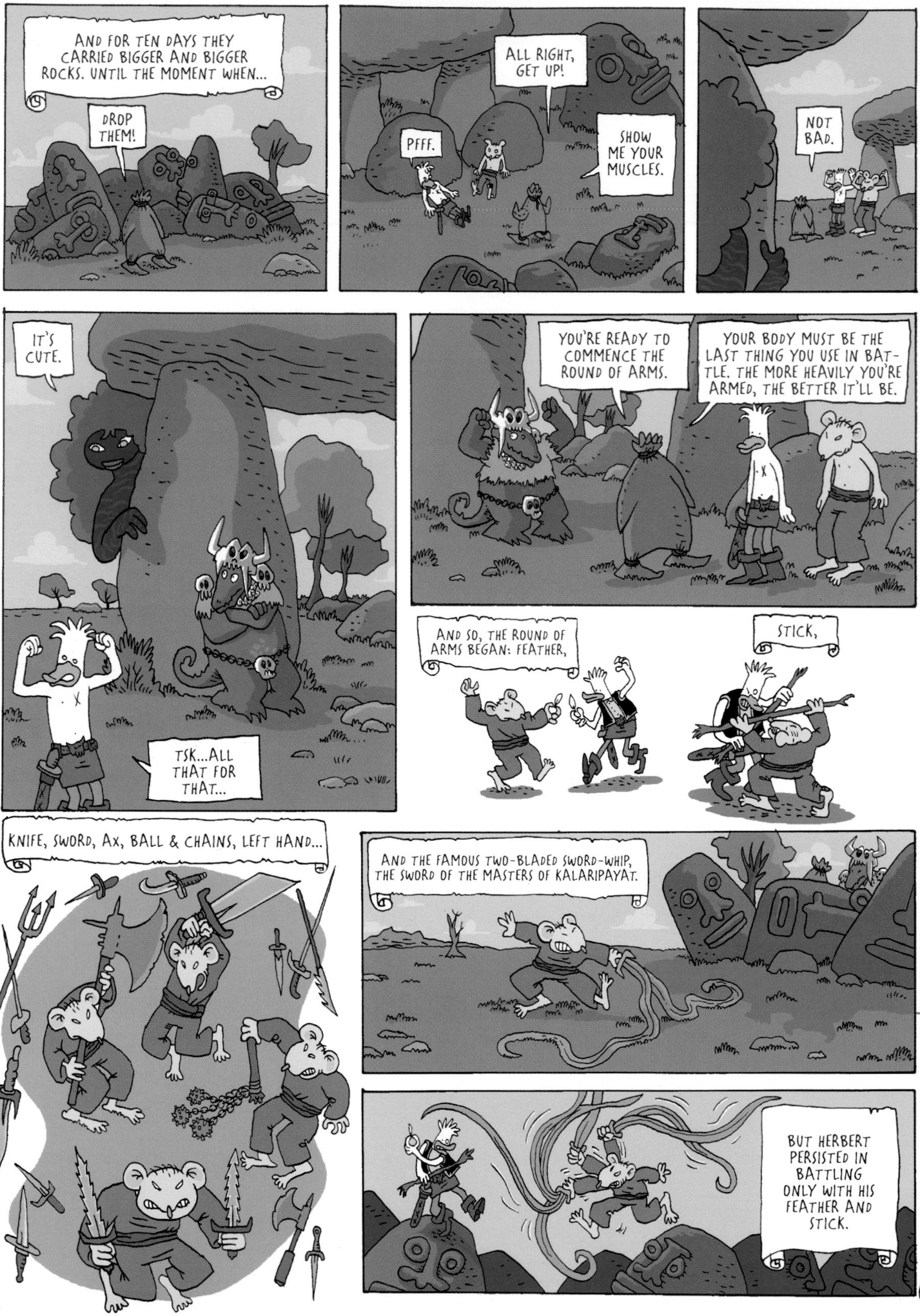
AND FOR TEN DAYS THEY CARRIED BIGGER AND BIGGER ROCKS. UNTIL THE MOMENT WHEN...
DROP THEM!
ALL RIGHT, GET UP!
PFFF.
SHOW ME YOUR MUSCLES.
NOT BAD.
IT'S CUTE.
TSK...ALL THAT FOR THAT...
YOU'RE READY TO COMMENCE THE ROUND OF ARMS.
YOUR BODY MUST BE THE LAST THING YOU USE IN BATTLE. THE MORE HEAVILY YOU'RE ARMED, THE BETTER IT'LL BE.
AND SO, THE ROUND OF ARMS BEGAN: FEATHER,
STICK,
KNIFE, SWORD, AX, BALL & CHAINS, LEFT HAND...
AND THE FAMOUS TWO-BLADED SWORD-WHIP, THE SWORD OF THE MASTERS OF KALARIPAYAT.
BUT HERBERT PERSISTED IN BATTLING ONLY WITH HIS FEATHER AND STICK.

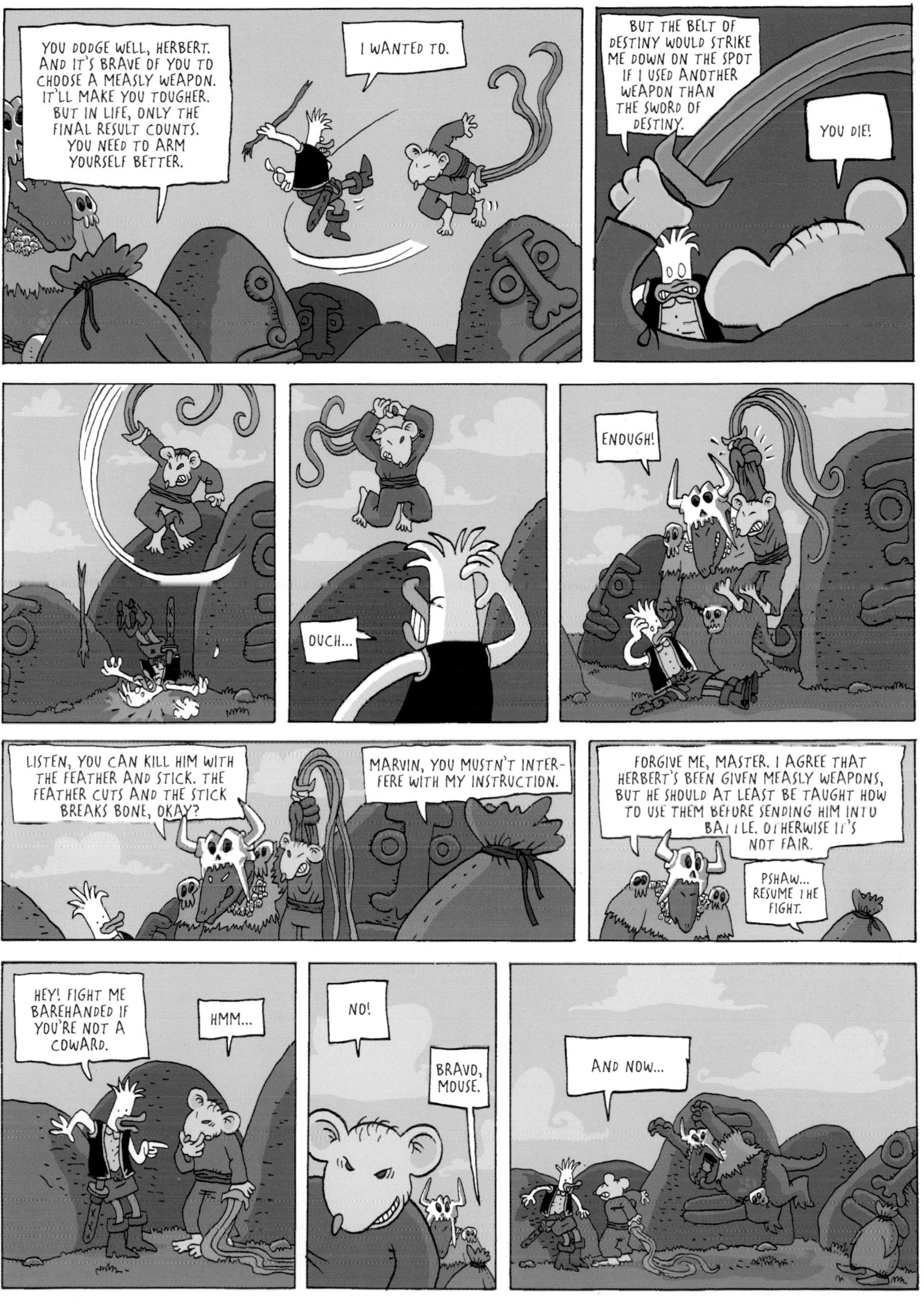
YOU DODGE WELL, HERBERT. AND IT'S BRAVE OF YOU TO CHOOSE A MEASLY WEAPON. IT'LL MAKE YOU TOUGHER. BUT IN LIFE, ONLY THE FINAL RESULT COUNTS. YOU NEED TO ARM YOURSELF BETTER.
I WANTED TO.
BUT THE BELT OF DESTINY WOULD STRIKE ME DOWN ON THE SPOT IF I USED ANOTHER WEAPON THAN THE SWORD OF DESTINY.
YOU DIE!
OUCH...
ENOUGH!
LISTEN, YOU CAN KILL HIM WITH THE FEATHER AND STICK. THE FEATHER CUTS AND THE STICK BREAKS BONE, OKAY?
MARVIN, YOU MUSTN'T INTERFERE WITH MY INSTRUCTION.
FORGIVE ME, MASTER. I AGREE THAT HERBERT'S BEEN GIVEN MEASLY WEAPONS, BUT HE SHOULD AT LEAST BE TAUGHT HOW TO USE THEM BEFORE SENDING HIM INTO BATTLE. OTHERWISE IT'S NOT FAIR.
PSHAW... RESUME THE FIGHT.
HEY! FIGHT ME BAREHANDED IF YOU'RE NOT A COWARD.
HMM...
NO!
BRAVO, MOUSE.
AND NOW...

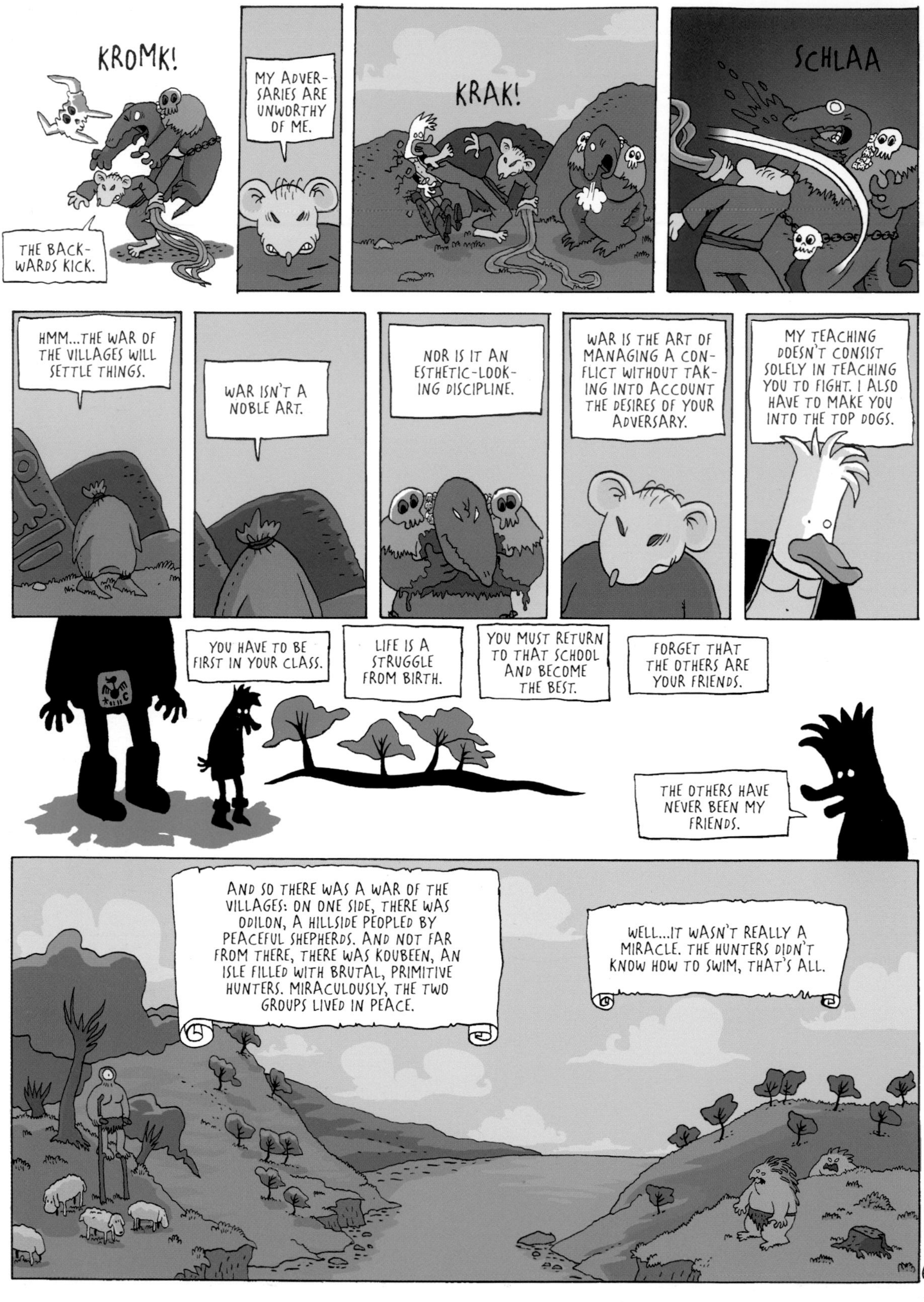

KROMK!
THE BACKWARDS KICK.
MY ADVERSARIES ARE UNWORTHY OF ME.
KRAK!
SCHLAA
HMM...THE WAR OF THE VILLAGES WILL SETTLE THINGS.
WAR ISN'T A NOBLE ART.
NOR IS IT AN ESTHETIC-LOOKING DISCIPLINE.
WAR IS THE ART OF MANAGING A CONFLICT WITHOUT TAKING INTO ACCOUNT THE DESIRES OF YOUR ADVERSARY.
MY TEACHING DOESN'T CONSIST SOLELY IN TEACHING YOU TO FIGHT. I ALSO HAVE TO MAKE YOU INTO THE TOP DOGS.
YOU HAVE TO BE FIRST IN YOUR CLASS.
LIFE IS A STRUGGLE FROM BIRTH.
YOU MUST RETURN TO THAT SCHOOL AND BECOME THE BEST.
FORGET THAT THE OTHERS ARE YOUR FRIENDS.
THE OTHERS HAVE NEVER BEEN MY FRIENDS.
AND SO THERE WAS A WAR OF THE VILLAGES: ON ONE SIDE, THERE WAS ODILON, A HILLSIDE PEOPLED BY PEACEFUL SHEPHERDS. AND NOT FAR FROM THERE, THERE WAS KOUBEEN, AN ISLE FILLED WITH BRUTAL, PRIMITIVE HUNTERS. MIRACULOUSLY, THE TWO GROUPS LIVED IN PEACE.
WELL...IT WASN'T REALLY A MIRACLE. THE HUNTERS DIDN'T KNOW HOW TO SWIM, THAT'S ALL.

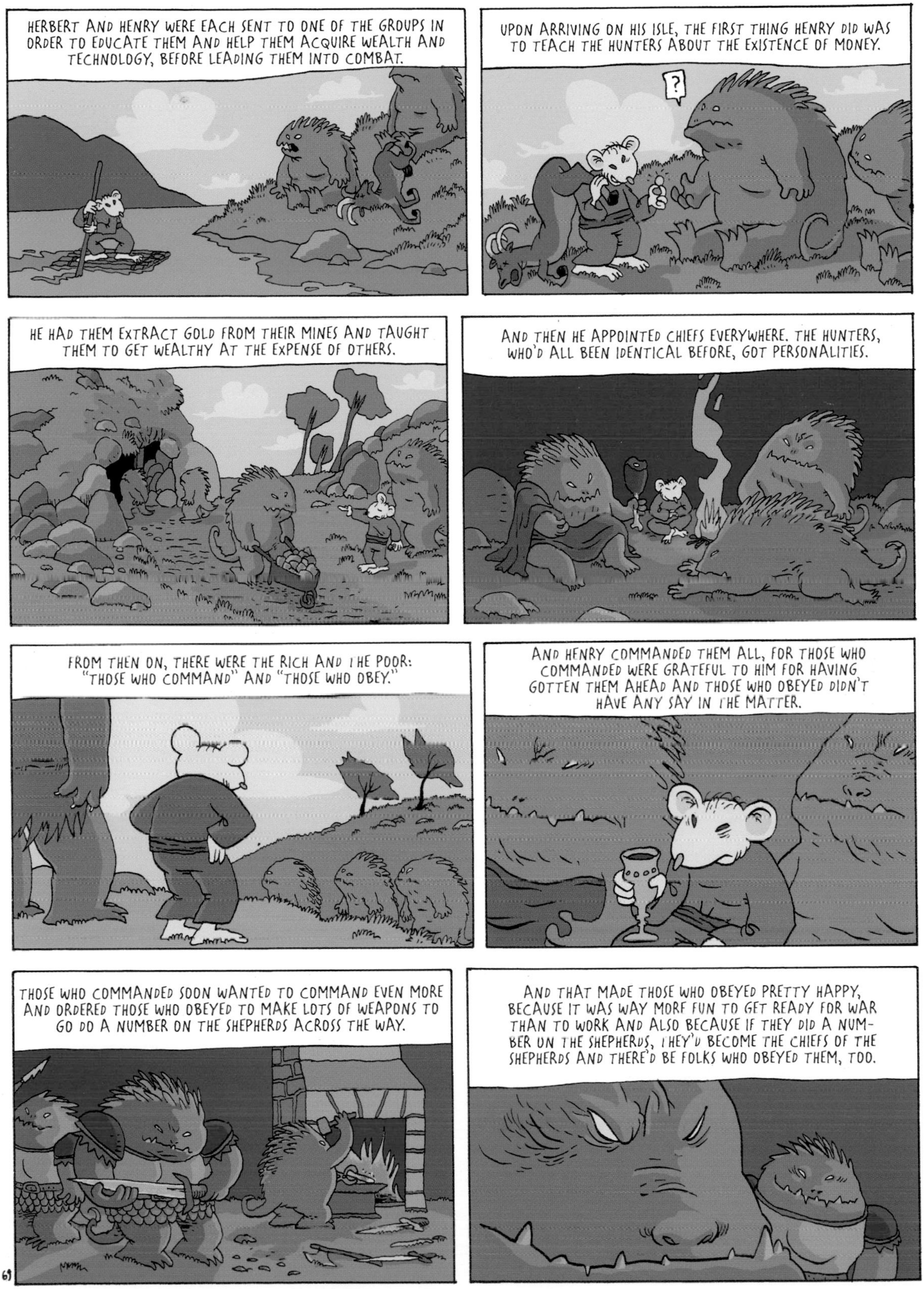

HERBERT AND HENRY WERE EACH SENT TO ONE OF THE GROUPS IN ORDER TO EDUCATE THEM AND HELP THEM ACQUIRE WEALTH AND TECHNOLOGY, BEFORE LEADING THEM INTO COMBAT.
UPON ARRIVING ON HIS ISLE, THE FIRST THING HENRY DID WAS TO TEACH THE HUNTERS ABOUT THE EXISTENCE OF MONEY.
?
HE HAD THEM EXTRACT GOLD FROM THEIR MINES AND TAUGHT THEM TO GET WEALTHY AT THE EXPENSE OF OTHERS.
AND THEN HE APPOINTED CHIEFS EVERYWHERE. THE HUNTERS, WHO'D ALL BEEN IDENTICAL BEFORE, GOT PERSONALITIES.
FROM THEN ON, THERE WERE THE RICH AND THE POOR: "THOSE WHO COMMAND" AND "THOSE WHO OBEY."
AND HENRY COMMANDED THEM ALL, FOR THOSE WHO COMMANDED WERE GRATEFUL TO HIM FOR HAVING GOTTEN THEM AHEAD AND THOSE WHO OBEYED DIDN'T HAVE ANY SAY IN THE MATTER.
THOSE WHO COMMANDED SOON WANTED TO COMMAND EVEN MORE AND ORDERED THOSE WHO OBEYED TO MAKE LOTS OF WEAPONS TO GO DO A NUMBER ON THE SHEPHERDS ACROSS THE WAY.
AND THAT MADE THOSE WHO OBEYED PRETTY HAPPY, BECAUSE IT WAS WAY MORE FUN TO GET READY FOR WAR THAN TO WORK AND ALSO BECAUSE IF THEY DID A NUMBER ON THE SHEPHERDS, THEY'D BECOME THE CHIEFS OF THE SHEPHERDS AND THERE'D BE FOLKS WHO OBEYED THEM, TOO.

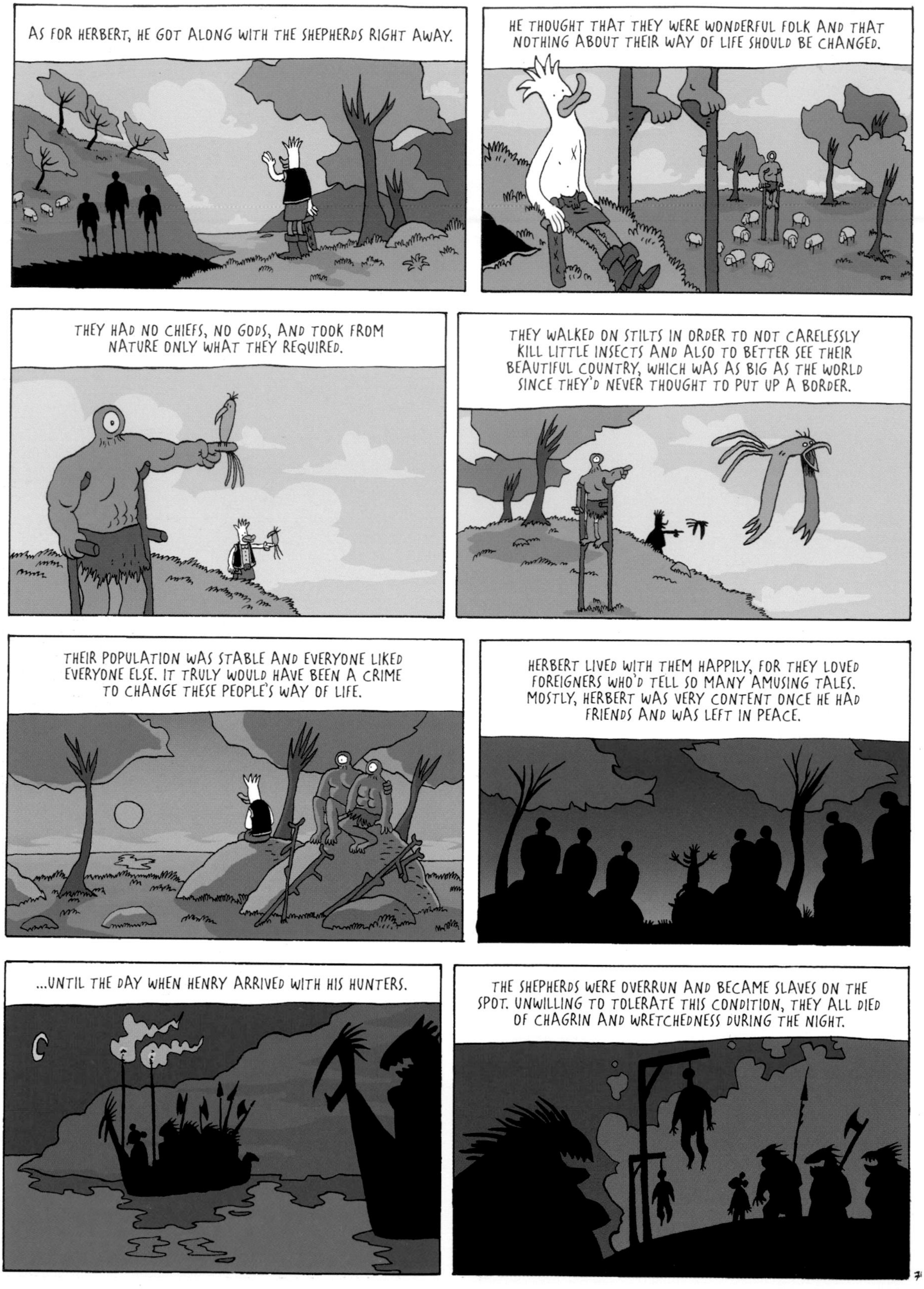
AS FOR HERBERT, HE GOT ALONG WITH THE SHEPHERDS RIGHT AWAY.
HE THOUGHT THAT THEY WERE WONDERFUL FOLK AND THAT NOTHING ABOUT THEIR WAY OF LIFE SHOULD BE CHANGED.
THEY HAD NO CHIEFS, NO GODS, AND TOOK FROM NATURE ONLY WHAT THEY REQUIRED.
THEY WALKED ON STILTS IN ORDER TO NOT CARELESSLY KILL LITTLE INSECTS AND ALSO TO BETTER SEE THEIR BEAUTIFUL COUNTRY, WHICH WAS AS BIG AS THE WORLD SINCE THEY'D NEVER THOUGHT TO PUT UP A BORDER.
THEIR POPULATION WAS STABLE AND EVERYONE LIKED EVERYONE ELSE. IT TRULY WOULD HAVE BEEN A CRIME TO CHANGE THESE PEOPLE'S WAY OF LIFE.
HERBERT LIVED WITH THEM HAPPILY, FOR THEY LOVED FOREIGNERS WHO'D TELL SO MANY AMUSING TALES. MOSTLY, HERBERT WAS VERY CONTENT ONCE HE HAD FRIENDS AND WAS LEFT IN PEACE.
...UNTIL THE DAY WHEN HENRY ARRIVED WITH HIS HUNTERS.
THE SHEPHERDS WERE OVERRUN AND BECAME SLAVES ON THE SPOT. UNWILLING TO TOLERATE THIS CONDITION, THEY ALL DIED OF CHAGRIN AND WRETCHEDNESS DURING THE NIGHT.

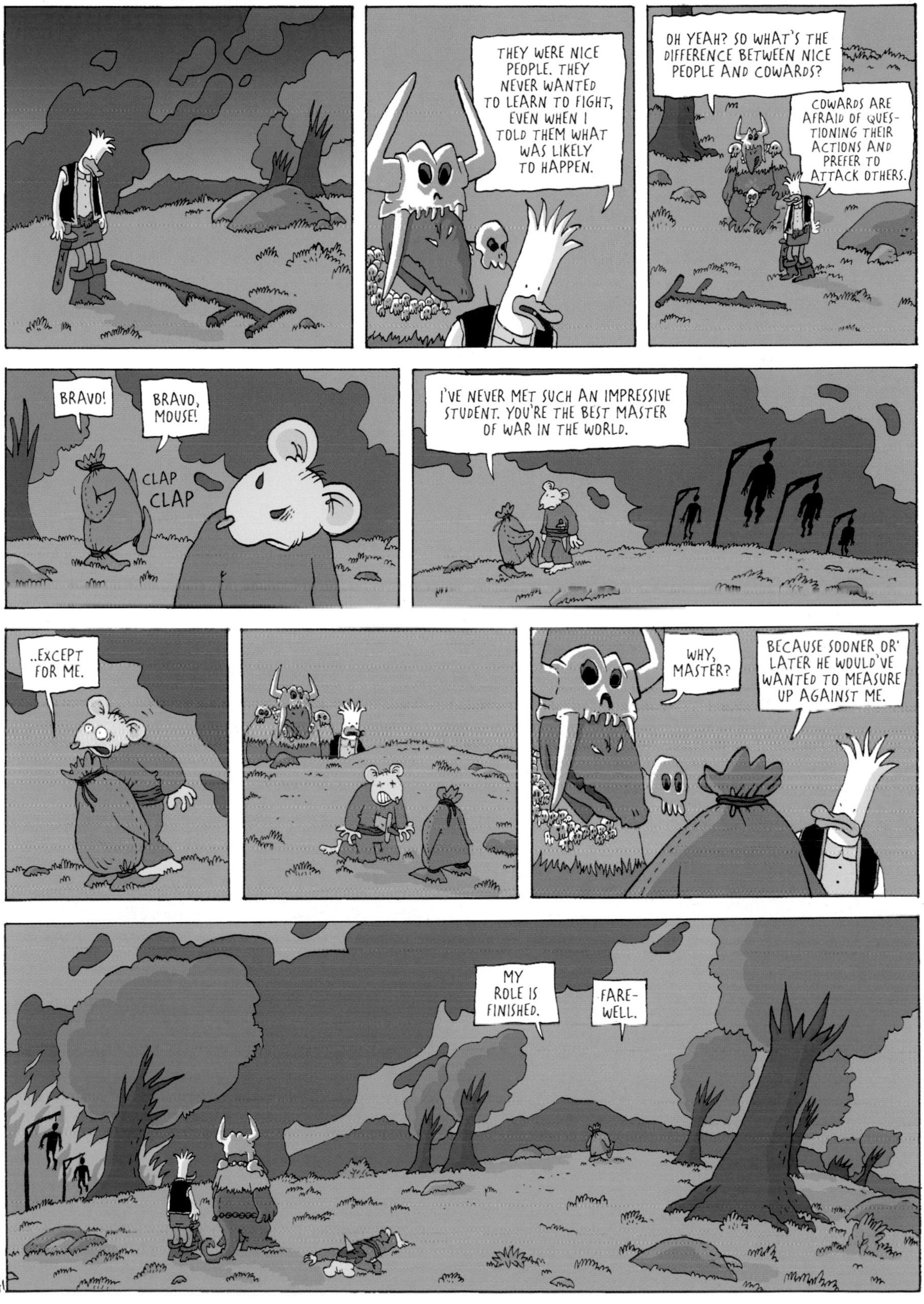
THEY WERE NICE PEOPLE. THEY NEVER WANTED TO LEARN TO FIGHT, EVEN WHEN I TOLD THEM WHAT WAS LIKELY TO HAPPEN.
OH YEAH? SO WHAT'S THE DIFFERENCE BETWEEN NICE PEOPLE AND COWARDS?
COWARDS ARE AFRAID OF QUESTIONING THEIR ACTIONS AND PREFER TO ATTACK OTHERS.
BRAVO!
BRAVO, MOUSE!
CLAP CLAP
I'VE NEVER MET SUCH AN IMPRESSIVE STUDENT. YOU'RE THE BEST MASTER OF WAR IN THE WORLD.
..EXCEPT FOR ME.
WHY, MASTER?
BECAUSE SOONER OR LATER HE WOULD'VE WANTED TO MEASURE UP AGAINST ME.
MY ROLE IS FINISHED.
FARE-WELL.

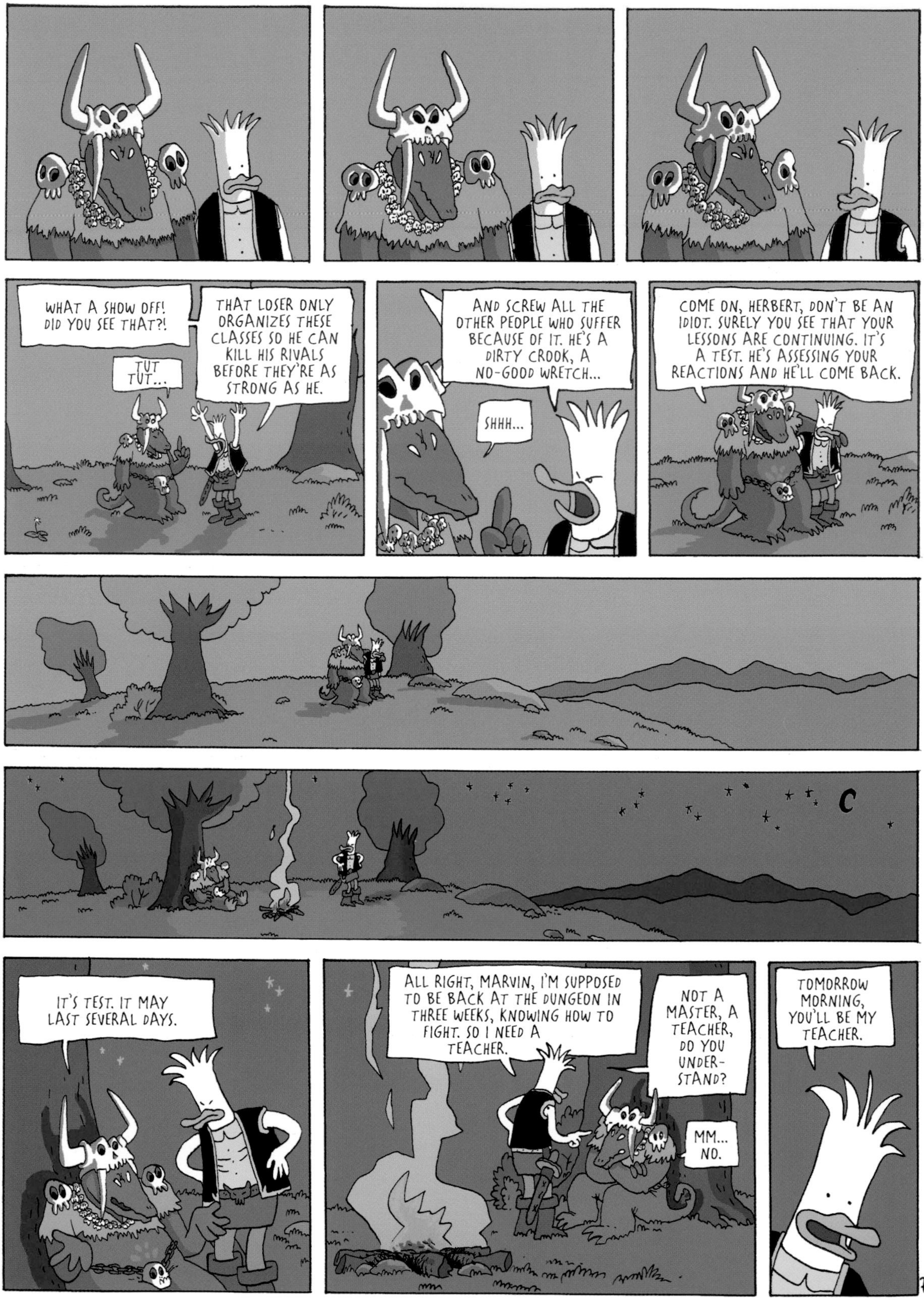
WHAT A SHOW OFF! DID YOU SEE THAT?!
TUT TUT...
THAT LOSER ONLY ORGANIZES THESE CLASSES SO HE CAN KILL HIS RIVALS BEFORE THEY'RE AS STRONG AS HE.
AND SCREW ALL THE OTHER PEOPLE WHO SUFFER BECAUSE OF IT. HE'S A DIRTY CROOK, A NO-GOOD WRETCH...
SHHH...
COME ON, HERBERT, DON'T BE AN IDIOT. SURELY YOU SEE THAT YOUR LESSONS ARE CONTINUING. IT'S A TEST. HE'S ASSESSING YOUR REACTIONS AND HE'LL COME BACK.
IT'S TEST. IT MAY LAST SEVERAL DAYS.
ALL RIGHT, MARVIN, I'M SUPPOSED TO BE BACK AT THE DUNGEON IN THREE WEEKS, KNOWING HOW TO FIGHT. SO I NEED A TEACHER.
NOT A MASTER, A TEACHER, DO YOU UNDER-STAND?
MM... NO.
TOMORROW MORNING, YOU'LL BE MY TEACHER.

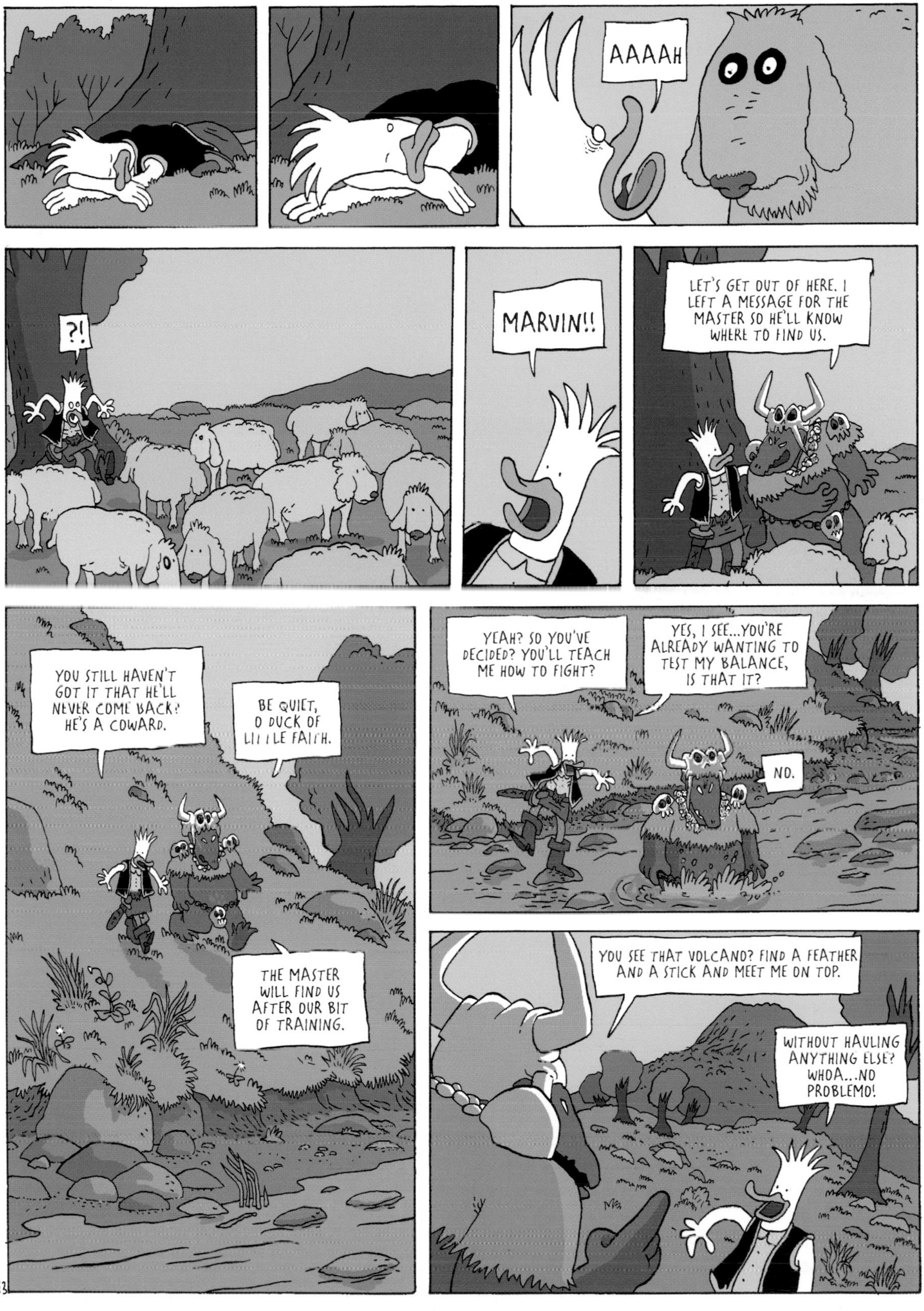
AAAAH
?!
MARVIN!!
LET'S GET OUT OF HERE. I LEFT A MESSAGE FOR THE MASTER SO HE'LL KNOW WHERE TO FIND US.
YOU STILL HAVEN'T GOT IT THAT HE'LL NEVER COME BACK? HE'S A COWARD.
BE QUIET, O DUCK OF LITTLE FAITH.
THE MASTER WILL FIND US AFTER OUR BIT OF TRAINING.
YEAH? SO YOU'VE DECIDED? YOU'LL TEACH ME HOW TO FIGHT?
YES, I SEE...YOU'RE ALREADY WANTING TO TEST MY BALANCE, IS THAT IT?
NO.
YOU SEE THAT VOLCANO? FIND A FEATHER AND A STICK AND MEET ME ON TOP.
WITHOUT HAULING ANYTHING ELSE? WHOA...NO PROBLEMO!

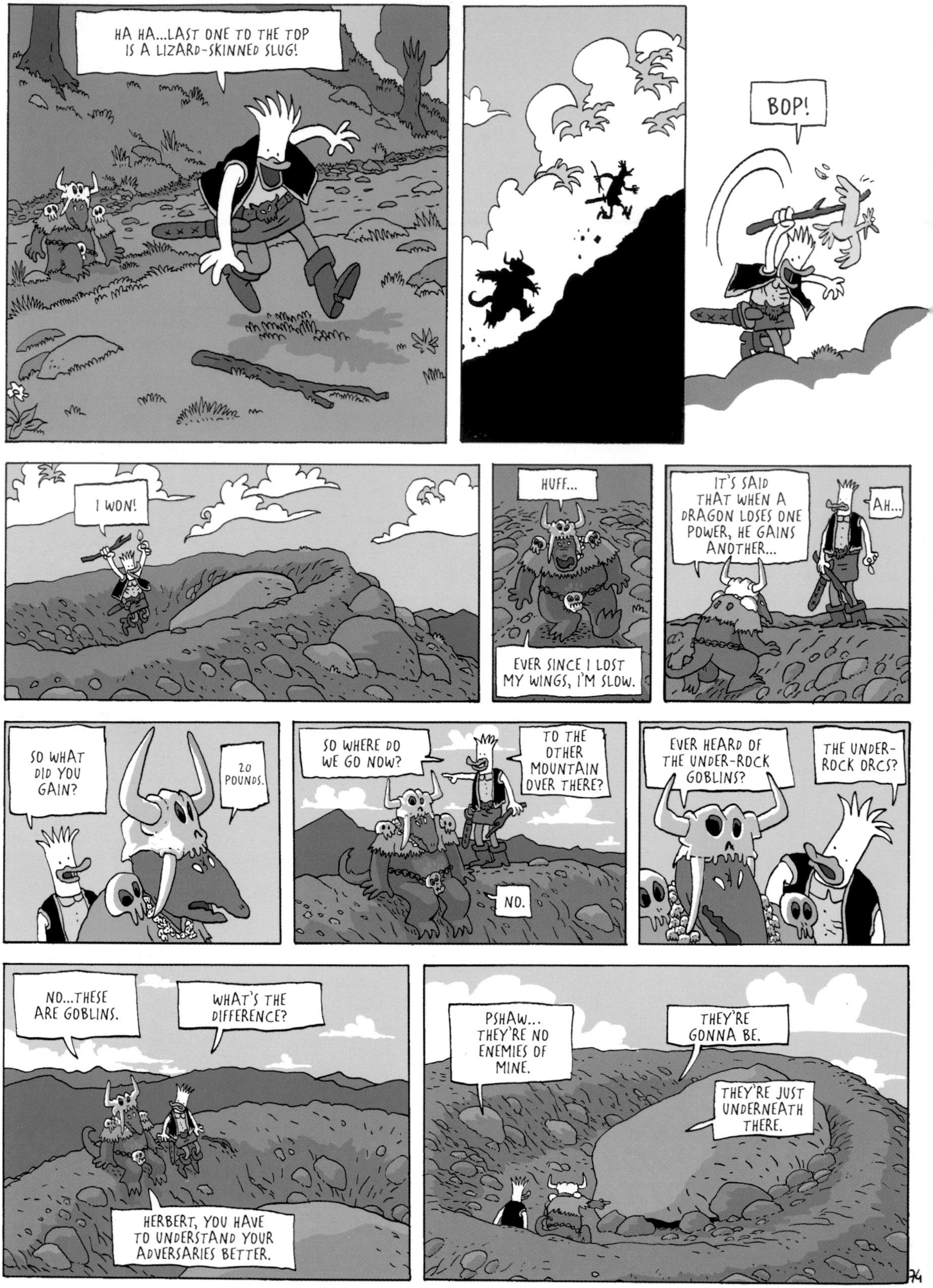
HA HA...LAST ONE TO THE TOP IS A LIZARD-SKINNED SLUG!
BOP!
I WON!
HUFF...
EVER SINCE I LOST MY WINGS, I'M SLOW.
IT'S SAID THAT WHEN A DRAGON LOSES ONE POWER, HE GAINS ANOTHER...
AH...
SO WHAT DID YOU GAIN?
20 POUNDS.
SO WHERE DO WE GO NOW?
TO THE OTHER MOUNTAIN OVER THERE?
NO.
EVER HEARD OF THE UNDER-ROCK GOBLINS?
THE UNDER-ROCK ORCS?
NO...THESE ARE GOBLINS.
WHAT'S THE DIFFERENCE?
HERBERT, YOU HAVE TO UNDERSTAND YOUR ADVERSARIES BETTER.
PSHAW... THEY'RE NO ENEMIES OF MINE.
THEY'RE GONNA BE.
THEY'RE JUST UNDERNEATH THERE.

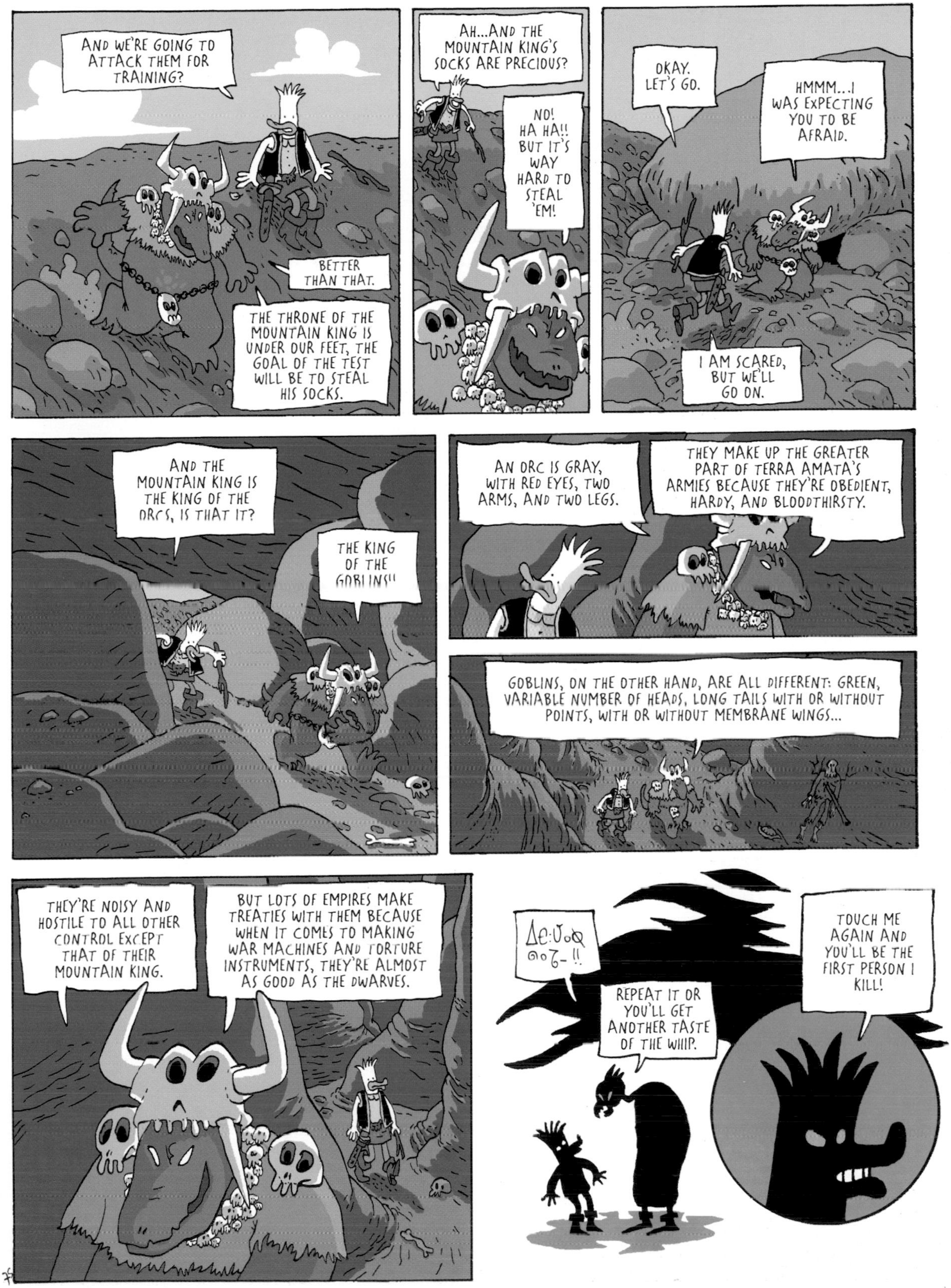

AND WE'RE GOING TO ATTACK THEM FOR TRAINING?
BETTER THAN THAT.
THE THRONE OF THE MOUNTAIN KING IS UNDER OUR FEET, THE GOAL OF THE TEST WILL BE TO STEAL HIS SOCKS.
AH...AND THE MOUNTAIN KING'S SOCKS ARE PRECIOUS?
NO! HA HA!! BUT IT'S WAY HARD TO STEAL 'EM!
OKAY. LET'S GO.
HMMM...I WAS EXPECTING YOU TO BE AFRAID.
I AM SCARED, BUT WE'LL GO ON.
AND THE MOUNTAIN KING IS THE KING OF THE ORCS, IS THAT IT?
THE KING OF THE GOBLINS!!
AN ORC IS GRAY, WITH RED EYES, TWO ARMS, AND TWO LEGS.
THEY MAKE UP THE GREATER PART OF TERRA AMATA'S ARMIES BECAUSE THEY'RE OBEDIENT, HARDY, AND BLOODTHIRSTY.
GOBLINS, ON THE OTHER HAND, ARE ALL DIFFERENT: GREEN, VARIABLE NUMBER OF HEADS, LONG TAILS WITH OR WITHOUT POINTS, WITH OR WITHOUT MEMBRANE WINGS...
THEY'RE NOISY AND HOSTILE TO ALL OTHER CONTROL EXCEPT THAT OF THEIR MOUNTAIN KING.
BUT LOTS OF EMPIRES MAKE TREATIES WITH THEM BECAUSE WHEN IT COMES TO MAKING WAR MACHINES AND TORTURE INSTRUMENTS, THEY'RE ALMOST AS GOOD AS THE DWARVES.
REPEAT IT OR YOU'LL GET ANOTHER TASTE OF THE WHIP.
TOUCH ME AGAIN AND YOU'LL BE THE FIRST PERSON I KILL!

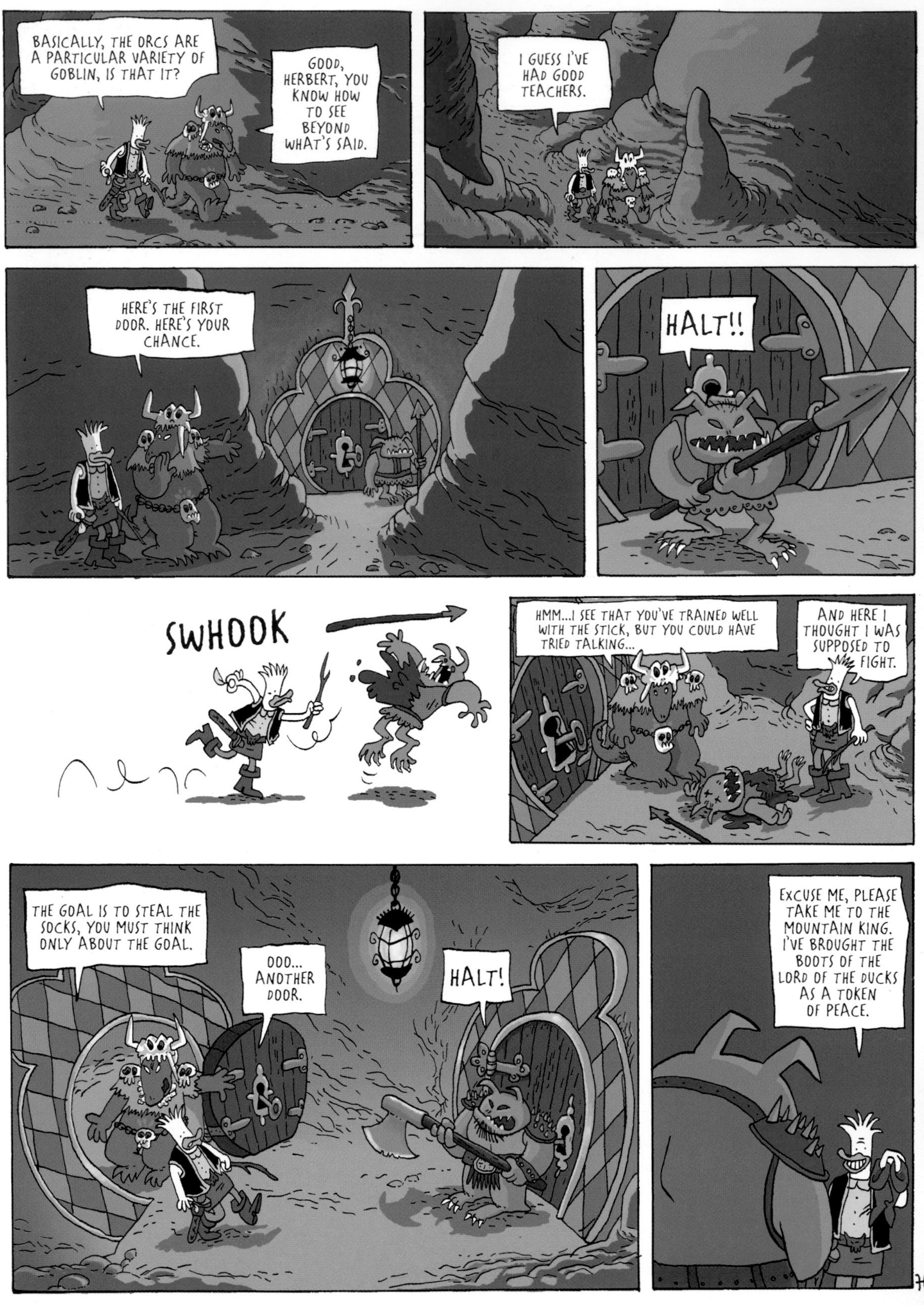

BASICALLY, THE ORCS ARE A PARTICULAR VARIETY OF GOBLIN, IS THAT IT?
GOOD, HERBERT, YOU KNOW HOW TO SEE BEYOND WHAT'S SAID.
I GUESS I'VE HAD GOOD TEACHERS.
HERE'S THE FIRST DOOR. HERE'S YOUR CHANCE.
HALT!!
SWHOOK
HMM...I SEE THAT YOU'VE TRAINED WELL WITH THE STICK, BUT YOU COULD HAVE TRIED TALKING...
AND HERE I THOUGHT I WAS SUPPOSED TO FIGHT.
THE GOAL IS TO STEAL THE SOCKS, YOU MUST THINK ONLY ABOUT THE GOAL.
OOO... ANOTHER DOOR.
HALT!
EXCUSE ME, PLEASE TAKE ME TO THE MOUNTAIN KING. I'VE BROUGHT THE BOOTS OF THE LORD OF THE DUCKS AS A TOKEN OF PEACE.

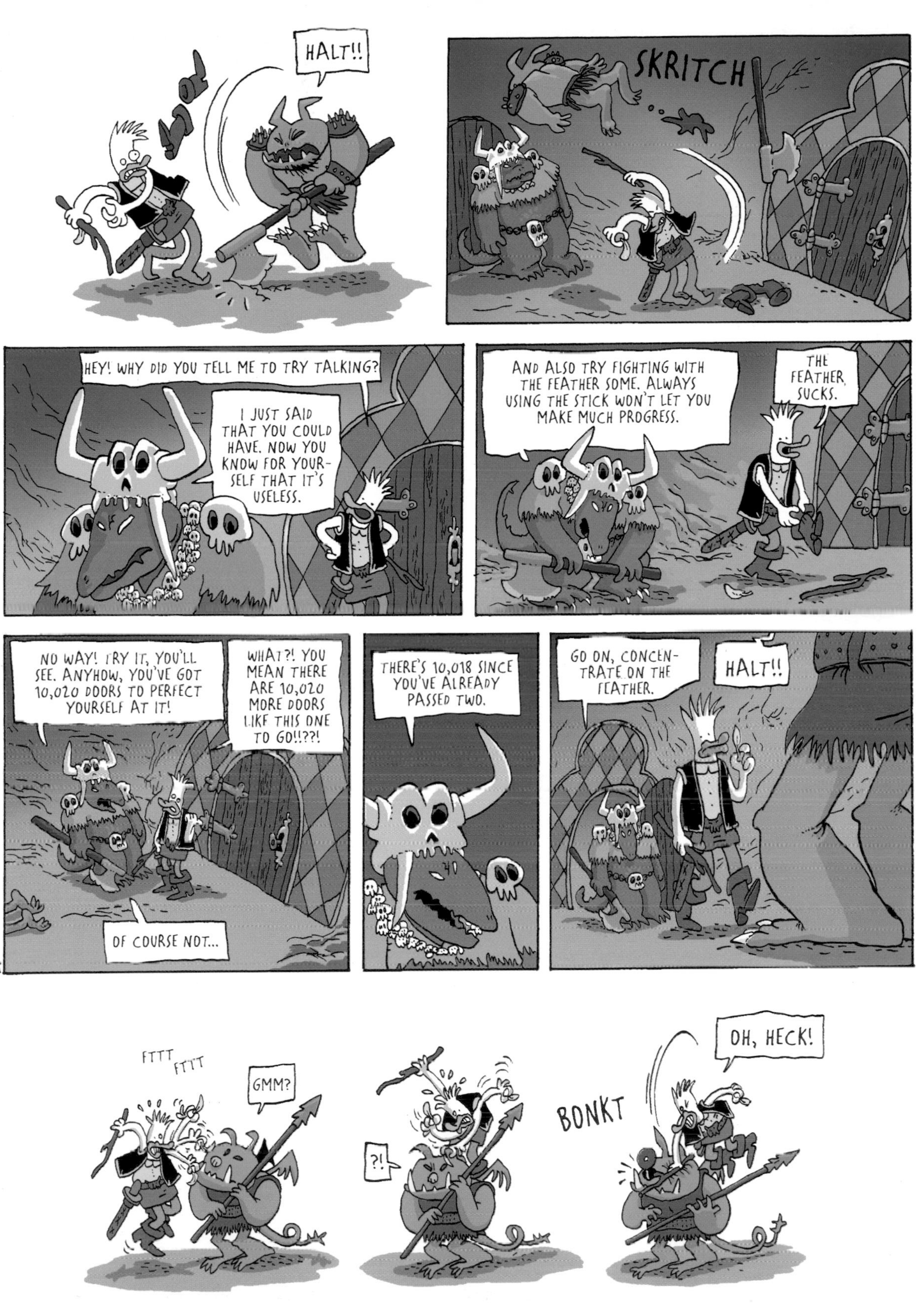

HALT!!
SKRITCH
HEY! WHY DID YOU TELL ME TO TRY TALKING?
I JUST SAID THAT YOU COULD HAVE. NOW YOU KNOW FOR YOURSELF THAT IT'S USELESS.
AND ALSO TRY FIGHTING WITH THE FEATHER SOME. ALWAYS USING THE STICK WON'T LET YOU MAKE MUCH PROGRESS.
THE FEATHER SUCKS.
NO WAY! TRY IT, YOU'LL SEE. ANYHOW, YOU'VE GOT 10,020 DOORS TO PERFECT YOURSELF AT IT!
WHAT?! YOU MEAN THERE ARE 10,020 MORE DOORS LIKE THIS ONE TO GO!!??!
OF COURSE NOT...
THERE'S 10,018 SINCE YOU'VE ALREADY PASSED TWO.
GO ON, CONCENTRATE ON THE FEATHER.
HALT!!
FTTT FTTT
GMM?
?!
BONKT
OH, HECK!

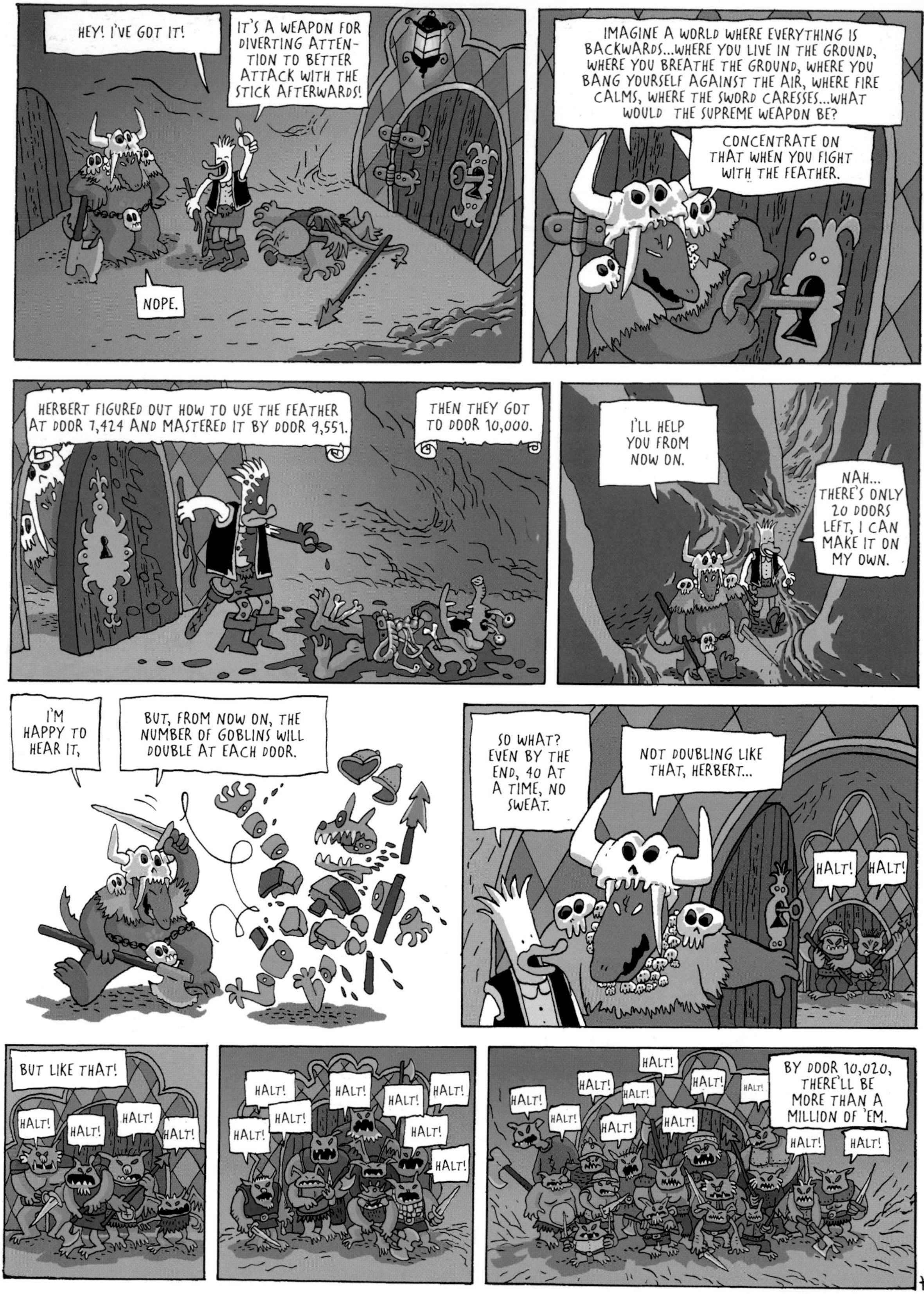
HEY! I'VE GOT IT!
IT'S A WEAPON FOR DIVERTING ATTENTION TO BETTER ATTACK WITH THE STICK AFTERWARDS!
NOPE.
IMAGINE A WORLD WHERE EVERYTHING IS BACKWARDS...WHERE YOU LIVE IN THE GROUND, WHERE YOU BREATHE THE GROUND, WHERE YOU BANG YOURSELF AGAINST THE AIR, WHERE FIRE CALMS, WHERE THE SWORD CARESSES...WHAT WOULD THE SUPREME WEAPON BE?
CONCENTRATE ON THAT WHEN YOU FIGHT WITH THE FEATHER.
HERBERT FIGURED OUT HOW TO USE THE FEATHER AT DOOR 7,424 AND MASTERED IT BY DOOR 9,551.
THEN THEY GOT TO DOOR 10,000.
I'LL HELP YOU FROM NOW ON.
NAH... THERE'S ONLY 20 DOORS LEFT, I CAN MAKE IT ON MY OWN.
I'M HAPPY TO HEAR IT,
BUT, FROM NOW ON, THE NUMBER OF GOBLINS WILL DOUBLE AT EACH DOOR.
SO WHAT? EVEN BY THE END, 40 AT A TIME, NO SWEAT.
NOT DOUBLING LIKE THAT, HERBERT...
HALT!
HALT!
BUT LIKE THAT!
HALT!
HALT!
HALT!
HALT!
HALT!
HALT!
HALT!
HALT!
HALT!
HALT!
HALT!
BY DOOR 10,020, THERE'LL BE MORE THAN A MILLION OF 'EM.

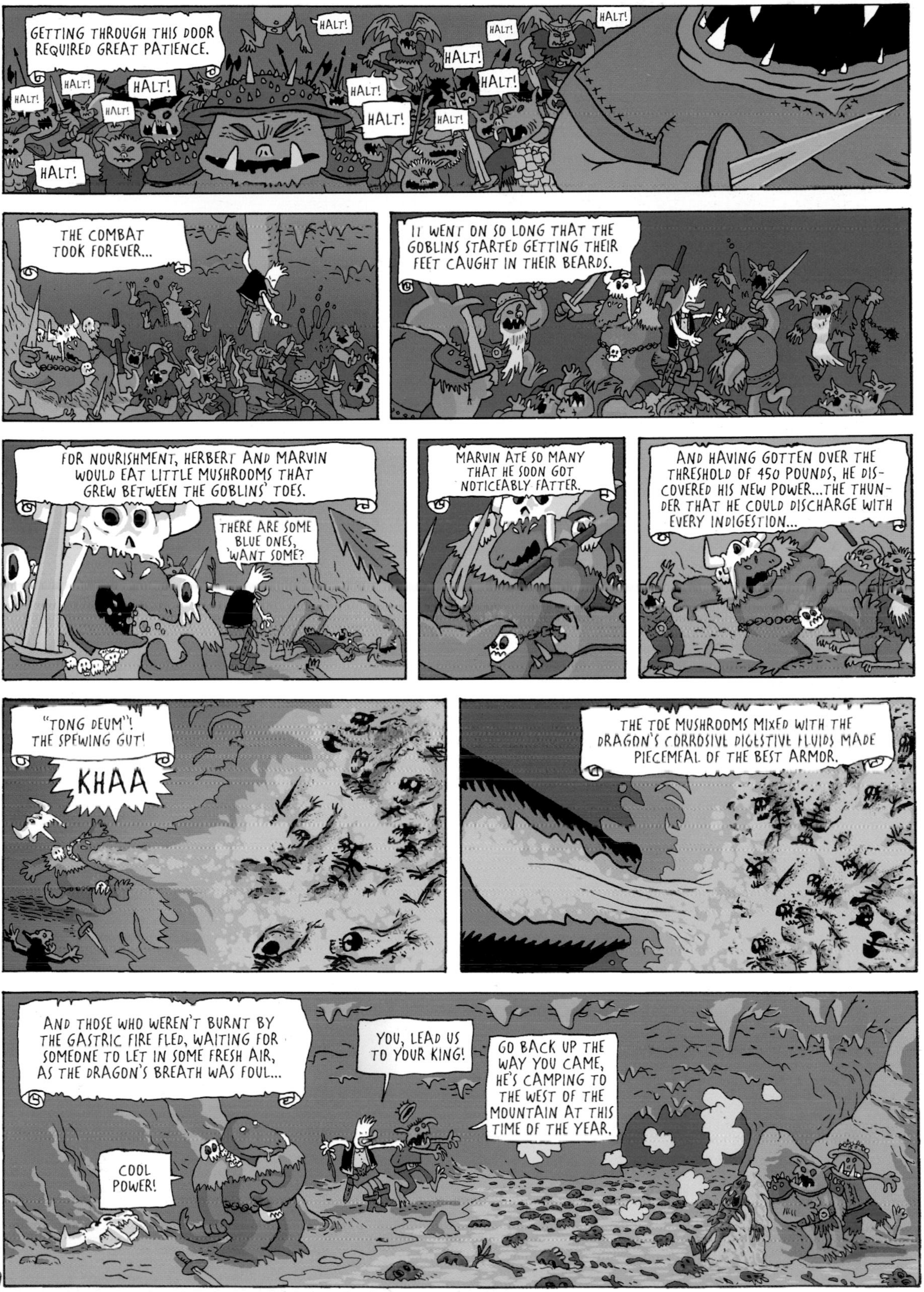

GETTING THROUGH THIS DOOR REQUIRED GREAT PATIENCE.
HALT!
HALT!
HALT!
HALT!
HALT!
HALT!
HALT!
HALT!
HALT!
HALT!
HALT!
HALT!
HALT!
THE COMBAT TOOK FOREVER...
IT WENT ON SO LONG THAT THE GOBLINS STARTED GETTING THEIR FEET CAUGHT IN THEIR BEARDS.
FOR NOURISHMENT, HERBERT AND MARVIN WOULD EAT LITTLE MUSHROOMS THAT GREW BETWEEN THE GOBLINS' TOES.
THERE ARE SOME BLUE ONES, WANT SOME?
MARVIN ATE SO MANY THAT HE SOON GOT NOTICEABLY FATTER.
AND HAVING GOTTEN OVER THE THRESHOLD OF 450 POUNDS, HE DISCOVERED HIS NEW POWER...THE THUNDER THAT HE COULD DISCHARGE WITH EVERY INDIGESTION...
"TONG DEUM"! THE SPEWING GUT!
KHAA
THE TOE MUSHROOMS MIXED WITH THE DRAGON'S CORROSIVE DIGESTIVE FLUIDS MADE PIECEMEAL OF THE BEST ARMOR.
AND THOSE WHO WEREN'T BURNT BY THE GASTRIC FIRE FLED, WAITING FOR SOMEONE TO LET IN SOME FRESH AIR, AS THE DRAGON'S BREATH WAS FOUL...
YOU, LEAD US TO YOUR KING!
GO BACK UP THE WAY YOU CAME, HE'S CAMPING TO THE WEST OF THE MOUNTAIN AT THIS TIME OF THE YEAR.
COOL POWER!

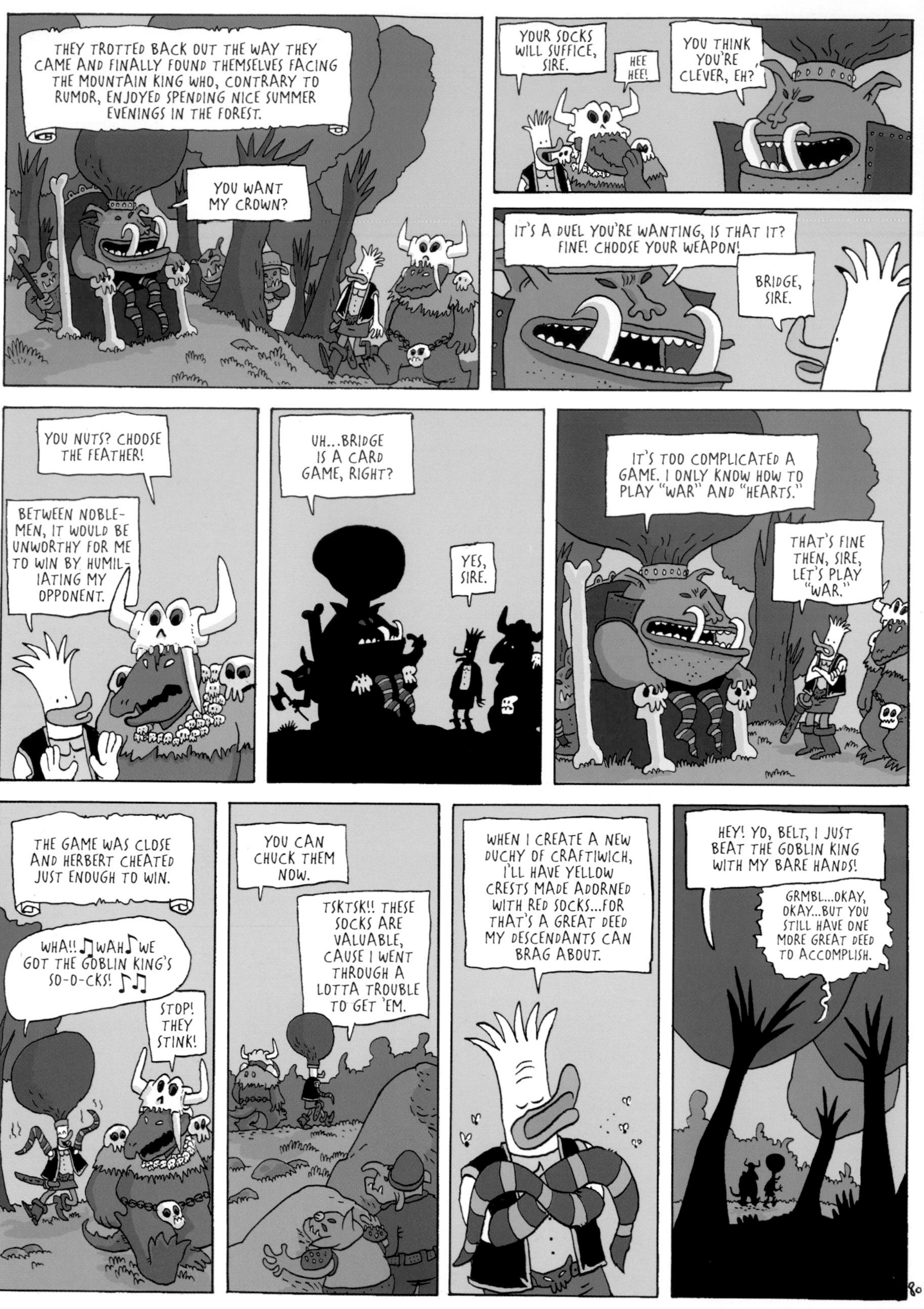
THEY TROTTED BACK OUT THE WAY THEY CAME AND FINALLY FOUND THEMSELVES FACING THE MOUNTAIN KING WHO, CONTRARY TO RUMOR, ENJOYED SPENDING NICE SUMMER EVENINGS IN THE FOREST.
YOU WANT MY CROWN?
YOUR SOCKS WILL SUFFICE, SIRE.
HEE HEE!
YOU THINK YOU'RE CLEVER, EH?
IT'S A DUEL YOU'RE WANTING, IS THAT IT? FINE! CHOOSE YOUR WEAPON!
BRIDGE, SIRE.
YOU NUTS? CHOOSE THE FEATHER!
BETWEEN NOBLEMEN, IT WOULD BE UNWORTHY FOR ME TO WIN BY HUMILIATING MY OPPONENT.
UH...BRIDGE IS A CARD GAME, RIGHT?
YES, SIRE.
IT'S TOO COMPLICATED A GAME. I ONLY KNOW HOW TO PLAY "WAR" AND "HEARTS."
THAT'S FINE THEN, SIRE, LET'S PLAY "WAR."
THE GAME WAS CLOSE AND HERBERT CHEATED JUST ENOUGH TO WIN.
WHA!! WAH WE GOT THE GOBLIN KING'S SO-O-CKS!
STOP! THEY STINK!
YOU CAN CHUCK THEM NOW.
TSKTSK!! THESE SOCKS ARE VALUABLE, CAUSE I WENT THROUGH A LOTTA TROUBLE TO GET 'EM.
WHEN I CREATE A NEW DUCHY OF CRAFTIWICH, I'LL HAVE YELLOW CRESTS MADE ADORNED WITH RED SOCKS...FOR THAT'S A GREAT DEED MY DESCENDANTS CAN BRAG ABOUT.
HEY! YO, BELT, I JUST BEAT THE GOBLIN KING WITH MY BARE HANDS!
GRMBL...OKAY, OKAY...BUT YOU STILL HAVE ONE MORE GREAT DEED TO ACCOMPLISH.

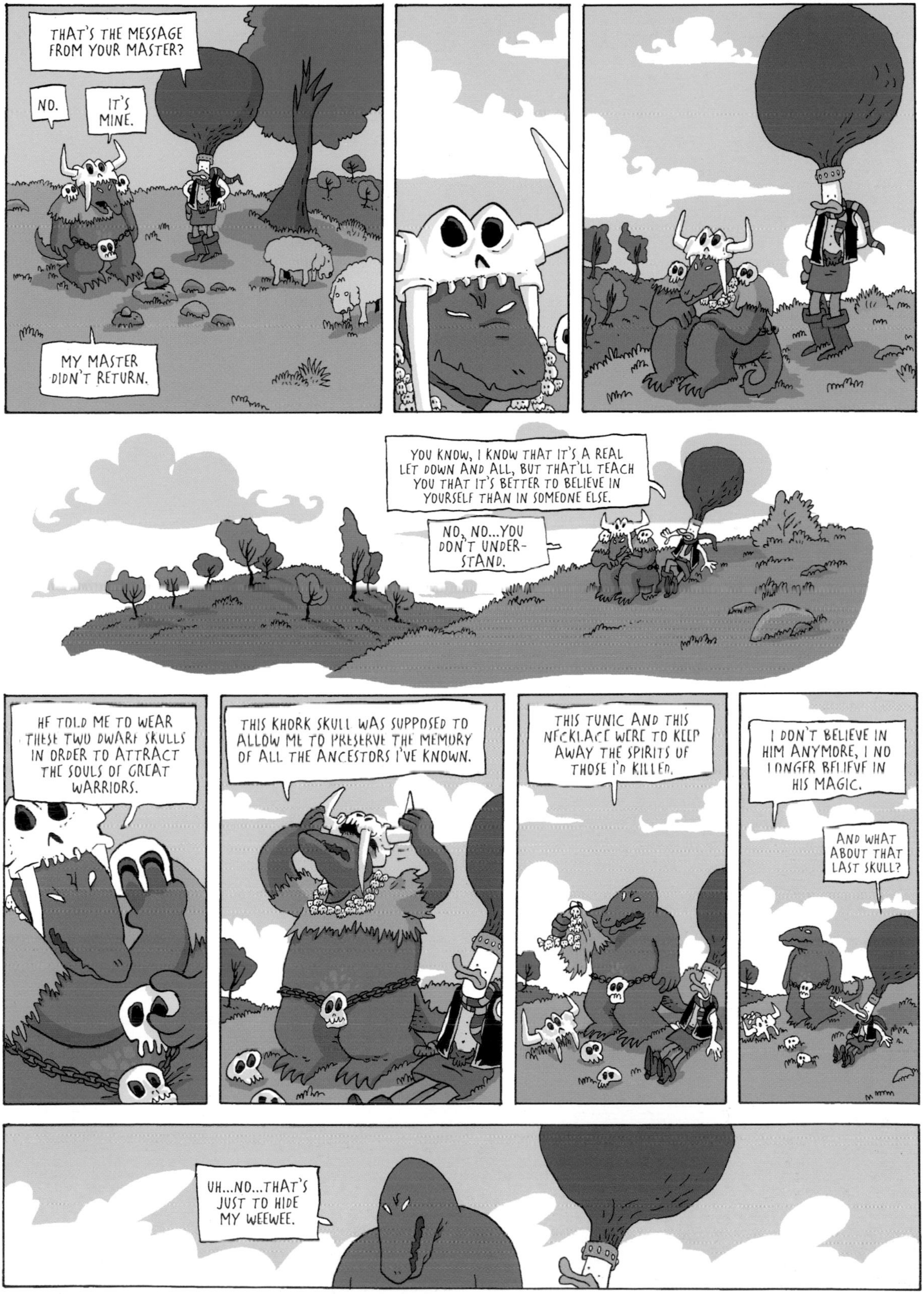
THAT'S THE MESSAGE FROM YOUR MASTER?
NO.
IT'S MINE.
MY MASTER DIDN'T RETURN.
YOU KNOW, I KNOW THAT IT'S A REAL LET DOWN AND ALL, BUT THAT'LL TEACH YOU THAT IT'S BETTER TO BELIEVE IN YOURSELF THAN IN SOMEONE ELSE.
NO, NO...YOU DON'T UNDER-STAND.
HE TOLD ME TO WEAR THESE TWO DWARF SKULLS IN ORDER TO ATTRACT THE SOULS OF GREAT WARRIORS.
THIS KHORK SKULL WAS SUPPOSED TO ALLOW ME TO PRESERVE THE MEMORY OF ALL THE ANCESTORS I'VE KNOWN.
THIS TUNIC AND THIS NECKLACE WERE TO KEEP AWAY THE SPIRITS OF THOSE I'D KILLED.
I DON'T BELIEVE IN HIM ANYMORE, I NO LONGER BELIEVE IN HIS MAGIC.
AND WHAT ABOUT THAT LAST SKULL?
UH...NO...THAT'S JUST TO HIDE MY WEEWEE.

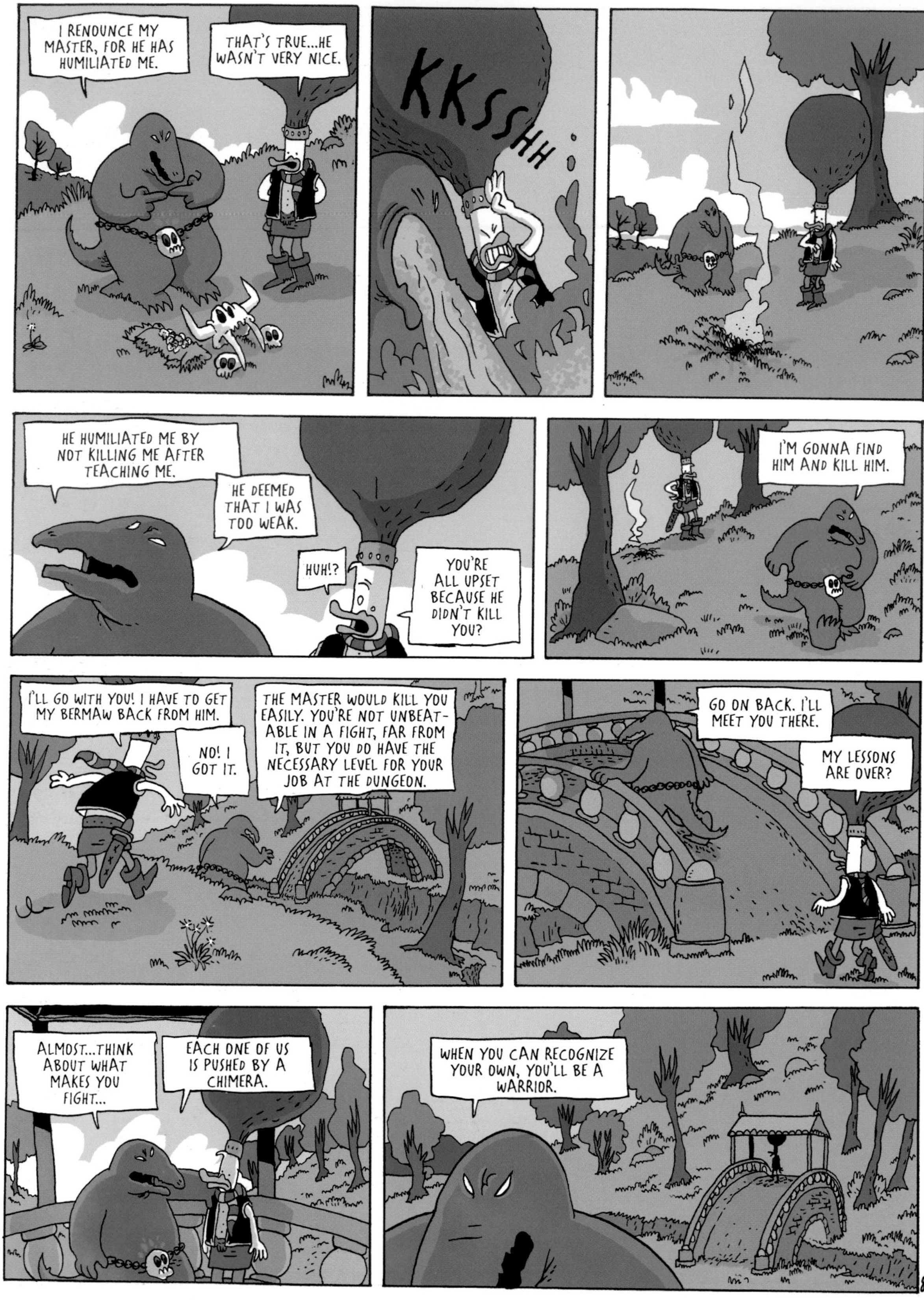
I RENOUNCE MY MASTER, FOR HE HAS HUMILIATED ME.
THAT'S TRUE...HE WASN'T VERY NICE.
KKSSHH
HE HUMILIATED ME BY NOT KILLING ME AFTER TEACHING ME.
HE DEEMED THAT I WAS TOO WEAK.
HUH!?
YOU'RE ALL UPSET BECAUSE HE DIDN'T KILL YOU?
I'M GONNA FIND HIM AND KILL HIM.
I'LL GO WITH YOU! I HAVE TO GET MY BERMAW BACK FROM HIM.
NO! I GOT IT.
THE MASTER WOULD KILL YOU EASILY. YOU'RE NOT UNBEATABLE IN A FIGHT, FAR FROM IT, BUT YOU DO HAVE THE NECESSARY LEVEL FOR YOUR JOB AT THE DUNGEON.
GO ON BACK. I'LL MEET YOU THERE.
MY LESSONS ARE OVER?
ALMOST...THINK ABOUT WHAT MAKES YOU FIGHT...
EACH ONE OF US IS PUSHED BY A CHIMERA.
WHEN YOU CAN RECOGNIZE YOUR OWN, YOU'LL BE A WARRIOR.

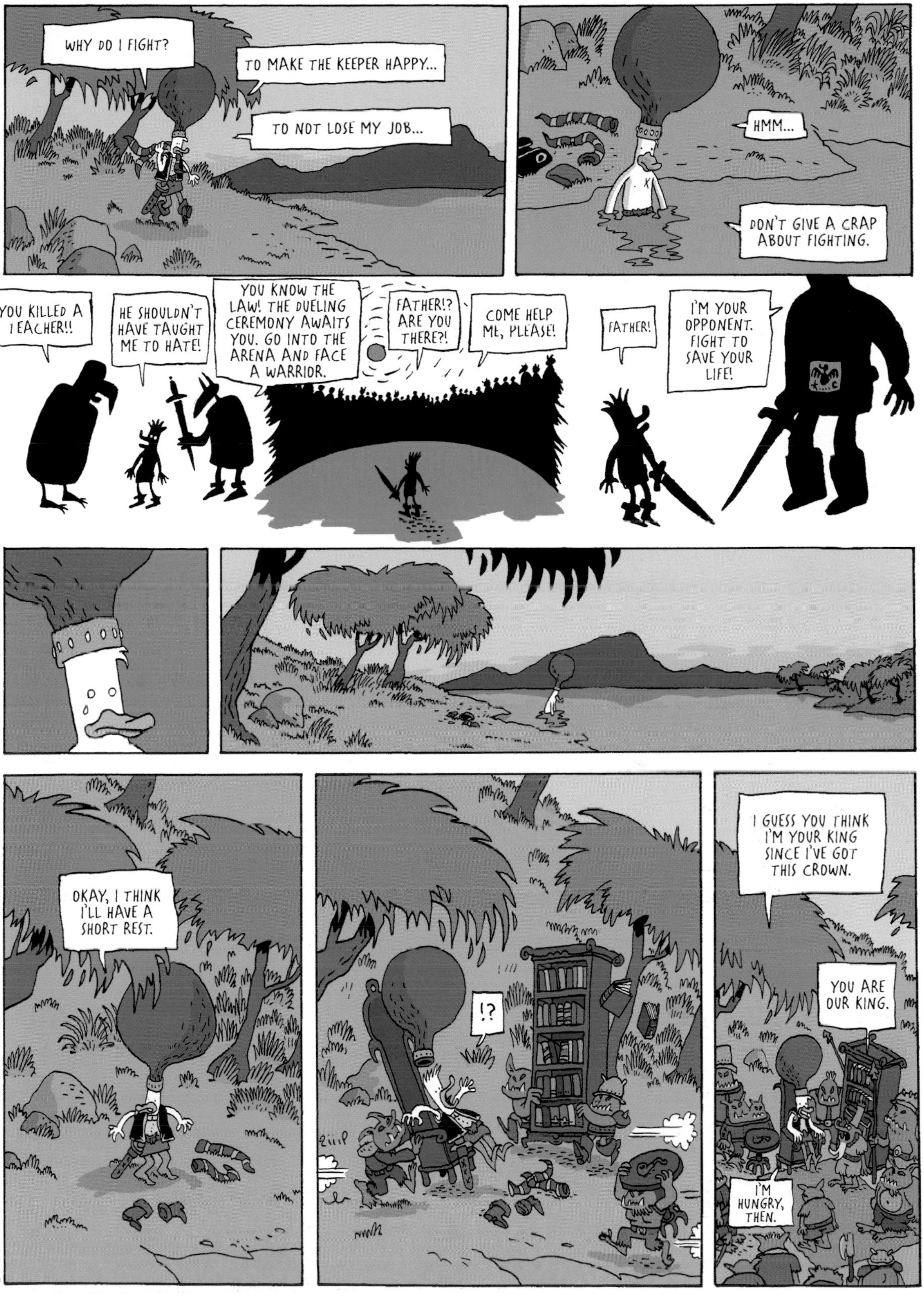
WHY DO I FIGHT?
TO MAKE THE KEEPER HAPPY...
TO NOT LOSE MY JOB...
HMM...
DON'T GIVE A CRAP ABOUT FIGHTING.
YOU KILLED A TEACHER!!
HE SHOULDN'T HAVE TAUGHT ME TO HATE!
YOU KNOW THE LAW! THE DUELING CEREMONY AWAITS YOU. GO INTO THE ARENA AND FACE A WARRIOR.
FATHER!? ARE YOU THERE?!
COME HELP ME, PLEASE!
FATHER!
I'M YOUR OPPONENT. FIGHT TO SAVE YOUR LIFE!
OKAY, I THINK I'LL HAVE A SHORT REST.
!?
I GUESS YOU THINK I'M YOUR KING SINCE I'VE GOT THIS CROWN.
YOU ARE OUR KING.
I'M HUNGRY, THEN.

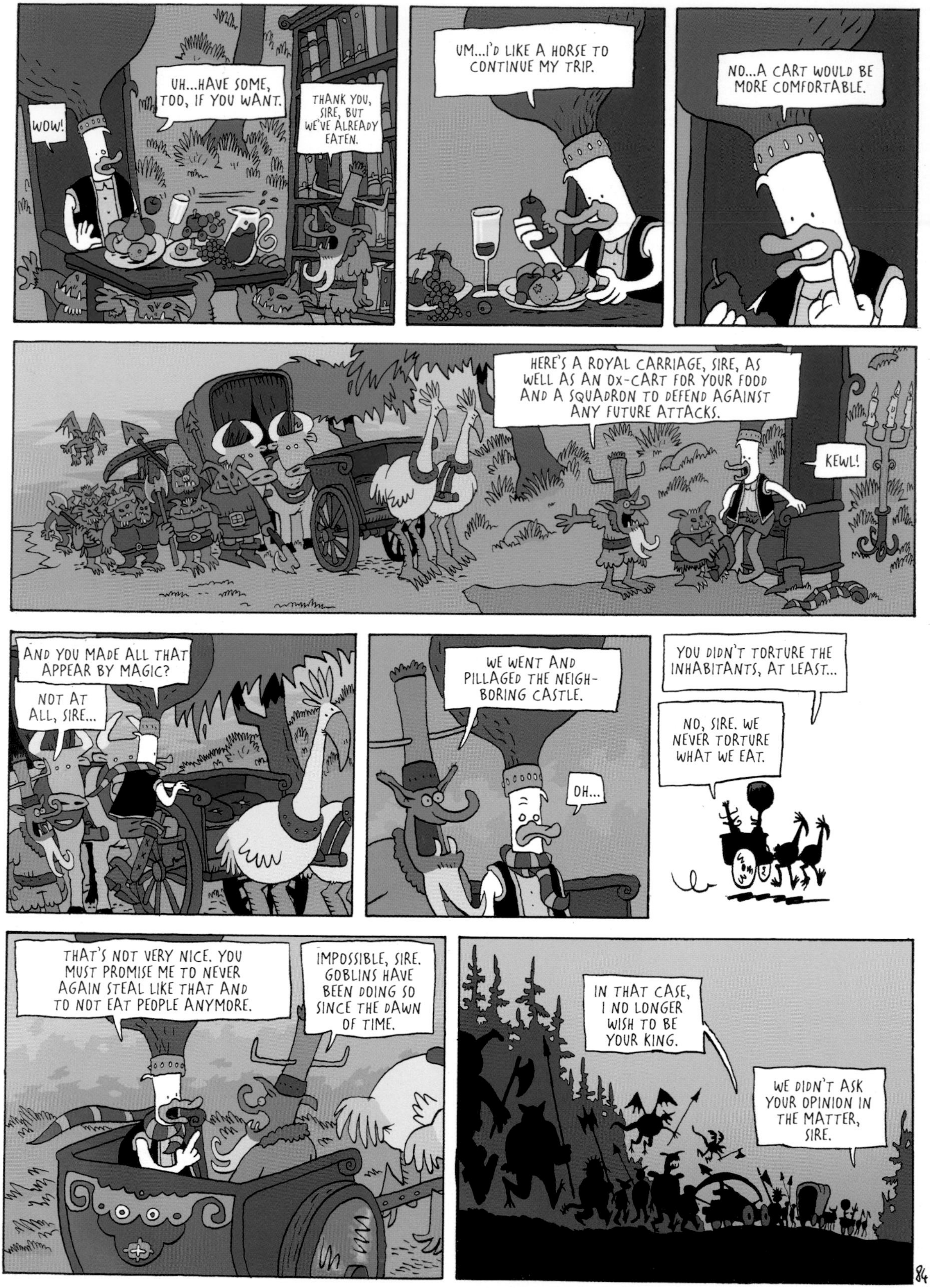
WOW!
UH...HAVE SOME, TOO, IF YOU WANT.
THANK YOU, SIRE, BUT WE'VE ALREADY EATEN.
UM...I'D LIKE A HORSE TO CONTINUE MY TRIP.
NO...A CART WOULD BE MORE COMFORTABLE.
HERE'S A ROYAL CARRIAGE, SIRE, AS WELL AS AN OX-CART FOR YOUR FOOD AND A SQUADRON TO DEFEND AGAINST ANY FUTURE ATTACKS.
KEWL!
AND YOU MADE ALL THAT APPEAR BY MAGIC?
NOT AT ALL, SIRE...
WE WENT AND PILLAGED THE NEIGH-BORING CASTLE.
OH...
YOU DIDN'T TORTURE THE INHABITANTS, AT LEAST...
NO, SIRE. WE NEVER TORTURE WHAT WE EAT.
THAT'S NOT VERY NICE. YOU MUST PROMISE ME TO NEVER AGAIN STEAL LIKE THAT AND TO NOT EAT PEOPLE ANYMORE.
IMPOSSIBLE, SIRE. GOBLINS HAVE BEEN DOING SO SINCE THE DAWN OF TIME.
IN THAT CASE, I NO LONGER WISH TO BE YOUR KING.
WE DIDN'T ASK YOUR OPINION IN THE MATTER, SIRE.

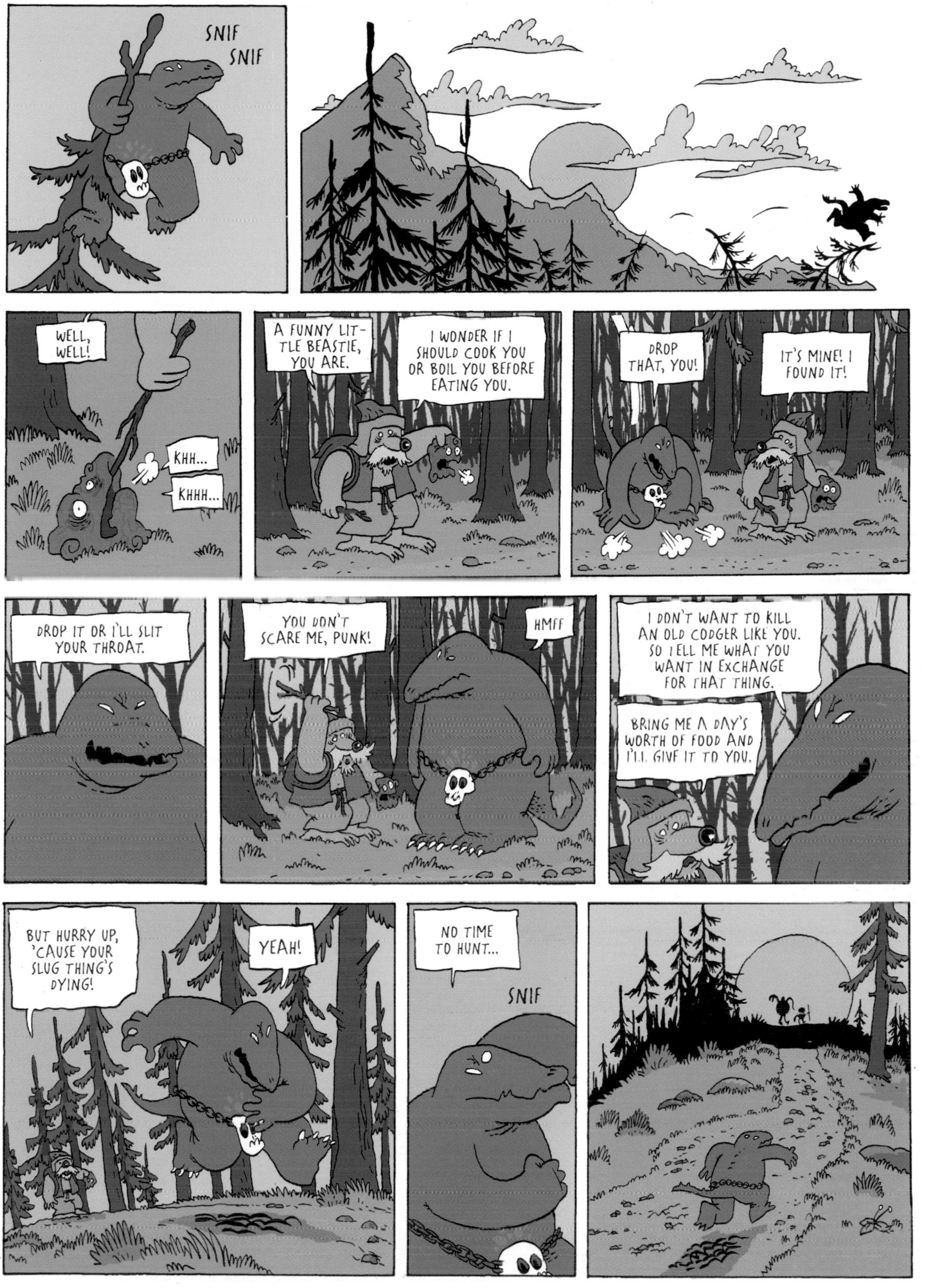
SNIF
SNIF
WELL, WELL!
KHH...
KHHH...
A FUNNY LITTLE BEASTIE, YOU ARE.
I WONDER IF I SHOULD COOK YOU OR BOIL YOU BEFORE EATING YOU.
DROP THAT, YOU!
IT'S MINE! I FOUND IT!
DROP IT OR I'LL SLIT YOUR THROAT.
YOU DON'T SCARE ME, PUNK!
HMFF
I DON'T WANT TO KILL AN OLD CODGER LIKE YOU. SO TELL ME WHAT YOU WANT IN EXCHANGE FOR THAT THING.
BRING ME A DAY'S WORTH OF FOOD AND I'LL GIVE IT TO YOU.
BUT HURRY UP, 'CAUSE YOUR SLUG THING'S DYING!
YEAH!
NO TIME TO HUNT...
SNIF

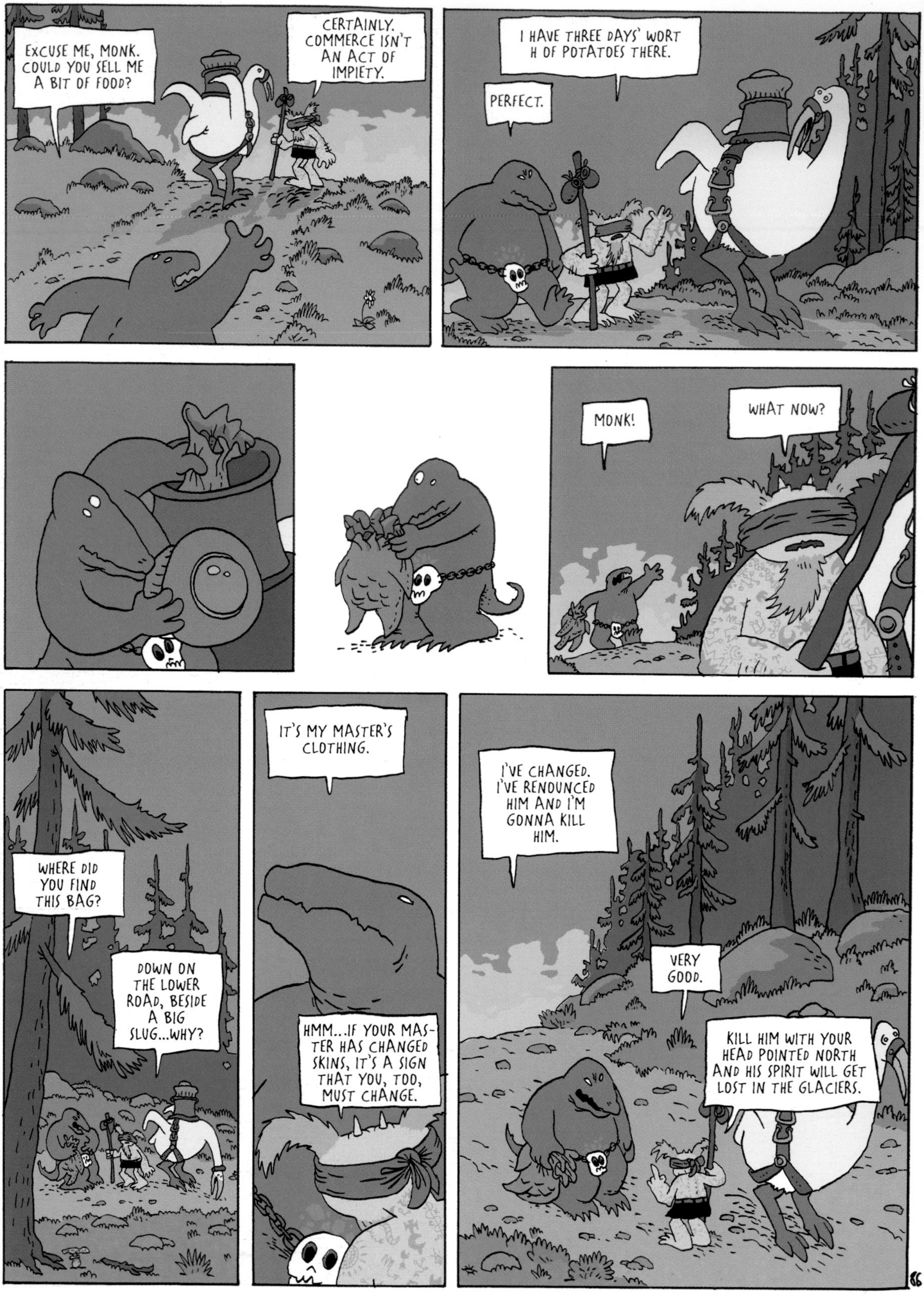

EXCUSE ME, MONK. COULD YOU SELL ME A BIT OF FOOD?
CERTAINLY. COMMERCE ISN'T AN ACT OF IMPIETY.
I HAVE THREE DAYS' WORT H OF POTATOES THERE.
PERFECT.
MONK!
WHAT NOW?
WHERE DID YOU FIND THIS BAG?
DOWN ON THE LOWER ROAD, BESIDE A BIG SLUG...WHY?
IT'S MY MASTER'S CLOTHING.
HMM...IF YOUR MASTER HAS CHANGED SKINS, IT'S A SIGN THAT YOU, TOO, MUST CHANGE.
I'VE CHANGED. I'VE RENOUNCED HIM AND I'M GONNA KILL HIM.
VERY GOOD.
KILL HIM WITH YOUR HEAD POINTED NORTH AND HIS SPIRIT WILL GET LOST IN THE GLACIERS.

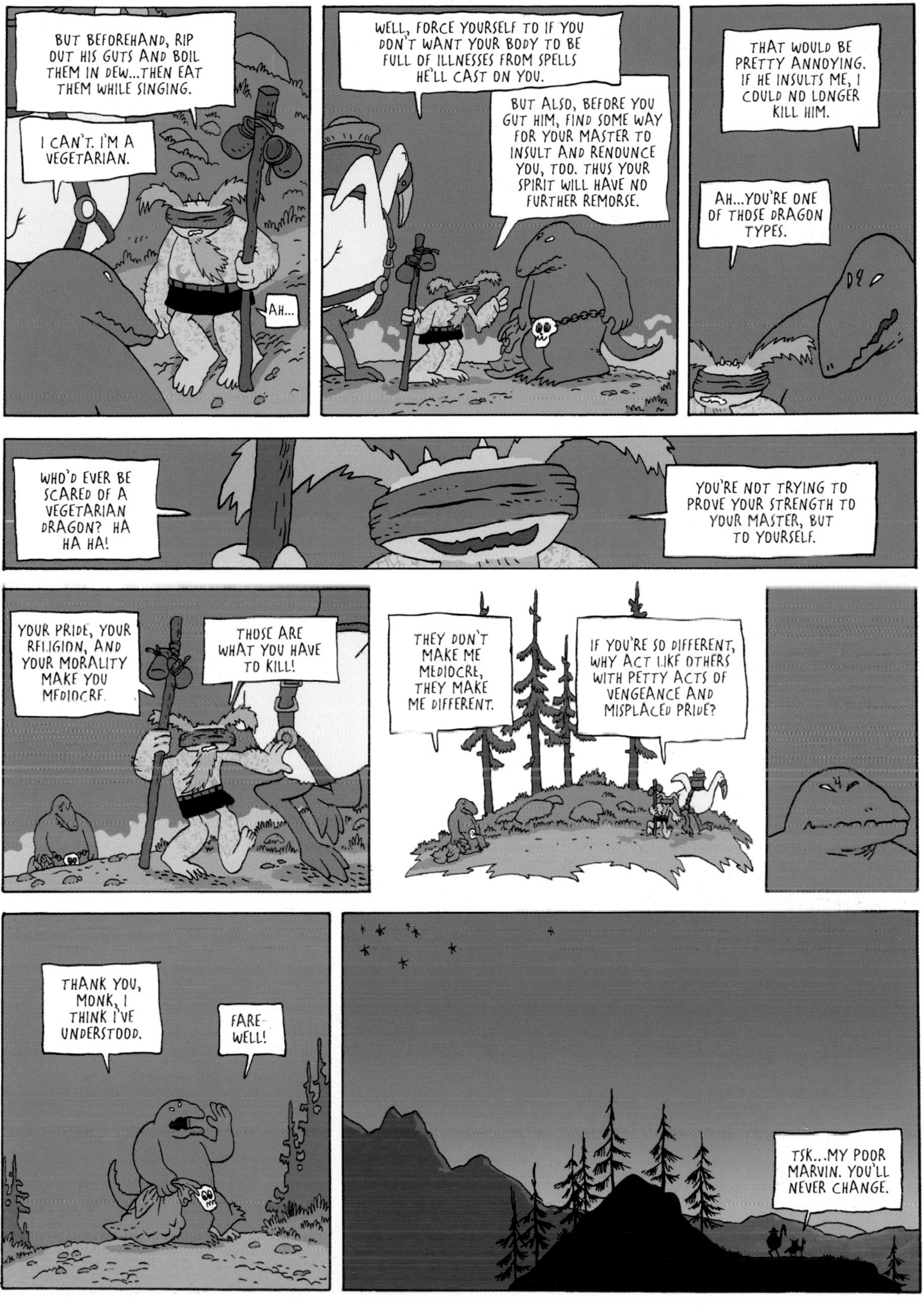
BUT BEFOREHAND, RIP OUT HIS GUTS AND BOIL THEM IN DEW...THEN EAT THEM WHILE SINGING.
I CAN'T. I'M A VEGETARIAN.
AH...
WELL, FORCE YOURSELF TO IF YOU DON'T WANT YOUR BODY TO BE FULL OF ILLNESSES FROM SPELLS HE'LL CAST ON YOU.
BUT ALSO, BEFORE YOU GUT HIM, FIND SOME WAY FOR YOUR MASTER TO INSULT AND RENOUNCE YOU, TOO. THUS YOUR SPIRIT WILL HAVE NO FURTHER REMORSE.
THAT WOULD BE PRETTY ANNOYING. IF HE INSULTS ME, I COULD NO LONGER KILL HIM.
AH...YOU'RE ONE OF THOSE DRAGON TYPES.
WHO'D EVER BE SCARED OF A VEGETARIAN DRAGON? HA HA HA!
YOU'RE NOT TRYING TO PROVE YOUR STRENGTH TO YOUR MASTER, BUT TO YOURSELF.
YOUR PRIDE, YOUR RELIGION, AND YOUR MORALITY MAKE YOU MEDIOCRE.
THOSE ARE WHAT YOU HAVE TO KILL!
THEY DON'T MAKE ME MEDIOCRE, THEY MAKE ME DIFFERENT.
IF YOU'RE SO DIFFERENT, WHY ACT LIKE OTHERS WITH PETTY ACTS OF VENGEANCE AND MISPLACED PRIDE?
THANK YOU, MONK, I THINK I'VE UNDERSTOOD.
FARE-WELL!
TSK...MY POOR MARVIN. YOU'LL NEVER CHANGE.

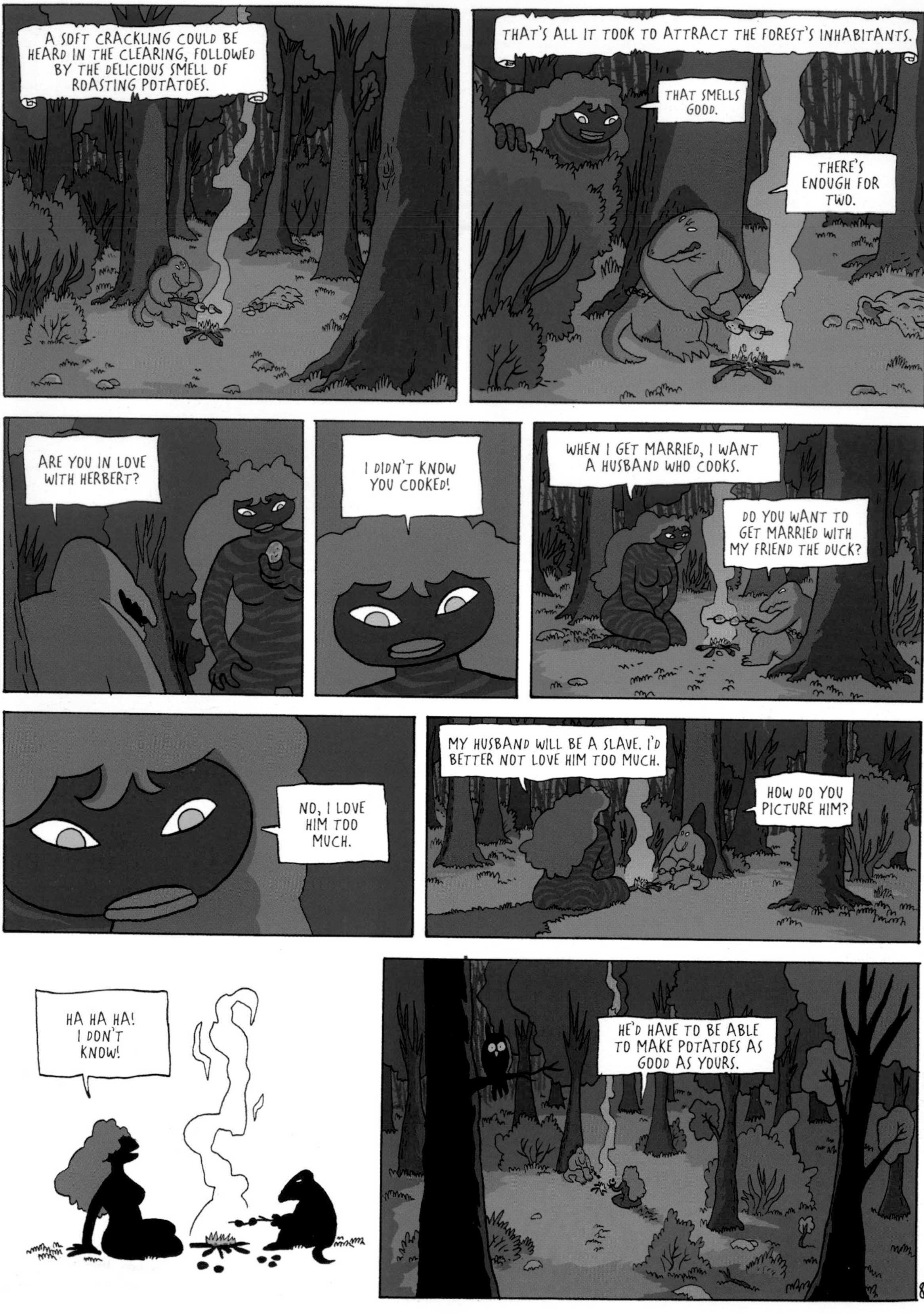
A SOFT CRACKLING COULD BE HEARD IN THE CLEARING, FOLLOWED BY THE DELICIOUS SMELL OF ROASTING POTATOES.
THAT'S ALL IT TOOK TO ATTRACT THE FOREST'S INHABITANTS.
THAT SMELLS GOOD.
THERE'S ENOUGH FOR TWO.
ARE YOU IN LOVE WITH HERBERT?
I DIDN'T KNOW YOU COOKED!
WHEN I GET MARRIED, I WANT A HUSBAND WHO COOKS.
DO YOU WANT TO GET MARRIED WITH MY FRIEND THE DUCK?
NO, I LOVE HIM TOO MUCH.
MY HUSBAND WILL BE A SLAVE. I'D BETTER NOT LOVE HIM TOO MUCH.
HOW DO YOU PICTURE HIM?
HA HA HA! I DON'T KNOW!
HE'D HAVE TO BE ABLE TO MAKE POTATOES AS GOOD AS YOURS.

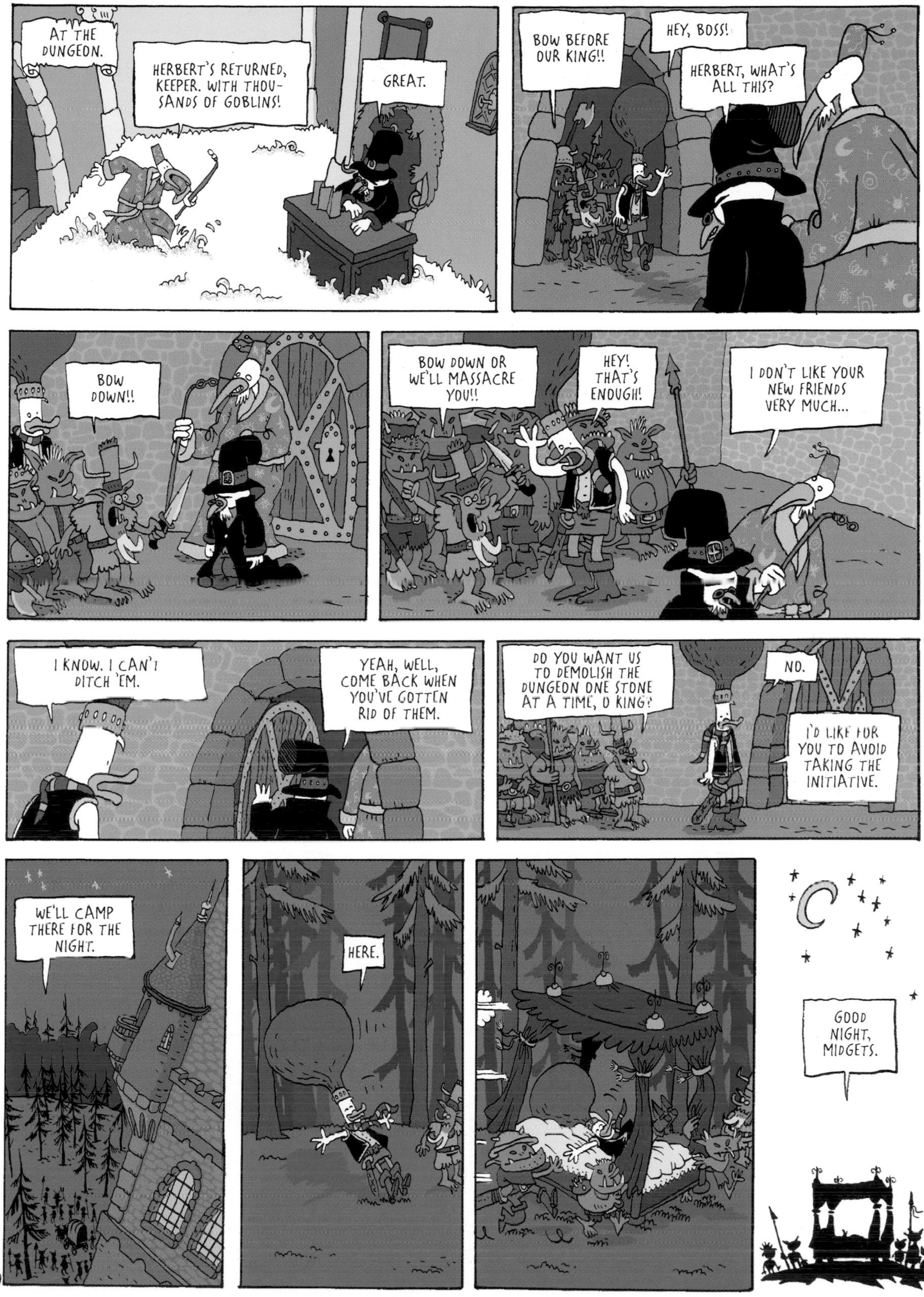
AT THE DUNGEON.
HERBERT'S RETURNED, KEEPER. WITH THOUSANDS OF GOBLINS!
GREAT.
BOW BEFORE OUR KING!!
HEY, BOSS!
HERBERT, WHAT'S ALL THIS?
BOW DOWN!!
BOW DOWN OR WE'LL MASSACRE YOU!!
HEY! THAT'S ENOUGH!
I DON'T LIKE YOUR NEW FRIENDS VERY MUCH...
I KNOW. I CAN'T DITCH 'EM.
YEAH, WELL, COME BACK WHEN YOU'VE GOTTEN RID OF THEM.
DO YOU WANT US TO DEMOLISH THE DUNGEON ONE STONE AT A TIME, O KING?
NO.
I'D LIKE FOR YOU TO AVOID TAKING THE INITIATIVE.
WE'LL CAMP THERE FOR THE NIGHT.
HERE.
GOOD NIGHT, MIDGETS.

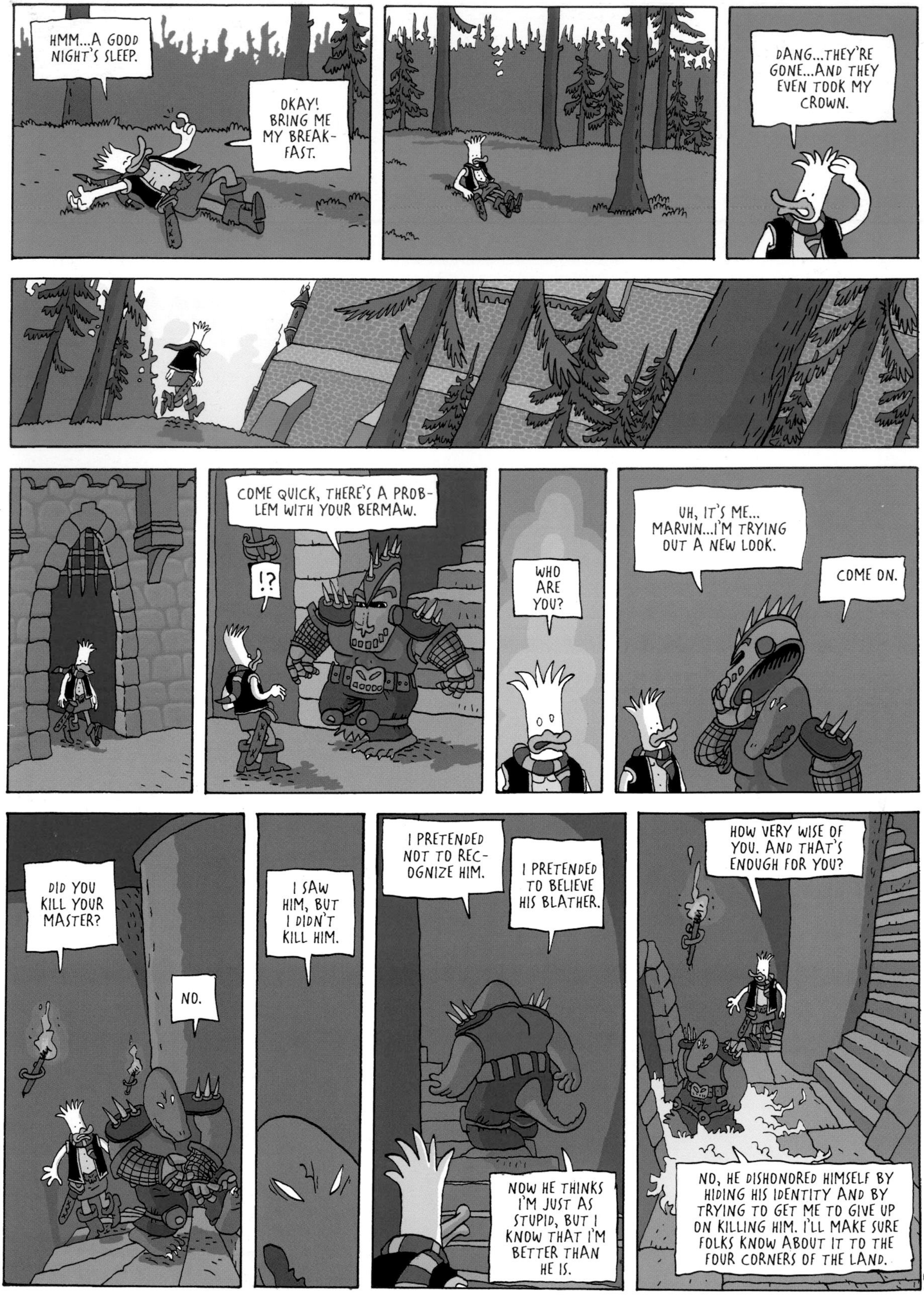
HMM...A GOOD NIGHT'S SLEEP.
OKAY! BRING ME MY BREAK-FAST.
DANG...THEY'RE GONE...AND THEY EVEN TOOK MY CROWN.
COME QUICK, THERE'S A PROB-LEM WITH YOUR BERMAW.
!?
WHO ARE YOU?
UH, IT'S ME... MARVIN...I'M TRYING OUT A NEW LOOK.
COME ON.
DID YOU KILL YOUR MASTER?
NO.
I SAW HIM, BUT I DIDN'T KILL HIM.
I PRETENDED NOT TO REC-OGNIZE HIM.
I PRETENDED TO BELIEVE HIS BLATHER.
NOW HE THINKS I'M JUST AS STUPID, BUT I KNOW THAT I'M BETTER THAN HE IS.
HOW VERY WISE OF YOU. AND THAT'S ENOUGH FOR YOU?
NO, HE DISHONORED HIMSELF BY HIDING HIS IDENTITY AND BY TRYING TO GET ME TO GIVE UP ON KILLING HIM. I'LL MAKE SURE FOLKS KNOW ABOUT IT TO THE FOUR CORNERS OF THE LAND.

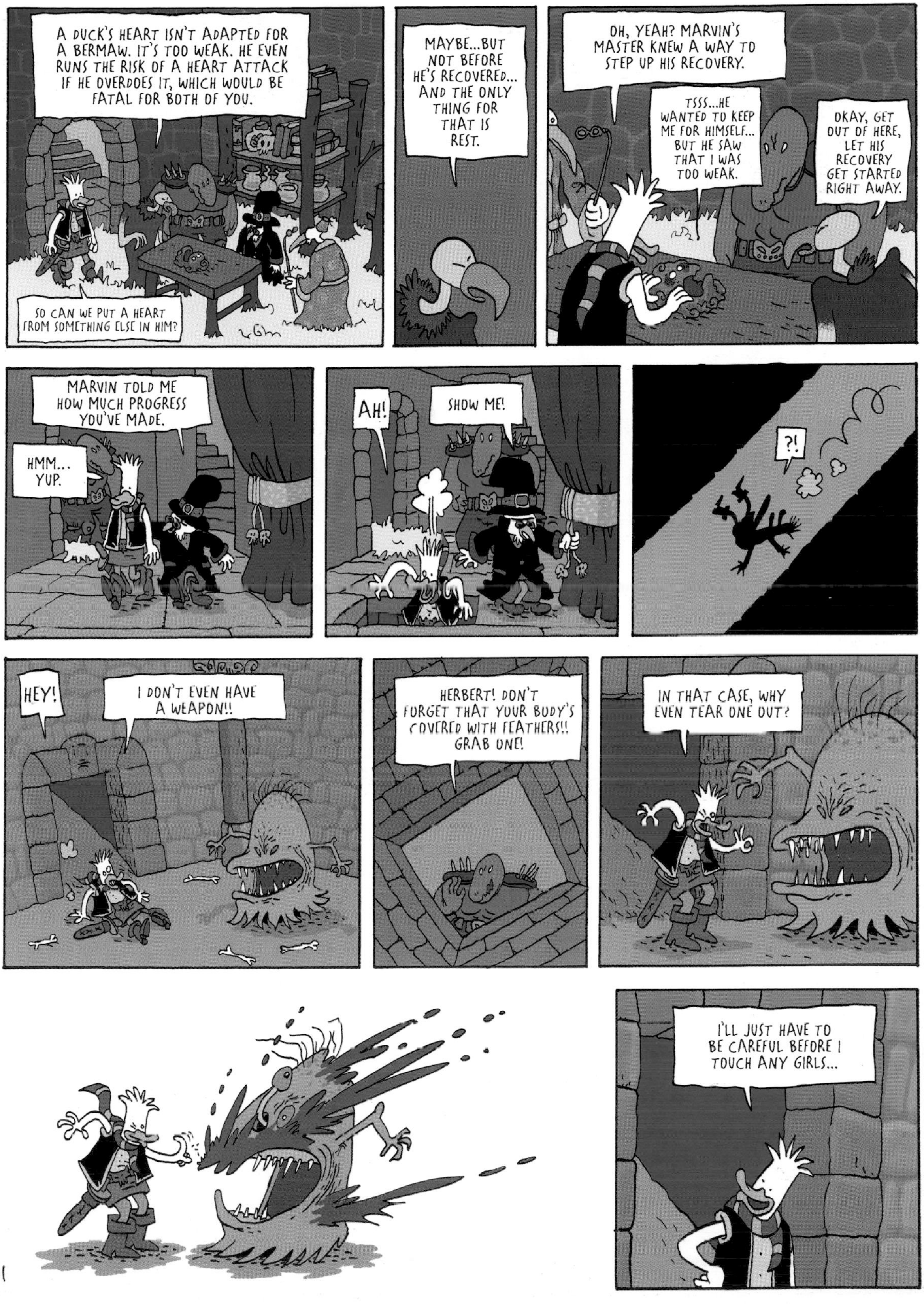
A DUCK'S HEART ISN'T ADAPTED FOR A BERMAW. IT'S TOO WEAK. HE EVEN RUNS THE RISK OF A HEART ATTACK IF HE OVERDOES IT, WHICH WOULD BE FATAL FOR BOTH OF YOU.
SO CAN WE PUT A HEART FROM SOMETHING ELSE IN HIM?
MAYBE...BUT NOT BEFORE HE'S RECOVERED... AND THE ONLY THING FOR THAT IS REST.
OH, YEAH? MARVIN'S MASTER KNEW A WAY TO STEP UP HIS RECOVERY.
TSSS...HE WANTED TO KEEP ME FOR HIMSELF... BUT HE SAW THAT I WAS TOO WEAK.
OKAY, GET OUT OF HERE, LET HIS RECOVERY GET STARTED RIGHT AWAY.
MARVIN TOLD ME HOW MUCH PROGRESS YOU'VE MADE.
HMM... YUP.
AH!
SHOW ME!
?!
HEY!
I DON'T EVEN HAVE A WEAPON!!
HERBERT! DON'T FORGET THAT YOUR BODY'S COVERED WITH FEATHERS!! GRAB ONE!
IN THAT CASE, WHY EVEN TEAR ONE OUT?
I'LL JUST HAVE TO BE CAREFUL BEFORE I TOUCH ANY GIRLS...

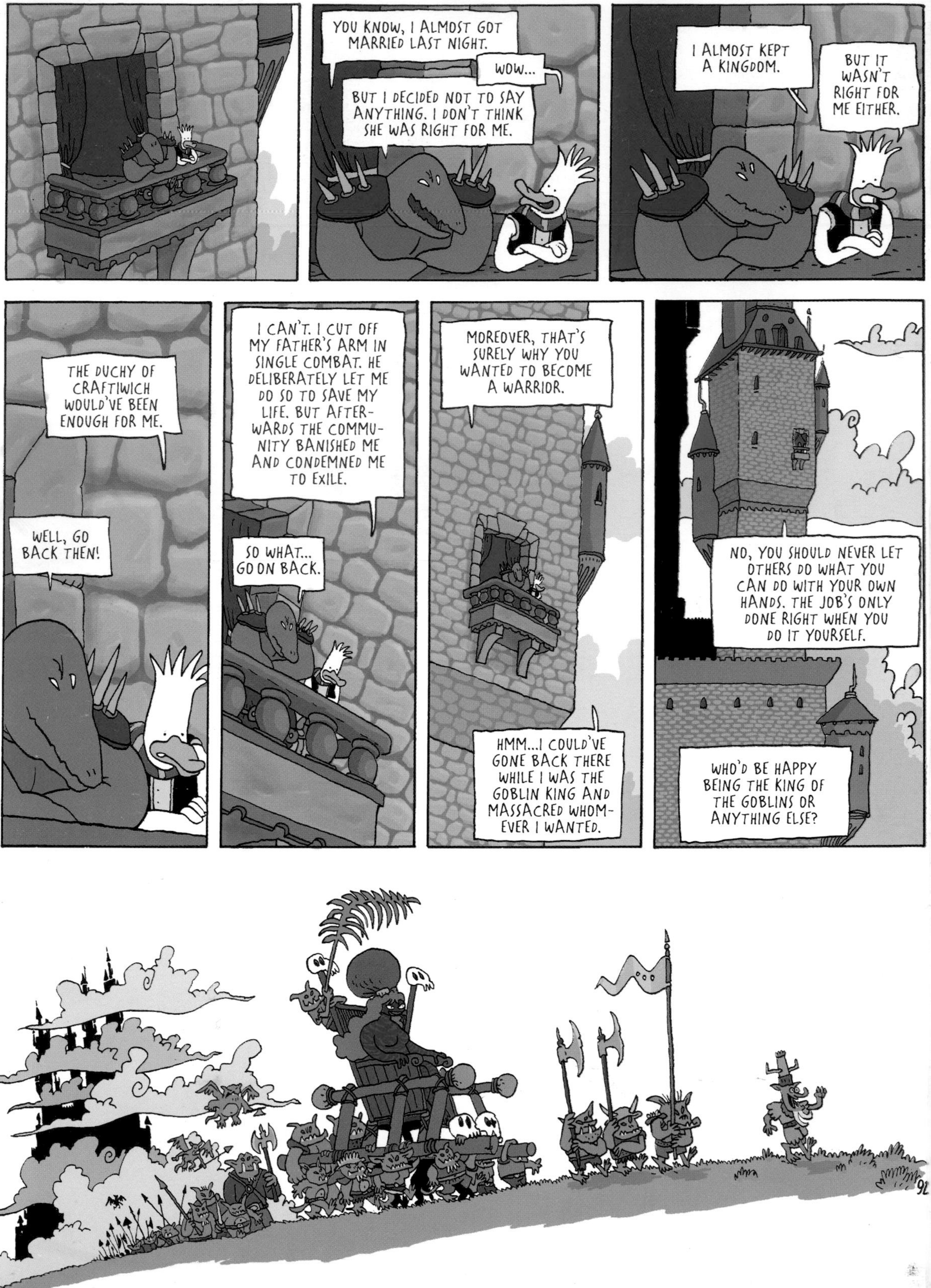

YOU KNOW, I ALMOST GOT MARRIED LAST NIGHT.
WOW...
BUT I DECIDED NOT TO SAY ANYTHING. I DON'T THINK SHE WAS RIGHT FOR ME.
I ALMOST KEPT A KINGDOM.
BUT IT WASN'T RIGHT FOR ME EITHER.
THE DUCHY OF CRAFTIWICH WOULD'VE BEEN ENOUGH FOR ME.
WELL, GO BACK THEN!
I CAN'T. I CUT OFF MY FATHER'S ARM IN SINGLE COMBAT. HE DELIBERATELY LET ME DO SO TO SAVE MY LIFE. BUT AFTER-WARDS THE COMMU-NITY BANISHED ME AND CONDEMNED ME TO EXILE.
SO WHAT... GO ON BACK.
MOREOVER, THAT'S SURELY WHY YOU WANTED TO BECOME A WARRIOR.
HMM...I COULD'VE GONE BACK THERE WHILE I WAS THE GOBLIN KING AND MASSACRED WHOM-EVER I WANTED.
NO, YOU SHOULD NEVER LET OTHERS DO WHAT YOU CAN DO WITH YOUR OWN HANDS. THE JOB'S ONLY DONE RIGHT WHEN YOU DO IT YOURSELF.
WHO'D BE HAPPY BEING THE KING OF THE GOBLINS OR ANYTHING ELSE?
Joann Sfar & Lewis Trondheim